PIPE FITTINGS

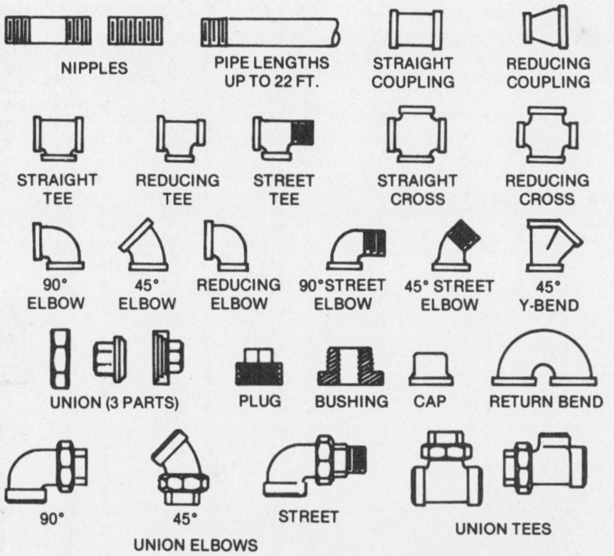

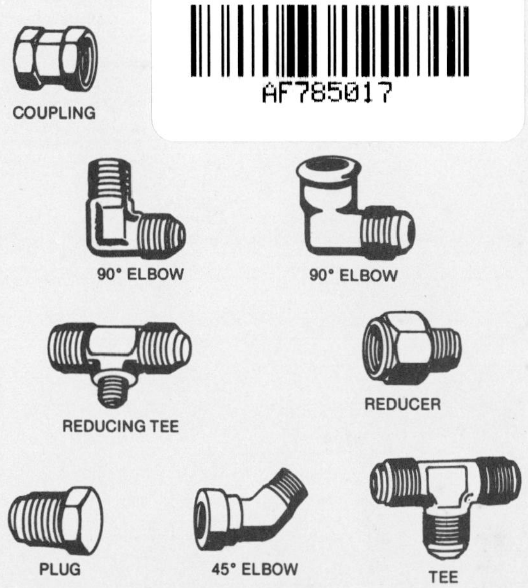

Here are the common steel pipe fittings. Nipples are simply short lengths of pipe threaded on both ends. Reducing fittings join two different sizes of pipe.

Compression fittings of the flared-tube type are the easiest for the novice to handle when working with copper tubing.

STANDARD STEEL PIPE (All Dimensions in Inches)					
Nominal Size	Outside Diameter	Inside Diameter	Nominal Size	Outside Diameter	Inside Diameter
1/8	0.405	0.269	1	1.315	1.049
1/4	0.540	0.364	1 1/4	1.660	1.380
3/8	0.675	0.493	1 1/2	1.900	1.610
1/2	0.840	0.622	2	2.375	2.067
3/4	1.050	0.824	2 1/2	2.875	2.469

SQUARE MEASURE

144 sq in = 1 sq ft
9 sq ft = 1 sq yd
272.25 sq ft = 1 sq rod
160 sq rods = 1 acre

VOLUME MEASURE

1728 cu in = 1 cu ft
27 cu ft = 1 cu yd

MEASURES OF CAPACITY

1 cup = 8 fl oz
2 cups = 1 pint
2 pints = 1 quart
4 quarts = 1 gallon
2 gallons = 1 peck
4 pecks = 1 bushel

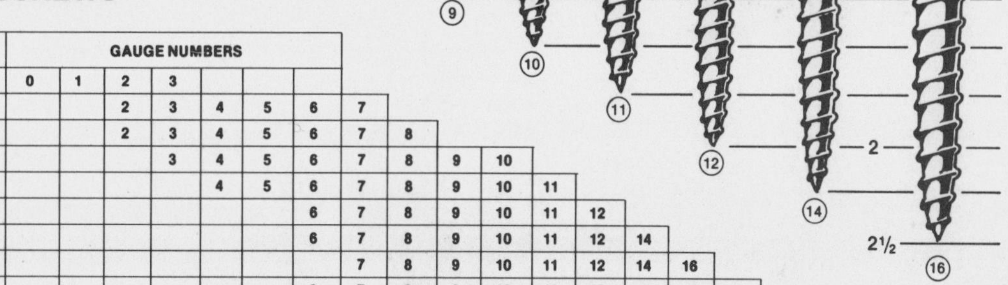

WOOD SCREWS

LENGTH	GAUGE NUMBERS																
1/4 INCH	0	1	2	3													
3/8 INCH			2	3	4	5	6	7									
1/2 INCH			2	3	4	5	6	7	8								
5/8 INCH				3	4	5	6	7	8	9	10						
3/4 INCH					4	5	6	7	8	9	10	11					
7/8 INCH							6	7	8	9	10	11	12				
1 INCH							6	7	8	9	10	11	12	14			
1 1/4 INCH								7	8	9	10	11	12	14	16		
1 1/2 INCH							6	7	8	9	10	11	12	14	16	18	
1 3/4 INCH									8	9	10	11	12	14	16	18	20
2 INCH									8	9	10	11	12	14	16	18	20
2 1/4 INCH										9	10	11	12	14	16	18	20
2 1/2 INCH													12	14	16	18	20
2 3/4 INCH														14	16	18	20
3 INCH															16	18	20
3 1/2 INCH																18	20	24
4 INCH																18	20	24

WHEN YOU BUY SCREWS, SPECIFY (1) LENGTH, (2) GAUGE NUMBER, (3) TYPE OF HEAD—FLAT, ROUND, OR OVAL, (4) MATERIAL—STEEL, BRASS, BRONZE, ETC., (5) FINISH—BRIGHT, STEEL BLUED, CADMIUM, NICKEL, OR CHROMIUM PLATED.

In this volume . . .

IMAGINE THIS attractive entertainment center, with its own built-in barbecue grill, in your own back yard. Build a cookout gazebo for much less than you would guess. See plans on page 1346.

CAN YOU BELIEVE this beautiful "hardwood" wall is hardboard? See page 1398.

THESE WALLS, TOO, are hardboard, combining elegance and practicability. Again, see page 1398.

AND HERE'S ANOTHER hardboard-finished room. There's an amazing array of finishes.

THIS ONCE WAS a garage! Here's one way *you* may add a beautiful room. See page 1316.

IF YOU TAKE PRIDE in your guns, you'll take pride in this cabinet. See plans on page 1378.

BUILD an authentic early American gossip bench. Crafted in solid cherry, this handsome piece is something you'll cherish for years to come. You'll find complete plans starting on page 1365.

Popular Mechanics

do-it-yourself encyclopedia

in 20 volumes

a complete how-to guide for the homeowner, the hobbyist—
and anyone who enjoys working with mind and hands!

All about:

home maintenance
home-improvement projects
wall paneling
burglary and fire protection
furniture projects
finishing and refinishing furniture
outdoor living
home remodeling
solutions to home problems
challenging woodworking projects
hobbies and handicrafts
model making
weekend projects
workshop shortcuts and techniques
hand-tool skills
power-tool know-how
shop-made tools
car repairs
car maintenance
appliance repair
boating
hunting
fishing
camping
photography projects
radio, TV and electronics know-how
clever hints and tips
projects just for fun

volume 9

ISBN 0-87851-074-5
Library of Congress Catalog Number 77 84920

MANUFACTURED IN THE UNITED STATES OF AMERICA

contents

VOLUME 9

Make rustic picture frames from barn siding

By JAMES A. LONG

■ AN OLD ABANDONED and weather-beaten farm building may be an eyesore to the countryside, but the boards in it are as good as gold. Weathered barn siding has become a popular and much-sought lumber for remodeling. I find the wood particularly appropriate for framing wildlife prints, nature paintings and landscapes. Its rustic look adds charm to the picture.

A few pieces of this rough-textured wood can usually be had for little or nothing. The thing to remember when you spot a weathered old building on its last legs is that it still belongs to someone and you should not just stop and help yourself. Get the owner's permission to remove a few boards. Probably he will be glad to get rid of them. Pick relatively straight boards and don't worry about nail holes—they add to the overall rustic look. If the boards are wet, they will have to be air-dried for a few days, maybe longer.

I have made some handsome picture frames from old weathered barn boards. You'll need a miterbox and four picture-frame corner clamps. A table saw makes it easy to run the bead on the inner molding. Follow the steps below and on page 1285 and you'll wind up with a beautiful frame that is a part of the picture.

AFTER CLEANING, rip boards 2 or 3 in. wide. Lay out picture size allowing ⅛ in. all around; miter to fit. Double check size. Butter ends with white glue.

PULL MITERED ends together with two-way picture-frame clamps and nail corners while the members are securely clamped together.

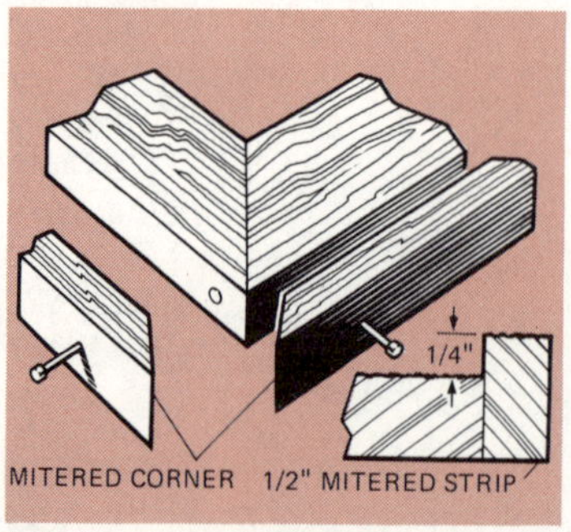

RIP ½ x 1-in. strips, miter ends and nail to outer edges of main frame. Gouge saw-cut edges here and there with a sharp knife.

ADD TO weather-beaten look of the frame by applying a light gray semi-transparent shingle stain. Brush with the grain.

SEE ALSO

Antique reproductions . . . Carving, wood . . . Chests . . . Clocks . . . Desk accessories . . . Dry sinks . . . Gossip benches . . . Hutch tables . . . Mirrors . . . Servers . . . Siding

WIPE OFF most of the stain with a coarse cloth; then while stain is still wet, brush lightly with oil colors that accent the picture's colors.

USE BURNT UMBER for rich brown tint, burnt sienna followed by a touch of yellow ochre here and there for a warm brown look. Experiment on scrap.

RIP ⅜ x ⅝-in. molding to shape shown for adding to inside of main frame from scrap stock. Sand the wood and miter the ends for an exact inside fit. The molding forms a rabbet for the glass.

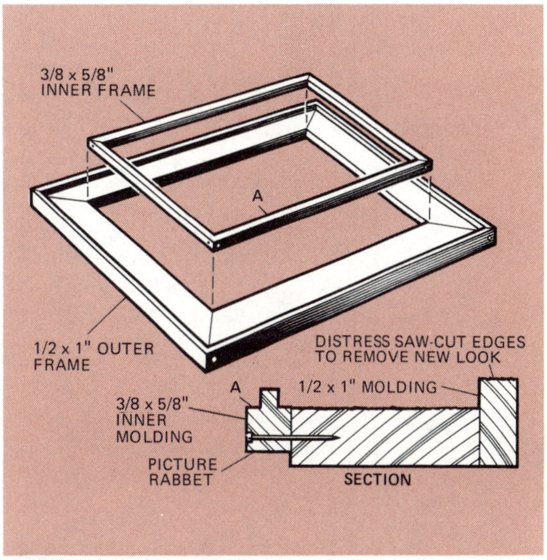

INNER FRAME adds decorative touch, also forms a rabbet for the picture and glass. Keep the shoulders of top bead on molding even with the textured surface of the main frame.

PICTURE-MOUNTING TRICK: When covering back of frame with brown paper, dampen paper first. Then apply glue to frame and lay paper in it. When the paper dries, it will shrink smooth and tight. Use screw eyes to attach picture wire to back, placing eyes about quarter way from top.

GLUE AND CLAMP inner molding together as a separate frame, using your picture-frame clamps to hold the four corners tight.

GIVE INNER FRAME two or more coats of a heavy white acrylic paint called gesso. You can purchase it at most art supply stores.

WHEN GESSO is dry, paint the top bead with two coats of gold paint. Finally insert the frame inside the main frame and nail.

How to fix a food freezer

Your home food freezer is not as complicated as you might think. Though problems with the sealed refrigeration system and compressor should be left to a qualified serviceman, by studying these diagrams and charts you can understand the basics

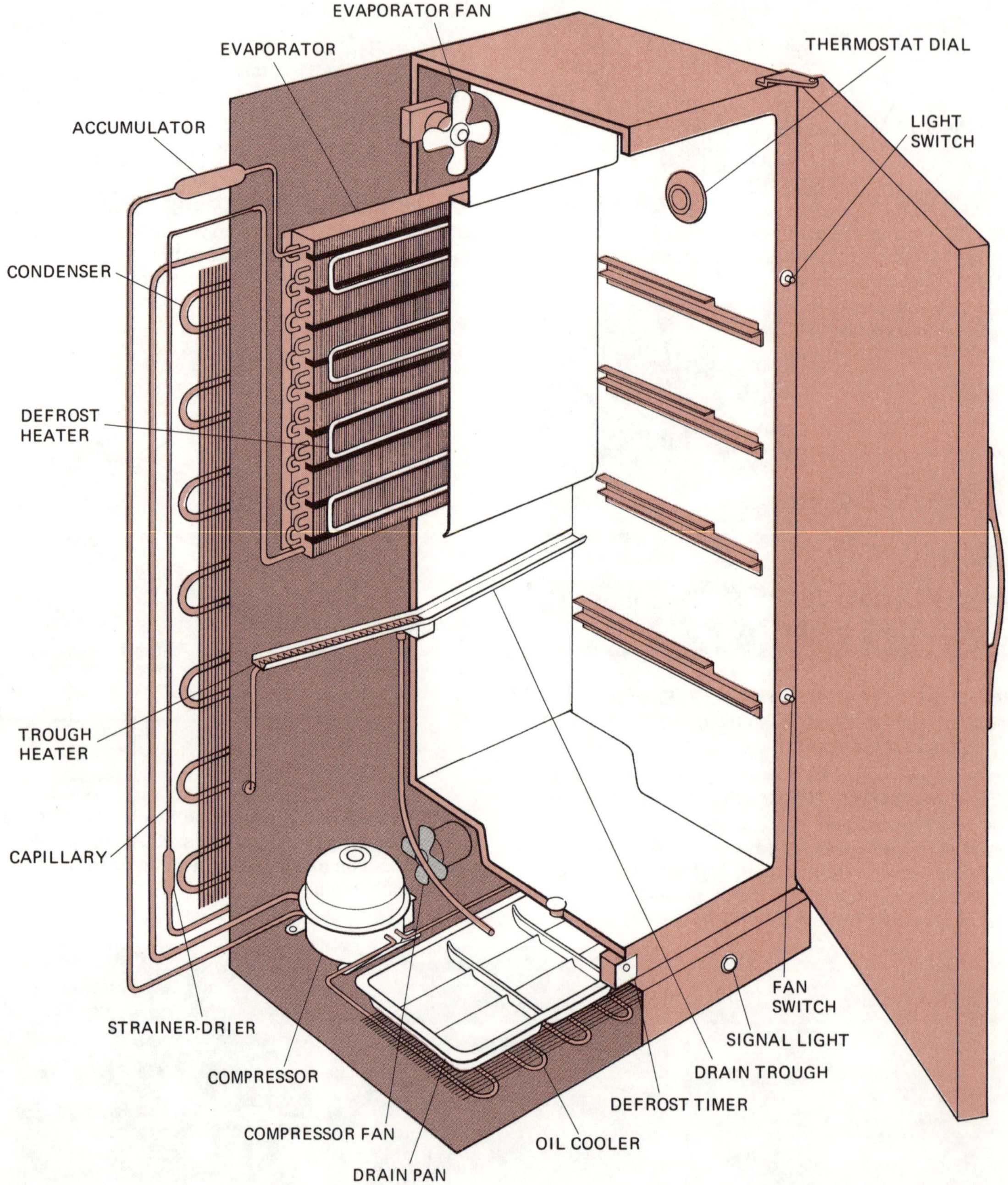

Typical freezer components

SEE ALSO

Appliance repair . . . Clothes dryers . . . Garbage disposers . . . Heaters, water . . . Humidifiers . . . Irons . . . Kitchens . . . Mixers, food . . . Oven hoods . . . Ranges . . . Vacuum cleaners . . . Washing machines

■ MANY OF THE PROBLEMS that may arise with home food freezers can be dealt with by consulting the 12 troubleshooting charts on this page and the following four pages. Many falsely believe that the home handyman cannot begin to understand his food freezer. Troubles that involve the sealed refrigeration system should be left to a qualified serviceman, but it will be helpful if the homeowner can recognize the symptoms when they occur.

In a normal system, refrigerant in a gaseous state is pumped by the compressor into the condenser, where it cools and changes into a liquid. It then passes through the extremely narrow capillary tube that leads to the evaporator. The change to larger tubing diameter at the evaporator inlet reduces the pressure on the refrigerant, allowing it to boil at low temperature, absorbing heat from the area surrounding the evaporator as it does. The vapor that results is drawn into the compressor to begin a new cycle.

During normal operation, the condenser will feel warm, the evaporator cold and the suction line from evaporator to compressor will be cool or at about room temperature. To work properly, the system must contain a specific amount (charge) of refrigerant and its lines must be unobstructed.

When a system is undercharged, the freezer lacks normal frost accumulation on walls or evaporator coil. The compressor runs continually or for longer periods than normal, drawing less current than normal, and temperatures inside the freezer rise. Evaporator and condenser both feel warmer than in normal operation.

leaks cause undercharge

Undercharge is most commonly the result of a leak. Oil stains around a joint will indicate a leak. Test for leaks by brushing a soapy water solution over joints on the system's high side (compressor, condenser, capillary) while the freezer is running, over joints on the low side (evaporator, suction line) while it is off. Any sign of bubbling at a joint indicates a leak.

When a system is overcharged, frost accumu-

text continued on page 1291

Compressor does not run

POSSIBLE CAUSES	WHAT TO TRY
1. Blown fuse or tripped circuit breaker.	Replace fuse or reset circuit breaker.
2. Defective relay.	Test for continuity between terminals L and R, S and L. Replace relay if there is no reading between L and R, or if there is a reading between S and L.
3. Defective overload protector.	Remove wires from overload protector and test for continuity across terminals. Replace overload protector if there is no reading at room temperature.
4. Defective temperature control (thermostat).	Remove wires from thermostat, turn control to coldest setting and test for continuity across terminals. Replace control if there is no reading.
5. Defective defrost timer.	Remove wires from defrost timer, and test for continuity across terminals for timer motor, defrost and compressor circuits (refer to unit's wiring diagram). Replace the timer if a circuit is open.
6. Defective compressor.	Direct-test compressor with test jumper. Have it replaced if it fails to operate properly.

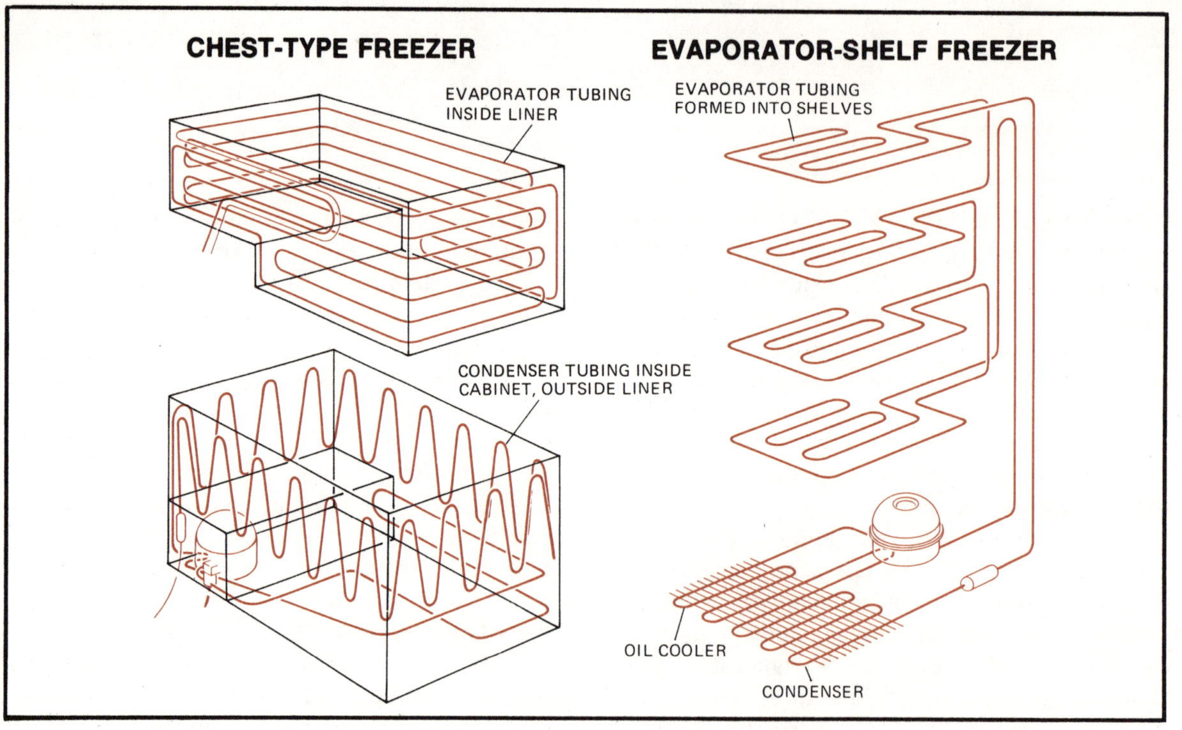

Compressor cycles on overload protector

POSSIBLE CAUSES	WHAT TO TRY
1. Low voltage.	Test voltage at wall outlet with a voltmeter. This should be within 10 percent of normal. If it's low, call power company.
2. Poor air circulation over condenser.	If condenser is dirty, vacuum-clean the coil and surrounding area.
3. Defective relay.	See No. 2 in chart titled "Compressor does not run" on page 1287.
4. Restricted system.	If signs of restriction (see text, page 1291) are present, contact a qualified serviceman.

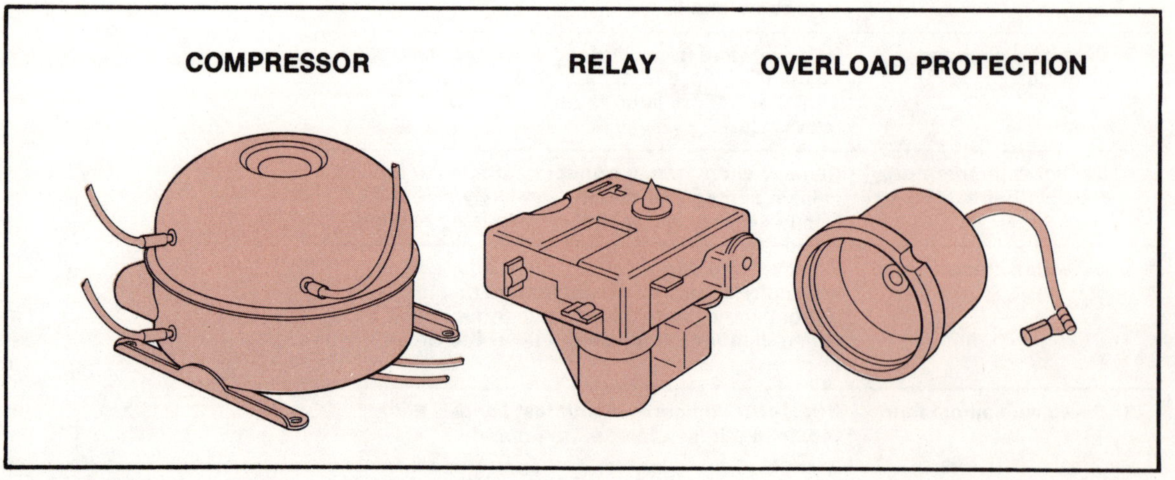

Compressor runs too much or constantly

POSSIBLE CAUSES	WHAT TO TRY
1. Thermostat is set too high or feeler bulb has worked loose.	Adjust thermostat to a warmer setting. Make sure that feeler bulb is secure in mounting.
2. Poor air circulation at condenser.	If condenser is dirty, use a vacuum cleaner on the coil and surrounding area.
3. Poor door seal.	Close the door on a dollar bill; there should be a slight tug when the bill is pulled out. If not, check the door and hinges for warp—if present, loosen the door-liner screws, push the door in until it seats against the gasket and retighten liner screws.
4. Undercharged or restricted system.	If signs of undercharge or restriction are present (see text, page 1287), call a qualified serviceman.

Freezer compartment too warm

POSSIBLE CAUSES	WHAT TO TRY
1. Poor door seal.	See No. 3 in chart titled "Compressor runs too much or constantly" above.
2. Defective freezer fan.	Disconnect wires from the fan and direct-test fan motor. Replace the motor if it fails to operate properly.
3. Defective defrost heater.	Disconnect wires from the heater and test it for continuity. Replace heater if no reading can be obtained.
4. Door opened too often.	Limit the number of door openings to reduce the amount of air at room temperature that can enter the freezer.
5. Defective defrost timer.	See chart titled "Compressor does not run" on page 1287.
6. Freezer overloaded with unfrozen food.	Add no more than 10 percent of freezer capacity at one time; remove some food or add dry ice.
7. Interior light on.	Push light-switch button in; the light should go out. If it does not, remove switch and test it for continuity. There should be a reading with button out, none with button in. Replace switch if defective.

Freezer does not defrost

POSSIBLE CAUSES	WHAT TO TRY
1. Insufficient time allowed for defrosting (manual).	Normal time to soften frost is 10 to 15 minutes. Repeat defrost cycle.
2. Defective defrost timer.	See chart titled "Compressor does not run" on page 1287.
3. Defective defrost heater.	See chart titled "Freezer compartment too warm" above.

THERMOSTAT

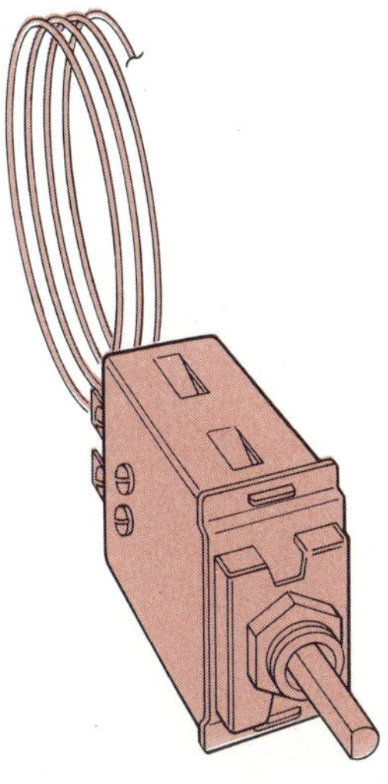

CAUTION: Be sure power is turned *off* before you handle components. Make all continuity tests with power *off*. When using a test lamp, keep power *off* while connecting and disconnecting the lamp. Use your manufacturer's manual to locate components, and use only replacement parts that meet his specifications. Do not open the refrigerant system.

continued

DEFROST TIMERS

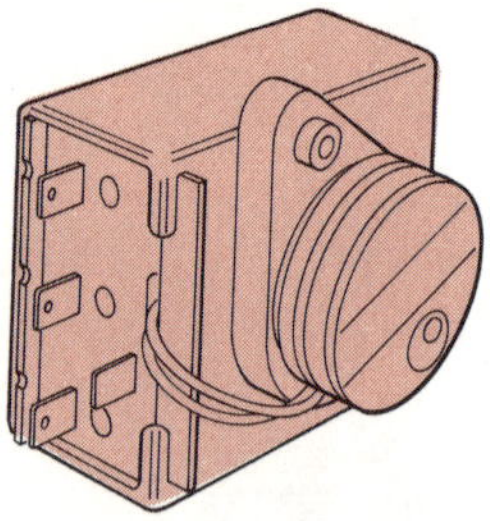

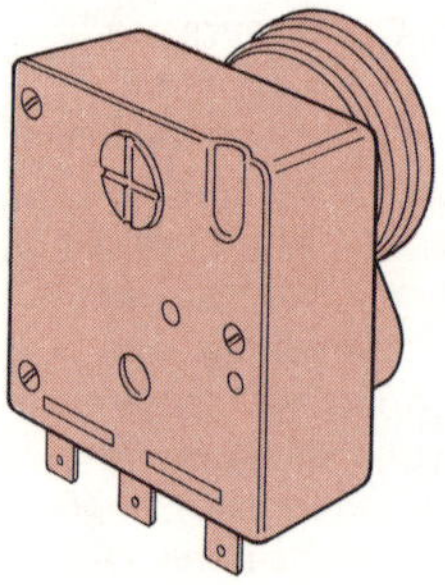

Freezer fan does not run

POSSIBLE CAUSES	WHAT TO TRY
1. Freezer defrosting.	Normal. Check again later.
2. Defective fan switch.	Remove wires from switch, test for continuity. There should be a reading with button in, none with button out. Replace switch if defective.
3. Defective fan motor.	Disconnect wires and direct-test fan motor. Replace it if it fails to operate properly.
4. Defective defrost timer.	See chart titled "Compressor does not run," page 1287.
5. Loose or defective wiring.	Check wiring against manufacturer's diagram. Tighten any loose wires.

Water freezes in drain trough

POSSIBLE CAUSES	WHAT TO TRY
1. Defective drain-trough heater.	Remove wires and test heater for continuity.
2. Defective defrost timer.	See chart "Compressor does not run," page 1287.
3. Loose or defective wiring.	Check wiring against manufacturer's diagram. Tighten any loose wires.

Moisture condenses on cabinet or door

POSSIBLE CAUSES	WHAT TO TRY
1. Poor door seal.	See chart titled "Compressor runs too much or constantly," page 1289.
2. Defective door heater.	Disconnect wires from door heater and test for continuity. Replace it if there is no reading.
3. Door opened too often.	Limit number of door openings to keep air at room temperature out of freezer.
4. Thermostat setting.	Thermostat left on too cold a setting for too long a time. Turn to warmer setting.

Freezer short cycles

POSSIBLE CAUSES	WHAT TO TRY
1. Low voltage.	Test voltage at wall outlet with a voltmeter. This should be within 10 percent of normal. Call power company if it's low.
2. High room temperature.	Lower the temperature or move the freezer to a cooler place.
3. Freezer overloaded with unfrozen food.	Add no more than 10 percent of freezer capacity at one time; remove some food or add dry ice.
4. Defective relay or overload protector.	See chart, "Compressor does not run," page 1287.

Excessive current draw

POSSIBLE CAUSES	WHAT TO TRY
1. Door opened too often.	Limit number of door openings to keep air at room temperature out of the freezer.
2. Heavy warm-food loads.	Do not overload freezer. See manufacturer's instructions for correct freezer capacity; do not exceed it.
3. Thermostat set too low.	Move thermostat to warmer setting.

DEFROST THERMOSTAT

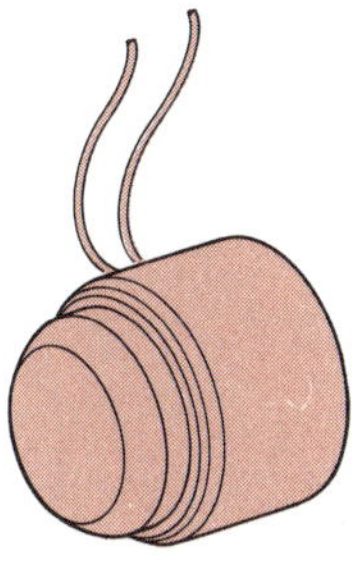

Noisy operation

POSSIBLE CAUSES	WHAT TO TRY
1. Freezer not level.	Level freezer.
2. Tubing vibrating.	Adjust tubing slightly so that it does not rub against cabinet.
3. Loose compressor mounting.	Tighten leg mountings of compressor.

Door does not open or close properly

POSSIBLE CAUSES	WHAT TO TRY
1. Freezer not level.	Level freezer.
2. Latch mechanism worn or out of adjustment.	Examine latch mechanism. If worn, replace it. If not, adjust it according to manufacturer's specifications.
3. Hinge mounting screws loose.	Realign and retighten mounting screws. Replace any worn bushings.
4. Door vacuum.	Normal. This occurs when there is a brief interval between door openings; inrush or air at room temperature contracts when cooled to create partial vacuum.

LIGHT AND FAN SWITCH

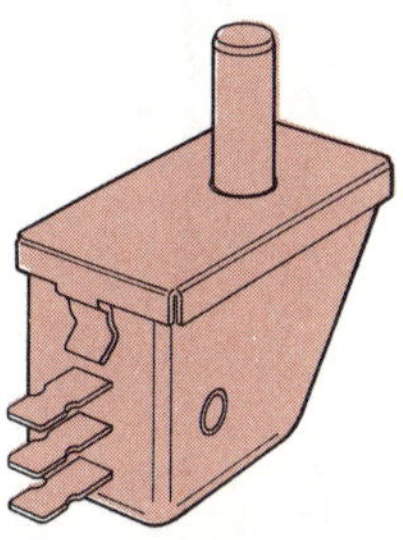

lates on the suction line between evaporator and compressor, and the compressor may run longer than normal or continually. Overcharge will exist only when the sealed system has been broken into. In the case of either undercharge or overcharge, the system must be evacuated and recharged with the correct amount of refrigerant. This is a job for a qualified serviceman who has the knowledge and the equipment to do a good job.

causes of line restriction

A partial or complete restriction in a line interrupts the normal flow of refrigerant through the system. It may be caused by moisture frozen in the capillary tube, by wax resulting from a breakdown of oil in the compressor or particles of dirt or lacquer from compressor windings.

A partial restriction produces symptoms like those of an undercharged system, plus frost buildup between the restriction and the suction line. It may clear itself when the compressor shuts off but reappear when the compressor starts again.

With a complete restriction there is no refrigerant flow at all. Evaporator and condenser remain at room temperature, the compressor refuses to start and cycles on the overload protector.

compressor problems

The compressor itself may be subject to shorting, grounding, jamming or open windings (it will hum with one open winding). Continuity tests, using the manufacturer's wiring diagram, can isolate these problems, but compressor repair or replacement should not be attempted by the homeowner.

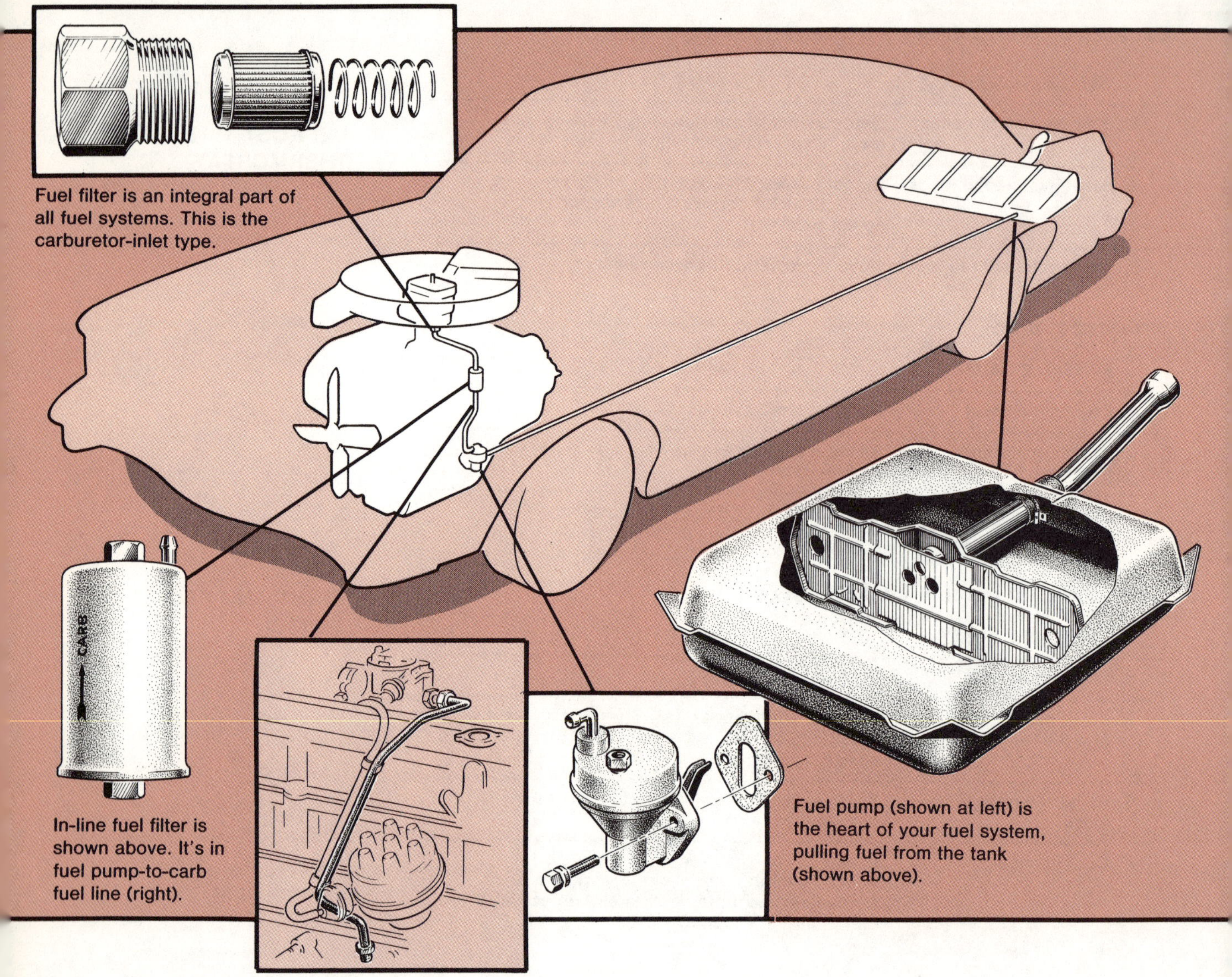

Fuel filter is an integral part of all fuel systems. This is the carburetor-inlet type.

In-line fuel filter is shown above. It's in fuel pump-to-carb fuel line (right).

Fuel pump (shown at left) is the heart of your fuel system, pulling fuel from the tank (shown above).

What you should know about your fuel system

By MORT SCHULTZ

■ A CONVENTIONAL fuel system (neither fuel-injected nor diesel) contains several key components:

■ The fuel tank.

■ A fuel pump that pumps gasoline from fuel tank to carburetor.

SEE ALSO

Autos, gas mileage . . . Autos, maintenance . . .
Carburetors, auto . . . Chokes, auto . . .
Dieseling, auto . . . Engines, auto . . .
Ignition systems, auto . . . Misfiring, auto . . .

■ Tubes (lines) that carry gasoline from fuel tank to carburetor.

■ Filters that cleanse impurities from gasoline before it enters the carburetor.

■ A carburetor that combines gasoline and air in order to make a combustible fuel mixture which enters the engine.

This article discusses roles played by each part, except the carburetor.

the fuel tank

The fuel tank is normally placed in the rear of

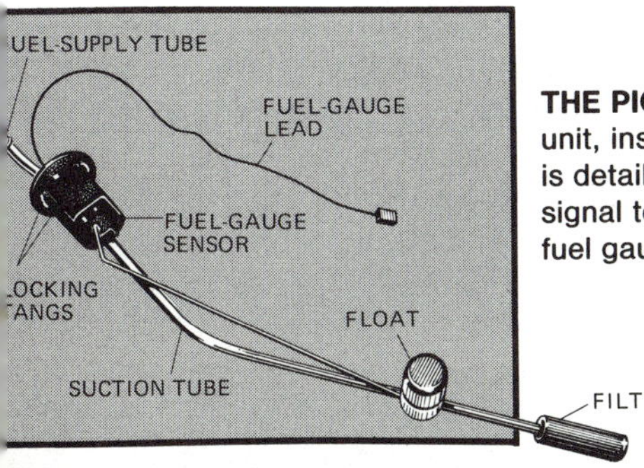

THE PICKUP and sending unit, inside your gas tank, is detailed at left. It sends a signal to your dashboard fuel gauge.

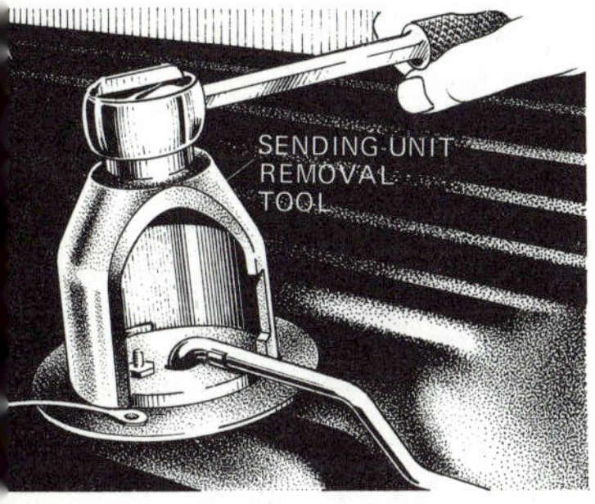

YOU CAN remove pickup and sending unit for repair or replacement, but this may call for a special tool.

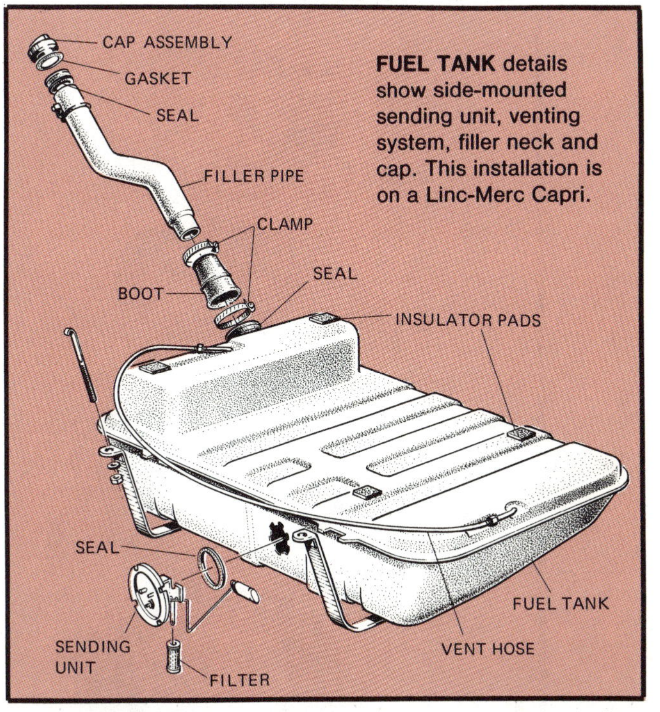

FUEL TANK details show side-mounted sending unit, venting system, filler neck and cap. This installation is on a Linc-Merc Capri.

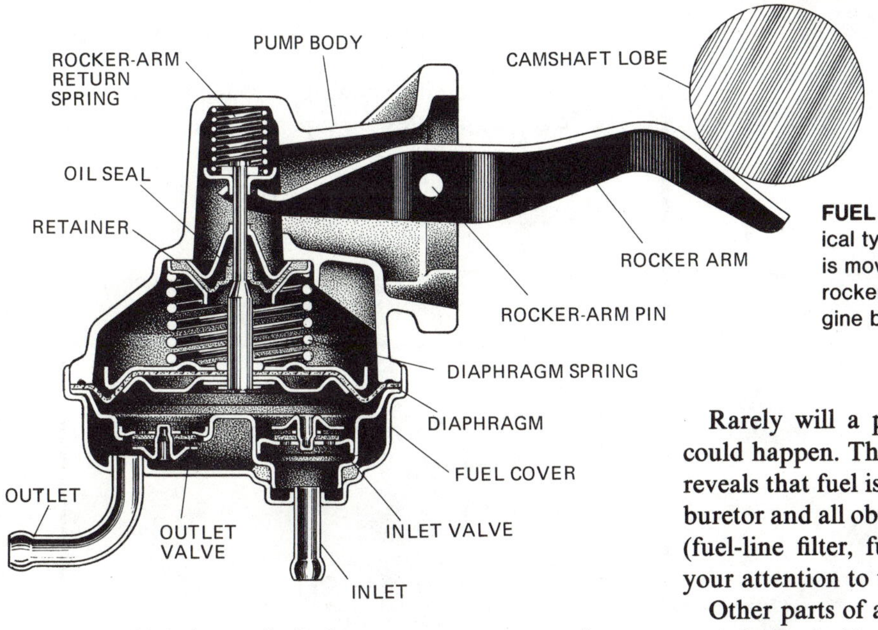

FUEL PUMP shown here is the mechanical type. Up and down pumping force is moved to diaphragm by camshaft via rocker arm. Pump bolts on side of engine block.

the vehicle beneath the luggage compartment. In cars having the engine in the rear, such as the old Corvair and the VW Beetle, the tank is placed in the forward compartment.

A tank has a filler pipe and an outlet, the latter consisting of a pickup that draws off gasoline sending it on its way to the carburetor.

Normally, a fiberglass filter having a relatively coarse mesh is positioned on the pickup. This end is usually placed about ½ inch off the bottom of the tank, allowing sediment that collects in the tank to settle on the bottom rather than be drawn into the fuel line.

Rarely will a pickup filter clog. However, it could happen. Thus, if a fuel-pump delivery test reveals that fuel is not being delivered to the carburetor and all obvious points have been checked (fuel-line filter, fuel pump and fuel line), turn your attention to the pickup filter.

Other parts of a conventional fuel tank are:

■ A baffle inside the tank that is welded to the sides and bottom to reinforce the tank and stop fuel from splashing and surging. A baffle has several holes in it to allow fuel to move freely.

■ A fuel-gauge sending unit, possessing a float to measure fuel level, and a low-voltage sensor. The unit is connected by wire to the fuel gauge on the instrument panel.

about fuel-tank venting

Fuel tanks are vented so air can enter the tank as gas is pumped out. Otherwise, vacuum formed in a tank could cause the walls to collapse.

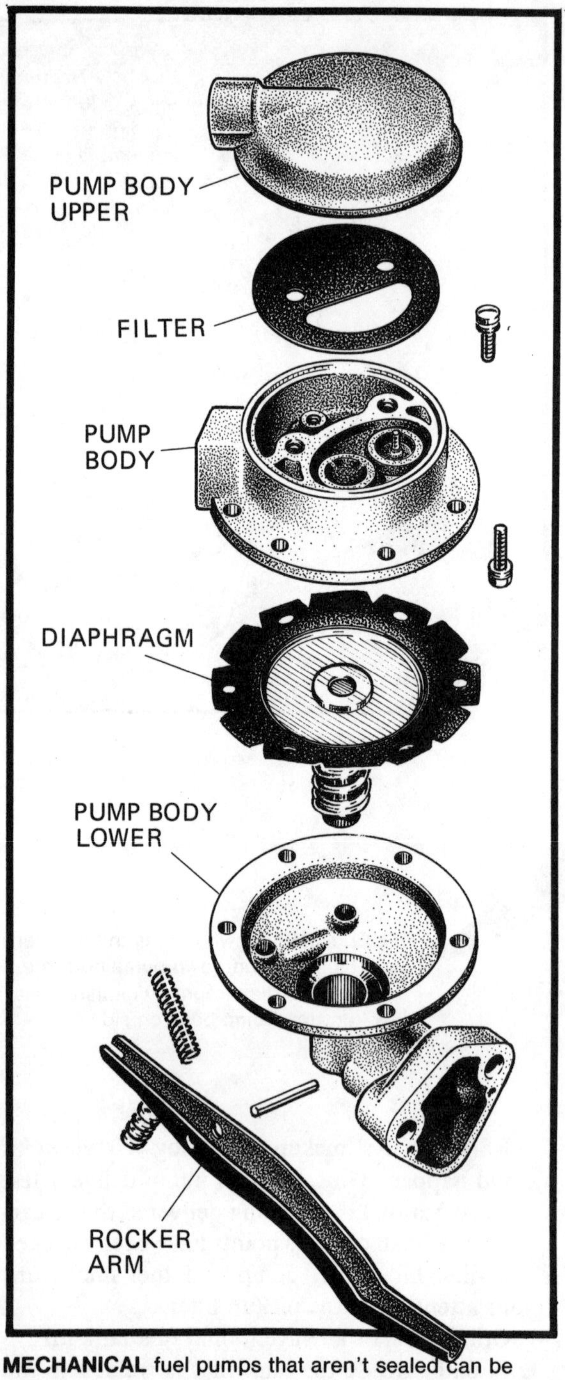

MECHANICAL fuel pumps that aren't sealed can be taken apart and restored with parts from a rebuild kit.

Some older cars had the vent in the gas cap. Other cars, including all present models with fuel evaporative control systems, have nonvented caps. A tube leading from inside the tank to the outside provides venting. In models with evaporative control, the vent line passes into the charcoal-filter canister in the engine compartment.

cleaning a fuel tank

If there is evidence of fuel tank contamination—that is, water in the fuel—the tank can be cleaned. In present domestically manufactured models, this involves dropping the tank. Some older and imported cars have a drain plug in the bottom of the tank. If you have one of these (the Triumph is one, for instance), draining the fuel and flushing the tank with alcohol while the tank remains on the car will usually decontaminate the tank.

To clean tanks without a built-in drain the general procedure is as follows:

Caution: Do this job in a well-ventilated area and away from everything that is likely to make a spark or flame. *No smoking.*

1. Disconnect the battery.
2. Siphon fuel tank.
3. Remove fuel tank (see below).
4. Remove the fuel sending-pickup assembly. A special wrench available from a car dealer or auto-tool dealer may be needed to get the plate off.
5. Inspect the pickup filter. Replace it if it is clogged with water.
6. Complete draining by rocking the tank and allowing fuel to pour out the fuel-sending-pickup assembly plate hole.
7. Pour running *hot* water through the tank for at least five minutes. Be sure all water is removed from the tank.
8. Allow the tank to air-dry thoroughly.
9. Reassemble everything.

FUEL FILTERS are designed into the fuel pump installed on many imported cars.

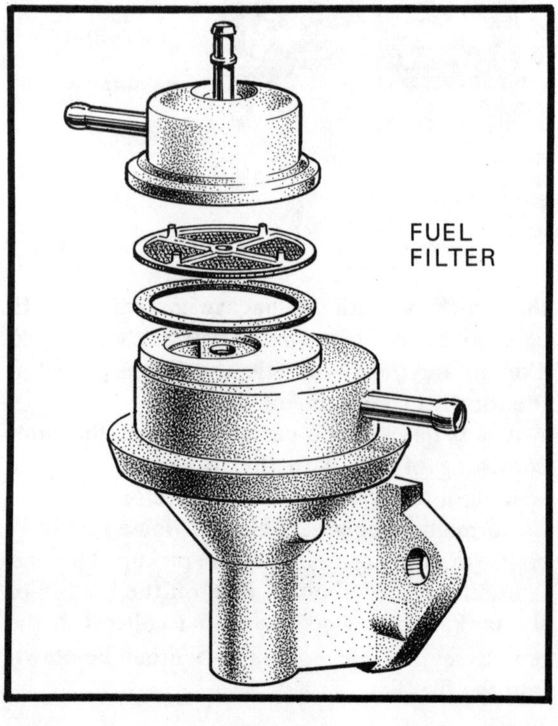

Note: If the tank shows evidence of rust, it should not be returned to service. Get another.

removing a fuel tank

The following will apply to your car although some variation in procedure may be required:

1. Disconnect the battery.
2. Siphon fuel from the tank.
3. Raise the car.
4. Disconnect all lines and wire at the tank, such as the sending unit wire and the fuel evaporative system line.
5. Support the tank by some method, such as a jack. However, be careful not to crush the tank. If you use a jack, place a block of wood between the top of the jack and the tank to serve as a pad.
6. Carefully remove the tank's supporting straps.
7. Lower the tank to the floor.

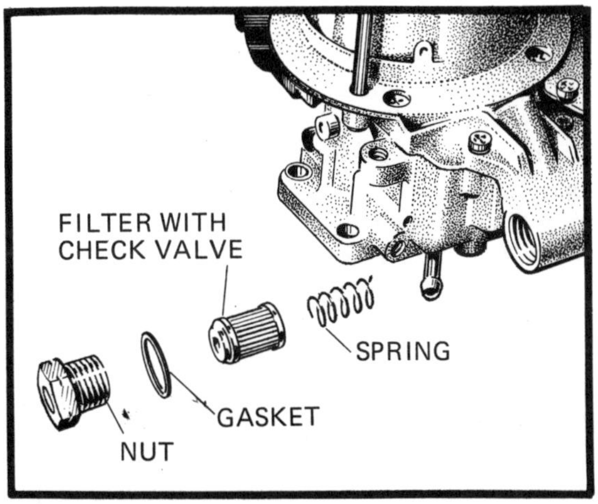

REMOVING carb-inlet-type filter requires care; don't lose the spring or gasket.

Caution: When installing a fuel tank, do not overtighten the support straps. Secure them until they bottom against the tank. Then torque the fasteners to about 25 ft.-lb.

types of fuel pumps

There are two kinds of fuel pumps: mechanical and electrical. Most American-made cars use the mechanical type, but there are exceptions. Chevrolet Vega is one.

The mechanical fuel pump is operated by a lobe of the camshaft. The pump's arm rests on this lobe. As the lobe revolves, pushing and relaxing the arm, suction is created inside the pump.

This suction draws gasoline from the fuel tank and pushes it to the carburetor. The critical parts of a mechanical fuel pump are:

- Inlet valve that opens to let fuel into the pump from the fuel tank.
- Outlet valve that opens to let fuel out of the pump to the carburetor.
- A flexible diaphragm that flutters alternately to draw in and push out fuel.
- A spring that controls diaphragm action.

In older domestic cars (pre-1968), it was possible to disassemble and overhaul a defective mechanical fuel pump. This can't be done with present-day fuel pumps, which are sealed. A bad pump has to be replaced.

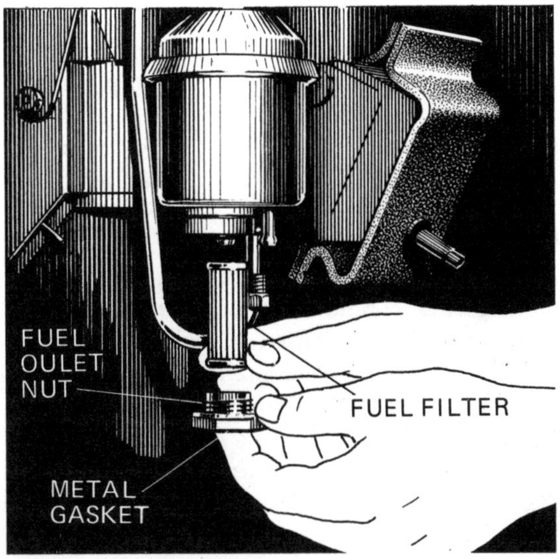

THE FUEL FILTER found on a Cadillac is installed at the bottom of the fuel pump.

Electric fuel pumps are used in many imported cars. They are normally placed close to the fuel tank, acting as pusher pumps rather than drawing pumps. In the Vega, for example, the fuel pump is in the fuel tank.

An electric fuel pump operates as long as the ignition switch is on, so be sure the switch is turned off when the car is not in use.

An electric fuel pump can fail because a mechanical part goes bad or because of an electrical malfunction. A mechanical defect requires that you replace the pump. Electrical failures require pinpointing the defect and repairing it.

testing the fuel pump

Testing is quite easy and may be done with nothing more esoteric in the way of equipment than a piece of vacuum hose and a glass graduate marked off in pints.

If you've been seeing gasoline on the ground under the fuel pump after the vehicle has been stationary, you don't even have to proceed with this test. Replace the pump. The diaphragm has gone bad.

To test fuel-pump delivery, disconnect the fuel line at the carburetor. Attach the hose, which should fit tightly. Place the end of the hose in the graduate.

Start the engine, running it for 30 to 45 seconds. The engine will run for at least this long on the fuel retained in the carburetor.

There should be at least one pint of gas in the graduate at the end of 45 seconds. If there isn't, the pump should be replaced.

Note: If your car is equipped with an electric fuel pump which has been giving failure signals, but the fuel delivery test proves satisfactory, the ignition-system output and fuel-pump electric circuit should be tested. A "failure signal" is engine cut-out that occurs during heavy acceleration or high speed because of fuel starvation.

replacing a fuel pump

Note: This procedure, which refers primarily to mechanical fuel pumps, may be used with variation to replace an electric fuel pump.

1. Disconnect the fuel line from the fuel tank.
2. Disconnect the fuel line going to the carburetor.
3. Remove the nuts holding the pump to the engine.
4. Turn the engine by turning the crankshaft pulley by hand until the pump's arm seems to be under the least pressure from the camshaft lobe.
5. Withdraw the pump slowly from the engine.
6. Scrape away old gasket material remaining on the engine.

Use a new gasket when fitting a new pump or returning the old pump to the engine. Apply a coating of gasket sealer to both sides of the gasket.

about those fuel lines

Two troubles, both rare, may strike a fuel line: foreign particles may clog the line or the line may spout a leak.

To clean out fuel lines, disconnect them at both ends—that is, at the fuel tank and fuel pump for one line, and at the fuel pump and carburetor for the other line. Blow compressed air through the lines in the direction opposite to fuel flow. Reconnect the lines.

If it becomes necessary to replace a fuel line, keep the following points in mind:

1. Use tubing that meets the manufacturer's specification, which is provided in the service manual.
2. Do not use copper or aluminum tubing to replace steel tubing. They can't stand the stress of normal vehicle vibration.
3. Be sure to locate tubing where tubing has been placed and hose where hose has been placed. Hose that has been accidentally placed near an exhaust-system part is a safety hazard.

fuel filters

With some exceptions, cars today possess one of two types of fuel filters: in-line or internal. The exceptions are cars having the fuel filter inside the fuel pump.

The fuel filter is the only part of the fuel system we are discussing that requires periodic maintenance. That maintenance is usually just to replace the filter. In one case (discussed below) the filter can be cleaned.

replacing a fuel filter

To replace an in-line filter, find the filter on the fuel line between the carburetor and fuel pump. It is a small chamber.

With the engine cold, move the retaining clips out of the way and slip the chamber off. Put a rag or receptacle under the filter to catch gas. Slip a new filter in place.

Caution: No smoking.

To replace an internal filter, with the engine cold:

1. Disconnect the fuel line at the carburetor inlet.
2. Remove the inlet filter nut.
3. Remove the filter and check the valve assembly. New fuel filters have a check valve to meet Motor Vehicle Safety Standards. The check valve prevents fuel discharge in case of a roll-over accident.
4. Remove the spring and examine it for damage and adequate tension. If it is okay, retain the spring for reuse.
5. Install the spring.
6. Install a new filter, making sure that the hole in the filter faces the nut.
7. Install a new gasket.
8. Install the inlet filter nut, tighten securely, and reconnect the fuel line tightly.

In the case of the Cadillac fuel filter, you will find it at the fuel pump outlet. You can reuse the metal gasket if it isn't damaged when replacing the filter.

A nylon-type filter in the fuel pump, such as those used by British Leyland, may be cleaned. To get at it, remove the fuel-pump dome retaining screw, remove the dome and sealing ring and lift out the filter. It's that easy.

TO KEEP abrasive paper on your orbital sander from breaking at the ends before the grit is worn out, try this stunt. Before installing the sandpaper, place two strips of masking tape across the paper at the ends. The tape will strengthen the paper at the points where it normally tears.—*Karl R. Timm, Jacksonville, FL.*

HERE'S A NOVEL use for loose-leaf rings. Use such rings to keep box-end wrenches together and in sequence, as well as keeping metrics from mixing with U.S. sizes. If possible, keep metrics on one ring, U.S. wrenches on a second.—*Gil Longwell, Hagerstown, MD.*

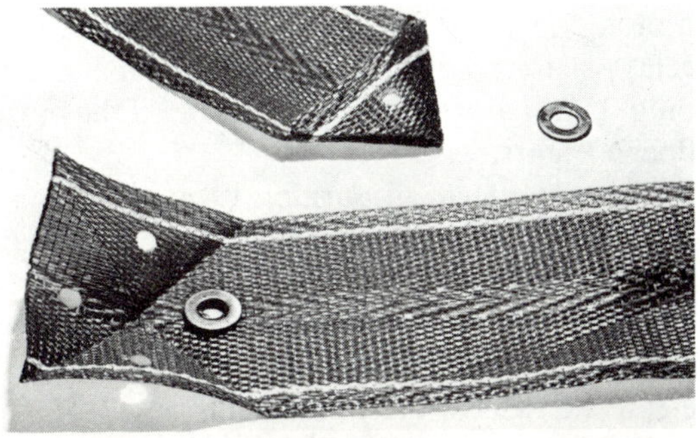

WHEN RENEWING the plastic webbing on folding lawn and patio chairs, increase the holding power of the cup screws by placing washers over the holes in the folded ends and inserting the screws through them. The washers help prevent raveling and tearing of the webbing at the holes.—*J. Carpenter, Williamstown, NJ.*

OLD NURSING BOTTLES make ideal glue or paint-applicator bottles. Simply insert the handle of a small modelmaker's brush through the hole in the nipple. The nipple provides an airtight seal around the brush, yet allows the brush to be pushed deeper into the bottle as glue level descends.—*William Butler, Liverpool, NY.*

A FILE TANG, preferably with sharply ground edges, can be used to enlarge holes in sheet metal if it's hardened first. Break off the flat file, heat the tang to cherry red, plunge it into cold water, then clamp it in a wooden slot. (A round file can be shortened and used in a regular file handle.)—*Peter Legon, Malden, MA.*

What to do until the serviceman comes? You can make many simple furnace repairs and temporarily restore heat by following these instructions

How to troubleshoot furnace failure

By STEPHEN J. HOWARD

■ IT'S A BITTER, 15-below night and the dawn is hours away—when suddenly you awake and realize the furnace isn't working.

At such times, the chances of getting a serviceman are pretty slim, but try anyway. Only instead of just shivering while waiting, do some troubleshooting yourself. You're likely to find the problem is a minor one you can fix nine out of ten times.

Before discussing what to do, let's define some terms to avoid confusion. Most heating systems consist of two sections. One is the burner portion where either gas or oil is burned to create heat. The other section delivers the heat to the rooms. Regardless of whether you have an oil or gas burner, the delivery will be made by hot water, steam or forced air. Thus, your first checks should be concerned with the source of heat, the burner.

checking an oil burner

If trouble hits your oil-fired furnace, try the following:

• *Check thermostat operation.* Set it 5° above the indicated room temperature and the burner should start. If you have an automatic day-night thermostat, be sure the cycle isn't reversed.

Open the thermostat cover. A mercury dial control is sealed and seldom gives trouble. But if you have a contact-point control, dirt on the points could prevent operation. Just pass a new dollar bill or a business card between the points.

• *Check all emergency switches.* Someone may have turned off one accidentally.

Most oil burners have two switches: One is usually on the burner; the other often at a distant location, such as near the head of the basement stairway or above the basement door leading to the yard. Know where these switches are and make sure they are turned on.

• *Check the two safety switches.* The overload and the stack control relay prevent damage if a problem develops in the electrical circuit.

The overload switch (usually painted red) is on the motor housing. Press it once only. If the motor doesn't start, activate the stack control relay (on the smoke pipe or burner housing) once only. Don't fool with these switches if the burner doesn't start.

Many modern oil-burning furnaces are controlled by a photoelectric cell. If dirty, it can prevent operation.

If you press the stack control relay and the furnace goes on and then off in about 30 seconds, clean the face of the photoelectric cell.

• *Check the fuse or circuit breaker.* Vibration can loosen a fuse, so make certain that it's tight.

If the fuse keeps blowing or a circuit breaker trips repeatedly, there's a malfunction in the electrical system, which should be checked out by a serviceman.

• *Check the oil valve.* Another malfunction in a late-model oil-burning furnace can be a delayed oil valve that's dirt-clogged or electrically faulty. You *can* run the burner without it in a pinch. Disconnect both input and output oil lines on the valve and remove the valve. Then connect the input directly to the output line.

• *Check oil supply.* Gauges on indoor tanks can stick, showing an oil reserve when there is none. Tap the gauge. If the cap of an outside tank is accessible, take a dipstick reading.

• *Check the nozzle.* Finally, the malfunction could be in the oil nozzle-and-electrode assembly inside the burner. Check them out but first be sure to turn off all emergency switches. *Never work inside the burner with the switches turned on.*

SEE ALSO
Basement remodeling . . . Emergencies . . . Family rooms . . . Fireplaces . . . Heating systems, home . . . Humidifiers . . . Stoves, wood-burning

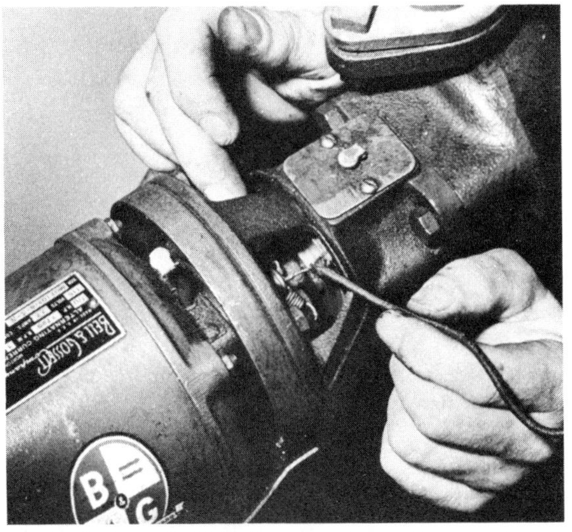

A BROKEN COUPLING in a circulator often can be repaired temporarily by wiring the parts together.

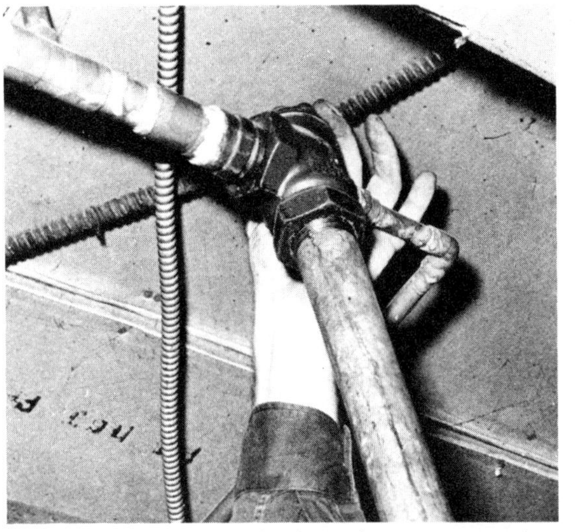

THE FLOW VALVE, usually hidden in a corner, can be opened to feed hot water through the system by gravity.

Remove the access plate, or unscrew and drop the transformer so you can reach inside the burner. Loosen the oil line connection with a wrench and disconnect the transformer and electrode wires. These are usually held by snap-on connectors. Take the electrode-nozzle assembly out of the burner, being careful not to change the setting of the electrodes.

Unscrew the nozzle. You'll find a filter inside. Unscrew that and wash it in warm water. (It could be clogged and blocking oil flow.) You'll find a small setscrew inside the nozzle. Unscrew that, too, and wash it.

Now blow into the nozzle. Air will pass through freely if it is clear and working. If not, you're out of luck unless you have a spare nozzle on hand.

Don't try to open the preset nozzle with an icepick. Probing will widen the hole, upset the fuel ratio and cause the burner to puff. Although this can't harm the system, the burner won't function.

Clean the electrodes carefully, using a rag or fine steel wool. Again, *do not disturb the setting* or puffing will occur. Put everything back together, turn on the emergency switches and

FILTERS in forced-air systems will greatly reduce available heat if dirty or clogged. Check them often.

IF AN OIL BURNER FAILS, locate the overload switch (usually found on the motor housing) and press.

THE STACK CONTROL RELAY is usually located on the smoke pipe or burner housing. Press it only once.

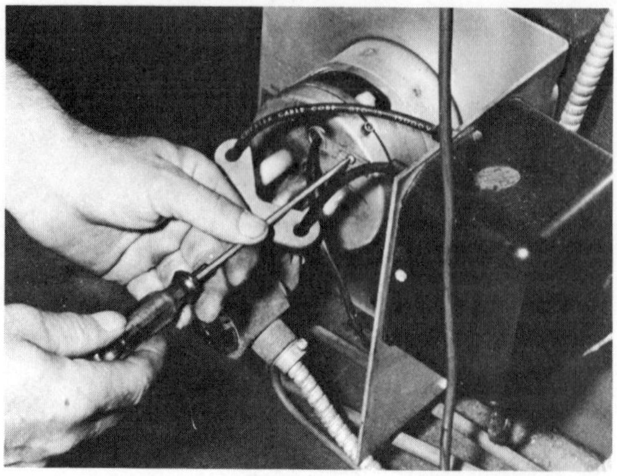

AN OIL BURNER may be controlled by a photoelectric cell. Just remove the small screw to gain access.

press the stack control relay.

If your burner is of the rotary type it won't have a nozzle. Just reach into the burner with a rag and carefully wipe the electrodes clean. And make sure that all emergency switches are off.

checking a gas burner

If you have a gas-fired heating system, check the thermostat, fuse or circuit breaker, and boiler, circulator or forced-air unit, the same as with an oil burner. A gas burner has but one electrical switch and that's mounted on the furnace. Check it to be sure that it's turned on.

• *Check the gas pilot.* If it's not burning, relight it as detailed on the instruction plate attached to the furnace. A pilot that refuses to light may be clogged with dirt or carbon. Shut off the electrical switch and the gas valves controlling the main burner as well as the pilot. Tap the pilot burner with a screwdriver, then turn on its control valve and try to light the pilot. Do not open the valve controlling the main burner before the pilot is lit, and do not try to light the main burner by hand—it could flare up when ignited.

checking delivery systems

If you haven't found the trouble by now, it's time to attack the delivery part of the setup. What we describe here applies to both oil and gas-fired furnaces.

• *Steam systems: Check the boiler gauge.* The burner will shut off automatically if the water level gets too low. But before refilling a hot boiler, let it cool down to avoid the chance of cracking. The burner should run again when the boiler gauge reaches the half-full mark.

• *Hot-water systems: Check the circulator.* One in need of lubrication won't circulate hot water, even though the burner itself will continue to run. However, relubricate only with grades of oil and/or cup grease recommended on the instruction plate found on the circulator body.

If there is a reset button on the circulator, press it once. If no button, try giving the unit a slap with your hand.

A circulator will stop heat delivery if it breaks a coupling. Put your ear close to a suspected part and listen for a sharp, rapping sound. To repair a broken coupling temporarily, remove the access cover and wire the broken crosspieces together.

If you can't fix the circulator and the burner is operating, you may still get some heat. Most hot-water systems have a flow valve on the water line that runs from the furnace to the heat-radiating components. Just open the valve and hot water will be fed through the system by gravity.

• *Forced-air system: Check for a clogged filter,* a major cause of reduced heat. If no spare, remove the filter (there may be more than one), take it outside and knock it against something hard to loosen the dirt. Better yet, go over the filter with the radiator attachment of your vacuum cleaner to pull out much of the dirt.

• *Check the blower fan belt.* The only practical solution for a broken fan belt on the blower-motor pulleys is replacement, so it's wise to keep a spare handy. Put it on the blower-motor pulleys and tighten the adjusting nut (usually behind the blower motor) until the belt has a ½ to ¾-in. play.

• *Check the blower motor.* A short is usually indicated by on-off cycling in short spurts or by its refusal to run at all. However, while waiting for the serviceman, you *can* get some heat, since the burner is still functioning. Just remove all filters from the furnace. Since hot air rises, some heat will go through the ducts to the registers.

USE A CLEAN CLOTH to wipe off the face of the cell. On-off cycling usually indicates a dirty unit.

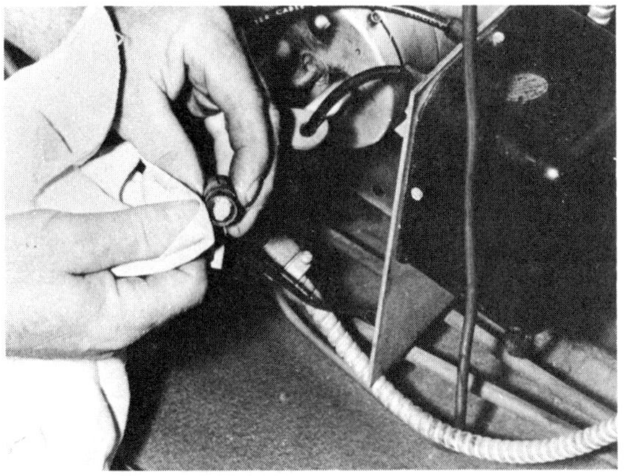

MODERN OIL BURNERS may have a delayed oil valve. In a pinch, remove the valve and connect the lines.

In the event of electrical failure in your area, you may still be able to produce heat in your home, provided your furnace is gas-fired. An oil burner requires power to pump oil from the storage tank to the furnace unit. It's easy with a self-energizing steam or hot-water system because the gas burner functions normally despite power failures. But a forced hot-water or forced-air system depends on electricity to operate a pump or blower. Also, a main burner that's not self-energizing won't ignite because it depends on an electrical impulse from the thermostat.

Does this mean you're out of luck? Not necessarily, for you can get the main burner going if it has a manual control on its motor-control valve. Simply press or turn the control or, in some cases, lift a lever protruding from the housing of the motorized valve until the burner is ignited by the pilot.

With the main burner of a forced hot-water system firing, open the flow valve on the water line to let hot water feed through the system by gravity.

With the main burner of a forced-air system on, remove the air filters from the cold-air return duct to induce circulation and let warm air be fed by gravity to the registers.

You can't sit back while this heat is getting to you, however. Watch that burner to make sure that excess pressure and temperature aren't building up. Some burners have a throttling device on the gas line to raise and lower the flame (like that on a kitchen range). Lower the flame every half-hour to let the burner cool down. If there is no throttle, shut off the manual control every half-hour for 10 minutes.

This is important! When power is restored, close that manual control.

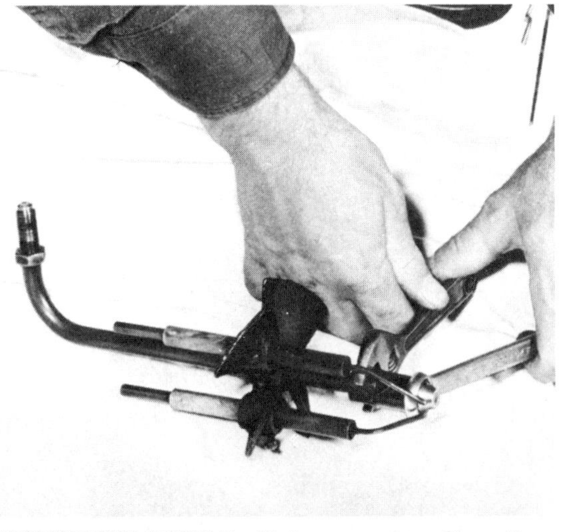

REMOVE THE NOZZLE with two wrenches. Clean the filter and setscrew, test the nozzle and then reassemble.

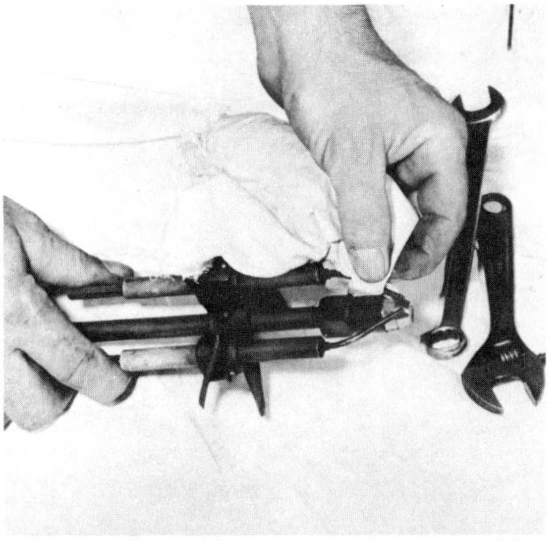

CARBON MAY BE FOULING the electrodes. Wipe them off with either a clean cloth or fine steel wool.

How to repair scratches in furniture

■ MARS IN FURNITURE—scratches, nicks and dents—often can be corrected by the owner. First, when you buy a new piece of furniture, you'll find that most manufacturers give specific instructions for the care of the finish. Save these booklets and follow the instructions. If you lack such aids, the information on these pages will help you keep your furniture looking its best, allowing it to age gracefully. Keep in mind that because of the variety of ways that different finishes can be damaged, you have no guarantee that results will always be successful. When attempting a repair, always test the planned repair on an inconspicuous area and make certain treatment is compatible with finish. If you have doubts, consult a professional refinisher.

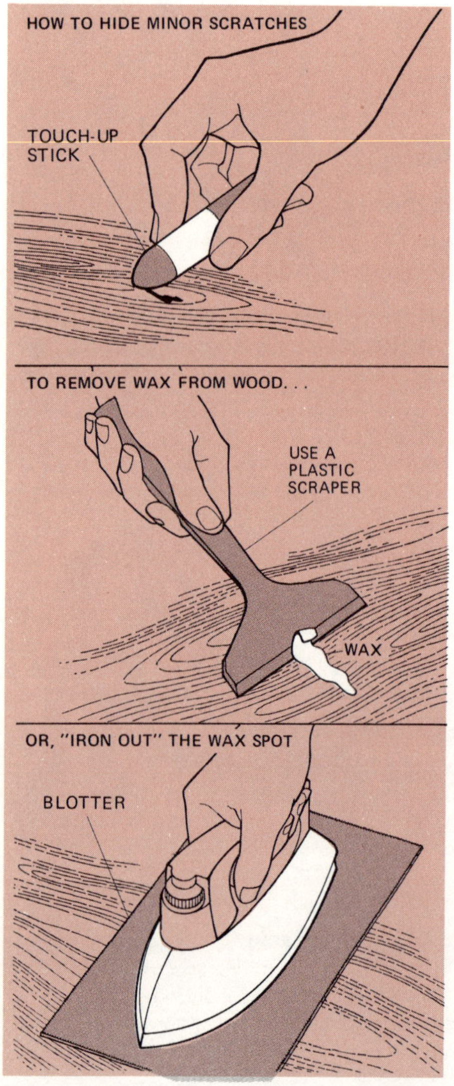

HOW TO CORRECT COMMON PROBLEMS

■ *Alcohol and other liquids* such as perfumes and medicines should be wiped up immediately. If the liquid remains on for a period of time, the finish may soften. Allow spot to dry, then use a staining polish of a shade close to the finish. If this doesn't do the job, try rubbing liquid or paste wax into the wood, using your fingers. For oil finishes, make a paste of finely powdered rotten-stone and boiled linseed oil and apply it to the damaged area, using a piece of felt or cotton swabs and rubbing lightly with grain. Then wipe the area dry with a clean cloth and polish the surface.

■ *Minor nicks and scratches* that have not penetrated the surface are called blemishes by professionals. These are more easily repaired. Your first try should be with a scratch-concealing (tinted) polish. If unsuccessful, apply a touch-up stick to the area (see top drawing). These are available in a variety of colors; if you cannot find a stick that comes close to the furniture color, try using a combination of two or more sticks to mix desired shade. Fill the scratch with this and rub well. Finally, polish with wax and a soft cloth. A couple of "home remedies" that work: shoe polish applied with a cotton swab and buffed dry. On cherry or mahogany pieces, iodine will sometimes conceal scratches.

■ *Minor burns* are a little more difficult to repair. Sometimes these can be hidden by rubbing with a poultice (paste) consisting of lemon juice and cigaret ashes. Apply with a gentle, circular rubbing motion and wipe clean. When dry, apply scratch-concealing polish. For major burns call in an expert.

■ *Candle wax* can be removed by chipping off as much as possible with a plastic scraper (center drawing). Follow by wiping with a cloth dampened with mineral spirits. On stubborn wax spots, place an ice cube over the spot for a few seconds to harden the wax, and repeat scraping. Frequently, wax can be ironed off. Place a heavy blotter on the spot and press with an iron set on "warm." The blotter absorbs the wax. Finish with liquid polish and a brisk rubbing. Water spots can usually be removed using same technique. To remove white rings, rub with a thin paste consisting of wax and mineral spirits. When dry, apply a thin coat of cleaning polish or paste wax.

CARE OF PLASTIC-LAMINATE FURNITURE

There are now available easy-to-use commercial plastic-laminate cleaners. Sold in a pressurized can, the cleaner is simply sprayed on the laminate and wiped with a clean, soft cloth. Before applying the cleaner/polish, first wash the surface using a mild soap or detergent and water solution to remove spots. Allow surface to dry before applying the polish. Although many homeowners mistakenly believe that plastic laminates are virtually indestructible, remember that they are not. Take precautions. Protect surface from hot vessels with trivets; do not use a kitchen countertop for slicing vegetables. Do your cutting on a cutting board.

ROUTINE FURNITURE CARE

Routine care means frequent dusting, occasional washing, periodic cleaning and waxing, and making minor repairs. *Dusting.* Should be done several times a week using a clean, lint-free absorbent cloth. *Washing.* At least annually use a mild, sudsy soap-and-water mix. Dip rag and wring out well. Take care so you do not overwet joints or glued parts will loosen. Work fast. Wash, rinse and dry a small area at a time; make certain you overlap washed areas. *Complete cleaning.* At least once a year, before applying a new coat of wax, give the wood finish a thorough cleaning. First remove old wax film with a clean cloth dampened with mineral spirits or, even better, a *synthetic turpentine* with an oily base. (Turpentine can leave a sticky residue.) Mineral spirits and synthetic turpentine are available at most paint stores. If many layers of wax have accumulated, use a cleanser-conditioner to completely remove dirt buildup. Do a small area at a time, drying worked areas as you go. To clean out crevices, such as in carvings, wrap absorbent cotton around a pointed stick (drawing, above left). Dampen cotton with mineral spirits and clean out desired areas. Wipe and dry the crevices as you proceed. Finish with a thin coat of liquid wax; rub thoroughly with piece of flannel.

SEE ALSO

Finishes, wood . . . Laminates, plastic . . . Sanding . . . Stains, removing . . . Wood finishes

SOME FURNITURE DOS AND DON'TS

Do immediately remove spilled liquids using a blotting rather than wiping action.
Do lift objects to move them. Lamps and ashtrays should not be dragged across a surface.
Do use trivets or pads to avoid burns.
Do use only polishes recommended for furniture. A self-polishing floor wax, for example, could soften and damage a wood finish.
Do use only soft, lintfree cloths for polishing. If using old shirts, remove all buttons and seams. Since some contain an abrasive starch, do not use cheesecloth to polish.
Do work *with* the grain of the wood whether washing, cleaning, polishing or waxing.
Don't use a new polish or cleaning agent without first testing on an inconspicuous area.
Don't use nail-polish remover on furniture.
Don't attempt the repair of badly damaged surfaces yourself. If you create a large damaged area, the inevitable calling-in of a pro will just up the cost of repair.
Don't place rubber or vinyl products (mats and coasters) on furniture surfaces unless the manufacturer states that they are intended for such purpose. Lacking this assurance, place a piece of felt under each lamp, ashtray and the like to serve as a protective pad for the furniture.
Don't wash painted furniture too frequently. Repeated washings or heavy scrubbings will eventually change the color.
Don't wax or polish a painted piece of furniture unless the product you plan to use is guaranteed not to discolor paint finishes.

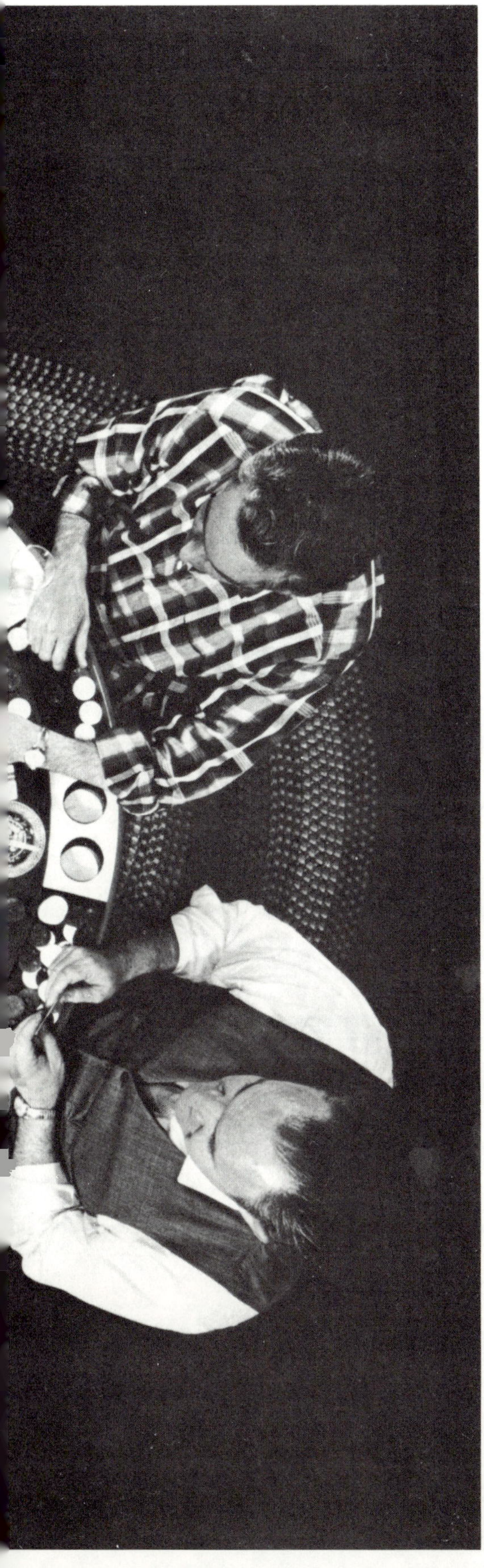

A game table for your playroom

From cards to bingo, this circular table is the ticket to more fun with family and friends in your home. It's easy to construct with standard materials and tools

■ HERE'S A WORKSHOP project that will provide hours of enjoyment for your family and friends. It's a family game table for most any game you want to play and, best of all, it's easy to construct with basic lumberyard materials.

Basically, the table consists of three circular assemblies—a bottom chip-and-glass tray, a center disc, and a felt-covered top—all cut from A-D plywood to nest one on top of the other.

You start with the center disc. If you have a router, you can cut a perfect circle by tethering it to a strip of wood with a nail in the end. If you don't have a router, use your sabre saw. Four quarter-circle segments are cut from 1/4-in.

SEE ALSO

**Air games . . . Basement remodeling . . .
Bridge tables . . . Caddies, table tennis . . .
Coffee tables . . . Dining tables . . .
Family rooms . . . Nesting tables . . .
Party tables . . . Pool tables . . .
Shuffleboard tables . . . Snack tables**

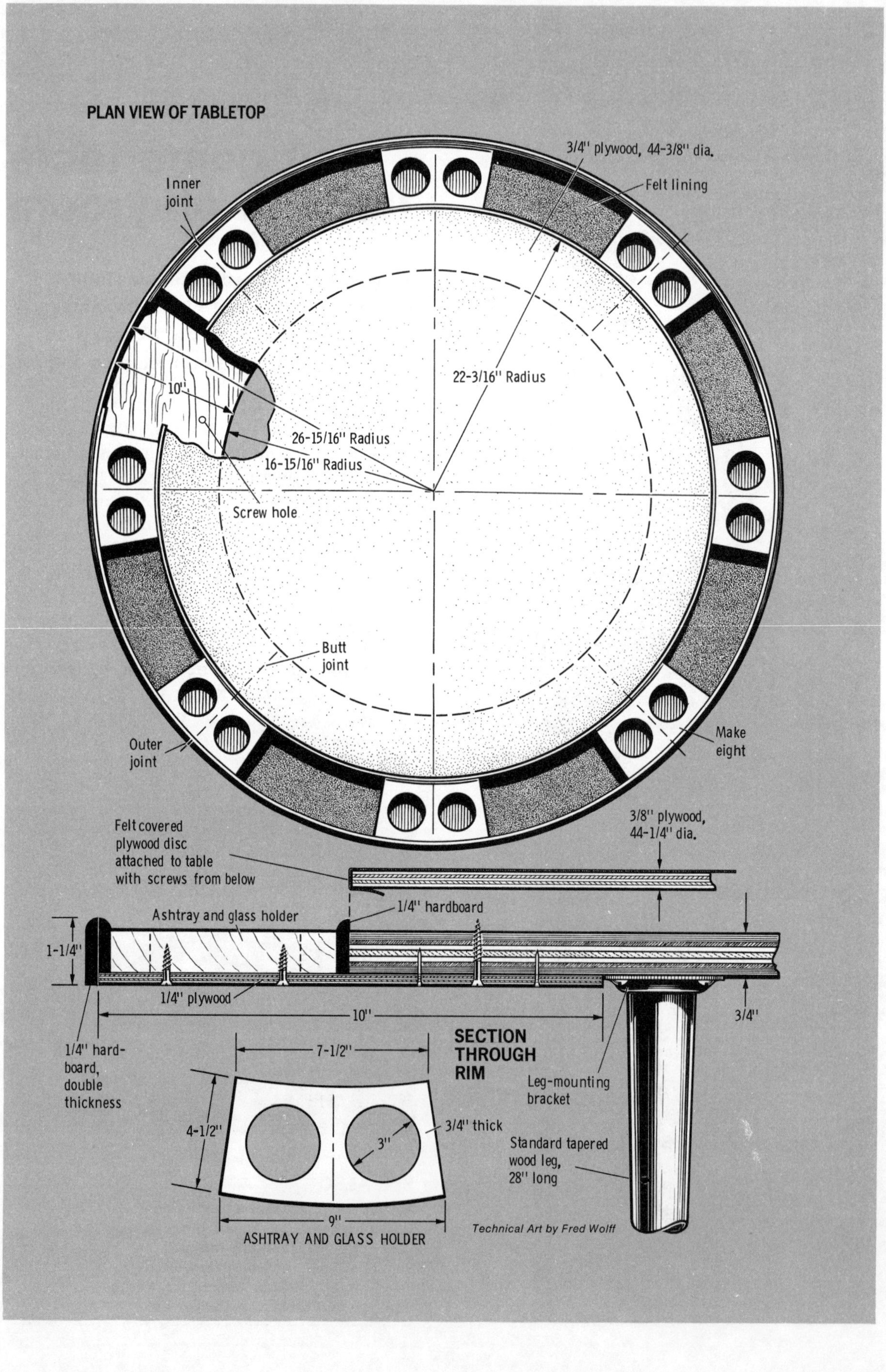
PLAN VIEW OF TABLETOP
3/4" plywood, 44-3/8" dia.
Felt lining
Inner joint
22-3/16" Radius
10"
26-15/16" Radius
16-15/16" Radius
Screw hole
Butt joint
Outer joint
Make eight
Felt covered plywood disc attached to table with screws from below
3/8" plywood, 44-1/4" dia.
1/4" hardboard
Ashtray and glass holder
1-1/4"
1/4" plywood
10"
3/4"
1/4" hard-board, double thickness
7-1/2"
SECTION THROUGH RIM
Leg-mounting bracket
4-1/2"
3"
3/4" thick
Standard tapered wood leg, 28" long
9"
ASHTRAY AND GLASS HOLDER
Technical Art by Fred Wolff

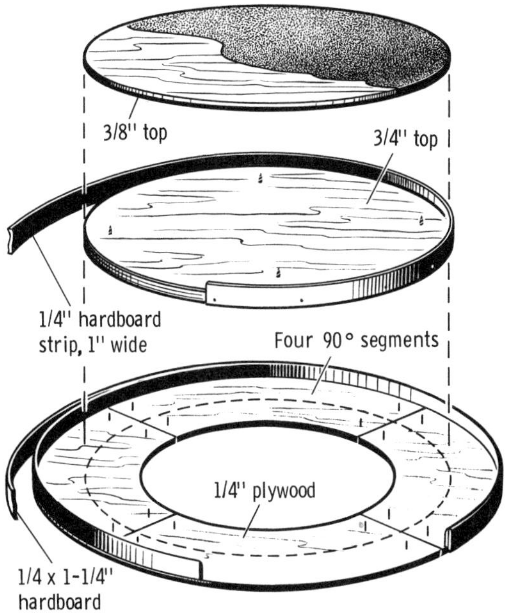

HOW THE PARTS SANDWICH TOGETHER

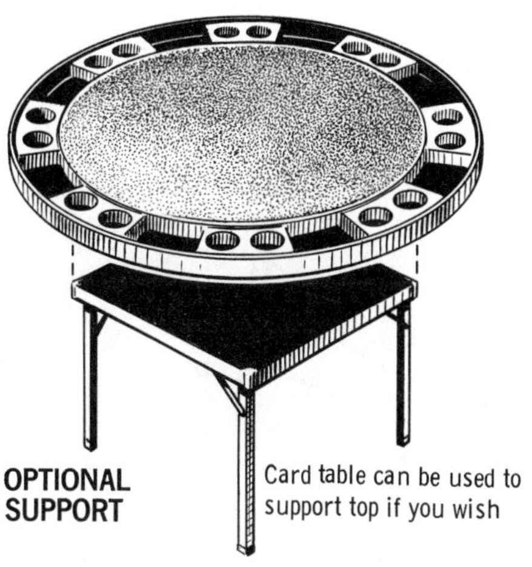

plywood and nailed to the underside of the center disc to form a tray. Then the edge of the disc is "wrapped" with a 1-in.-wide strip of ¼-in. hardboard and nailed and glued. Next, eight glass-holder dividers are added equidistant around the plywood tray, four of them being placed over the butted joints.

Finally, the outer edge is wrapped with a double strip of hardboard. Glue and nail one at a time and place the joints of the two strips 180° apart. The top playing surface is a ⅜-in. plywood disc, which is covered with green felt. The legs screw into metal mounting plates you can buy.

FELT CAN BE STRETCHED without puckering if you first staple one edge and then the edge opposite.

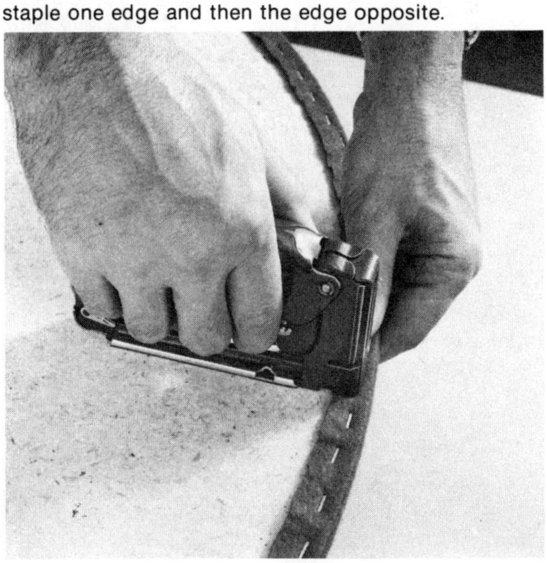

A CAN of spray paint is the best way of finishing ready-made legs in almost any color.

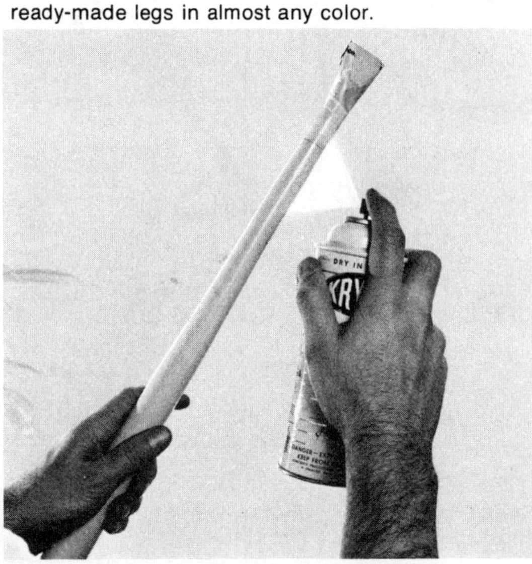

Keep your garage door rolling

By STEVEN J. HOWARD

There are eight basic problems that can keep your overhead garage door from swinging properly. You'll find them here plus some simple repairs that will help keep your door maintenance-free for many months

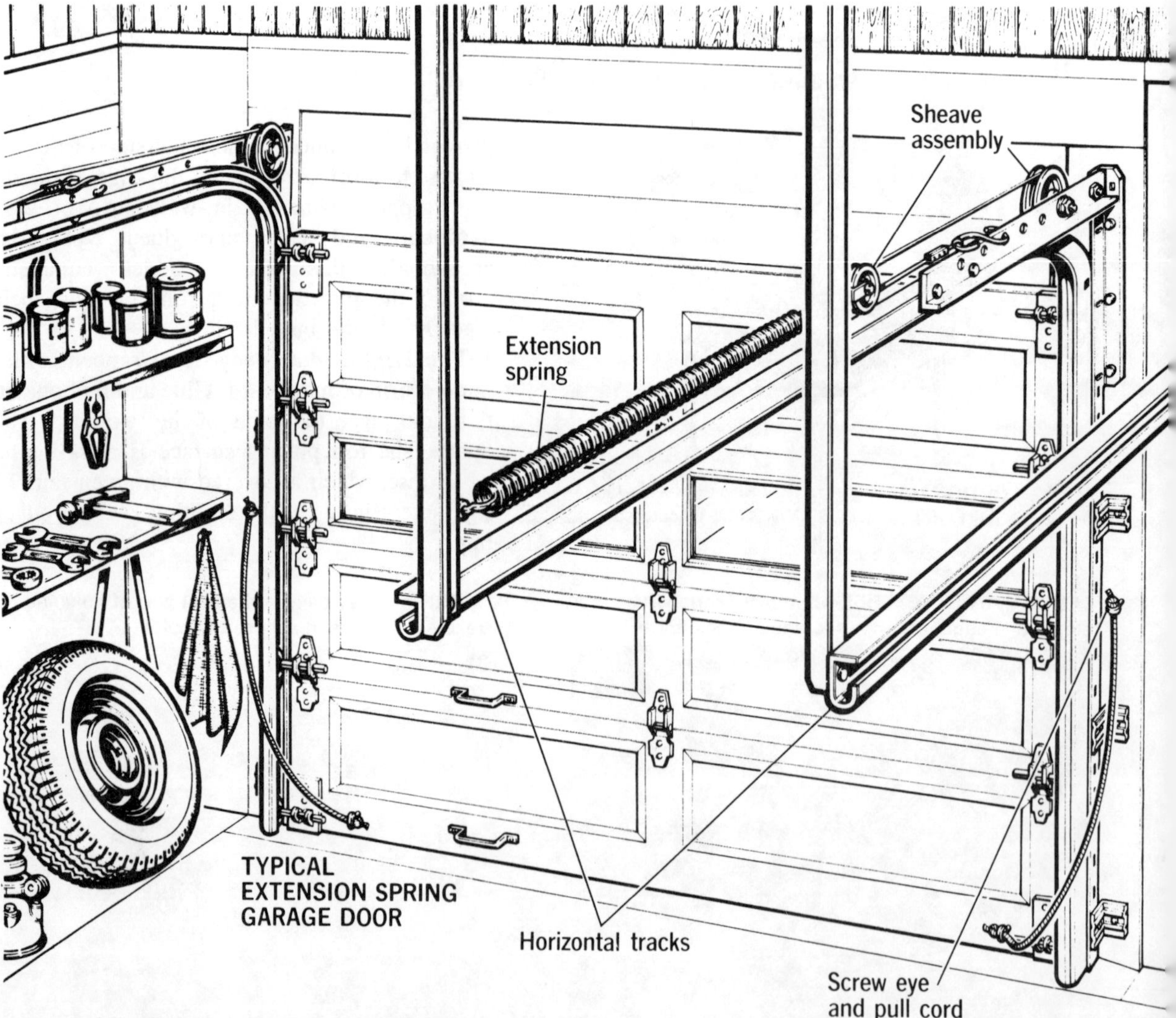

SEE ALSO
Garage remodeling . . . Garages, storage . . . Lubrication, home . . . Storage ideas

■ SOME PEOPLE NEVER have trouble with their garage doors. Others start having headaches the day the doors are installed.

Why? There are actually eight reasons.

1. Enough forces are working against a door to knock it out of adjustment.

2. Bolts, screws and lags holding hardware can loosen in time.

3. Wooden doors often absorb moisture and get too heavy for simple spring adjustment.

4. Rainy spells will also cause wooden doors and stops to swell, creating binding and friction.

5. Anything added to the door after initial adjustment and balance (such as glass, decorations, even paint) increases weight and can throw the springs out of balance.

6. Dirt in the tracks increases friction.

7. Lack of lubrication or dirty lubricant will also add to door problems.

8. Any physical damage to either the doors or tracks will affect their operation.

These eight factors will affect both extension-spring and torsion-spring overhead-type doors. The extension-spring type, identified by springs along both horizontal tracks, is the easiest to work on—you can repair and adjust it yourself.

The torsion-spring door is identified by torsion springs wrapped around a shaft that can be seen across the top of the door when it is closed. Cables in a torsion-spring setup wind on winch-like drums attached to the same shaft as the springs.

Here's the only rub—you shouldn't attempt to adjust torsion springs by yourself. According to

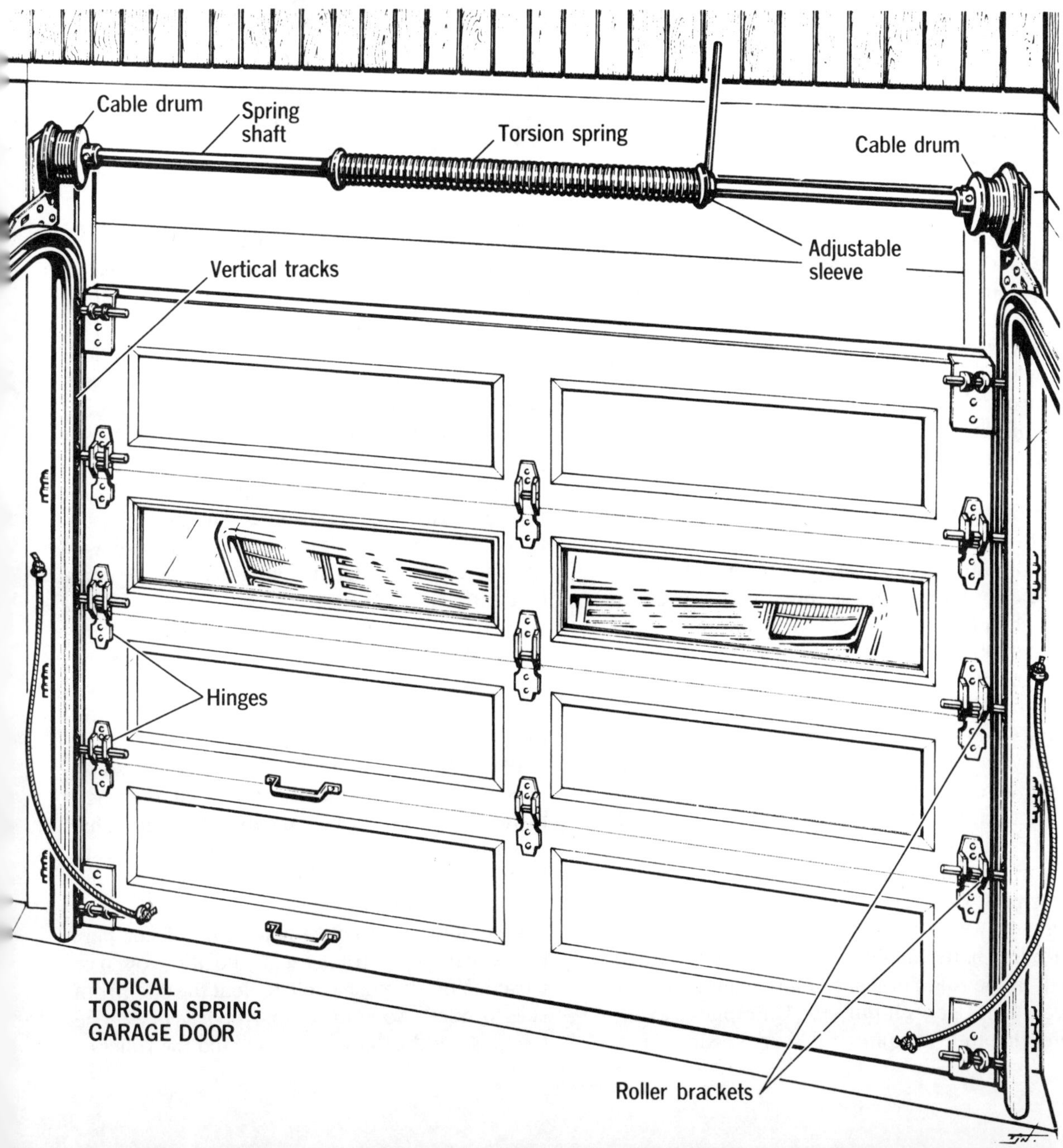

TYPICAL TORSION SPRING GARAGE DOOR

REDUCING FRICTION between the door and the track (left) or the door and the stop (right) requires bolt adjustment.

one door manufacturer, "The only way spring force of a torsion-spring door can be increased is by winding the springs additional turns. This requires two bars to hold the winding plugs. The springs are under tremendous tension and someone who has had no experience in the job can be seriously injured. We recommend a professional if adjustment is required to any torsion-spring setup, other than oiling and adjusting of hardware."

Before getting to service information I suggest you first get a diagram calling out the specific parts of your particular door. The manufacturer of the door will usually supply it if you give him the right information. Look for a name and serial number plate near the lock. Tell the manufacturer the width and height of the door, its material (wood, fiberglass, steel), model name (if available), serial number and approximate age.

Now let's take each major door problem and see how to handle it.

Friction, for instance, is the most prevalent. To cure it, use a fairly heavy grade of oil (No. 20 is best) on pulley, ball bearings, door rollers and hinge pins. Only a few drops are needed at each point.

Roller shafts should be free to slide back and forth in the roller bracket. Many manufacturers recommend general-purpose Lubriplate, available through automotive stores, since it's waterproof and unaffected by weather changes.

Another lubrication spot you shouldn't miss is inside the track where the rollers slide, especially around curved portions.

Should lubrication fail to solve the friction problem, check the door and door stops to see where and to what degree paint has been rubbed off. If you find evidence of excessive rubbing, you have two alternatives: You can move the stops away from the door if rubbing is localized in one or two areas, or you can move the door away from the stops if it is a general problem—that is, if rubbing occurs along most of the contact surface.

In the latter case, examine the hardware alongside of each track. Brackets holding the track away from the door may be spot-welded and not adjustable, or attached with bolts and fully adjustable.

If you have a door with adjustable brackets, loosen the bolts holding the track, pull the track toward you about ⅛ in. and tighten the nuts. This will usually alleviate the problem. If you find friction localized to a few smaller areas, plane the stop to remove high spots.

It is important to have ¼ to ½ in. of side play between door and tracks at any position, open or closed. You should be able to float the door from side to side ¼ to ½ in. If not, the tracks may be too close to the door edge and bind the rollers.

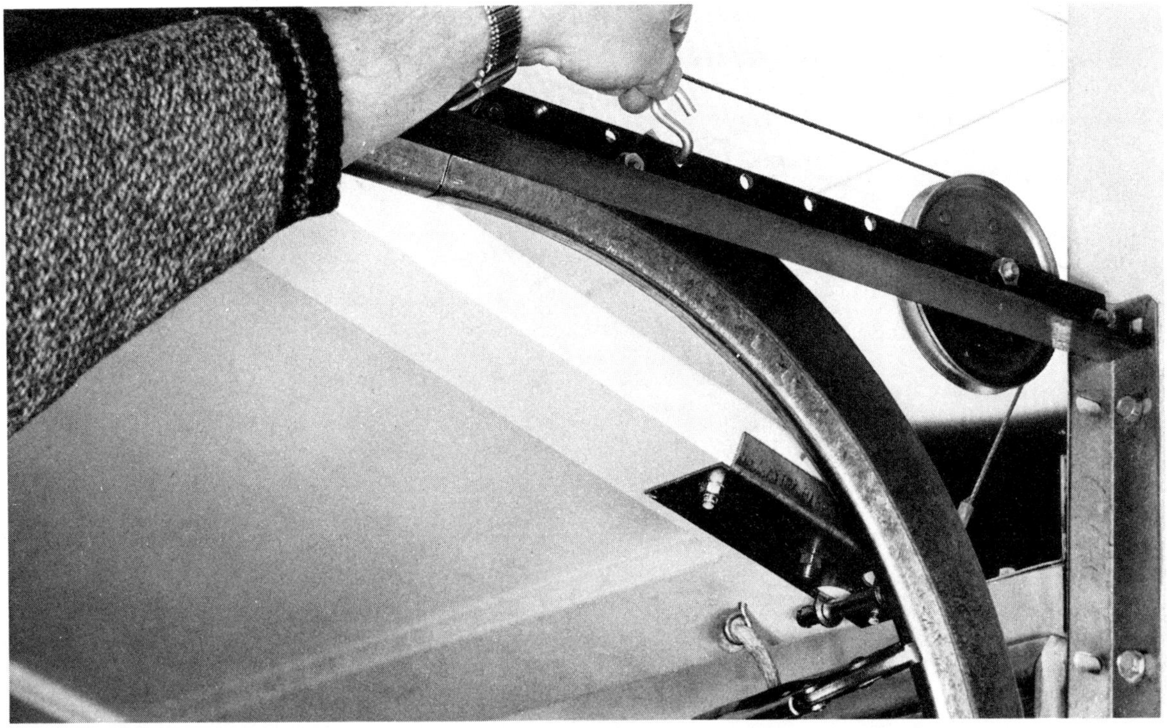

COMMON WAY to adjust spring tension is to change the S-hook placement. Vise clamps are used to hold the door.

To adjust, simply go back to the track brackets, back out the lags a few turns and move the tracks farther apart. Make sure tracks are vertical and evenly spaced by checking with a carpenter's level.

Spacing tracks too far apart is not a good idea. This could permit one side to reach higher than the other during open cycles. The condition, called "racking," wedges the door in the track and stops it.

The next problem is the door that is overweight due to moisture. Tip-offs to a moisture problem are surface checks and small cracks in panels. Springs can be adjusted to compensate for added weight, but during a dry spell you should thoroughly sand panels and repaint *both sides* with a quality exterior paint.

Adjusting for weight is done by putting more stretch in springs. But remember—do this only on extension-spring doors.

Most extension-spring doors are adjusted from the cable's dead end fastened to the horizontal track reinforcing member near the door opening headers.

No matter how springs are adjusted, the door must be opened and propped, since springs will be detached and the door can fall. Prop the door open with clamps or by putting a strong ladder beneath it.

Many doors are anchored by S-hooks. To increase spring tension, first move one hook forward a few holes, then move the hook on the other side the same amount.

On some doors, spring adjustment is made by moving the back end of the extension spring over a notched bar. On still others, adjustments are made with an eyebolt and nut through the rear track hanger.

Next check for the proper balance point. With the bottom of the door 1 to 2 ft. off the floor, it should neither tend to raise or fall by itself. Above this position, a well-balanced door will tend to rise slowly by itself. Below it, the door should fall by itself.

If it's no longer possible to balance the door with the present springs, they should be replaced with stronger ones. If you can identify the make of door, you can probably get them from a dealer. If not, weigh the door (detach the springs and lower the door onto a bathroom scale placed under the center of the door).

You'll probably need help. A one-car garage door weighs up to 150 pounds; two-car sizes weigh 300 pounds and more. When you know the weight, ask a dealer to get workable springs.

To keep a working door troublefree, lubricate all moving and turning parts once every six months. At that time, tighten all loose bolts, check the cables for fraying or wear and make sure one hasn't slipped off its sheave.

THE REMODELED EXTERIOR shows windows chosen to fill the old garage-door opening. Interior can be duplicated by a careful craftsman.

This was once an attached garage

By HARRY WICKS

THE FIREPLACE and hearth form the focal center of the room. Decorative panel-inserts flanking fireplace have dimmer-controlled lights behind.

SEEKING A SPACIOUS family entertainment center close to the kitchen, Mr. and Mrs. Robert M. Skare of Golden Valley, Minn., chose to utilize the already attached garage for that "addition." The decision not only eliminated architectural design problems, but, in fact, improved the exterior appearance because the garage doors—which faced the street—were replaced with windows that are completely compatible with those in the existing house. And, as can be seen from these pictures, what the owners saved on structural costs they used for a detailed, and very elegant, interior-finish treatment.

The Skares decided that the creation of a cathedral ceiling meant that the joists (called collar beams in a garage) would have to go. Without them, the roof would very likely sag under a heavy load, so they called in contractor William Schneck & Sons to solve the problem.

The first thing done was to snake in a 6 x 12-in. beam beneath the ridgeboard. This transferred the roof load to the ground via spiked-together 2 x 10-in. headers over the studs. The existing rafters were then tied into the new beam. [*PM's architect simplifies construction even further (as shown in the drawing on page 1315), and he assures us it is equally sound structurally. Either way, after drafting your plans, you are well advised to discuss the project with your local building department. Proper weight transferral to the ground is too important to leave to guesswork. And almost every job is different because of variables such as length of ridge, rafter-run and the like.*]

SEE ALSO

Basement remodeling . . . Family rooms . . . Fireplaces . . . Floors . . . Garage doors . . . House additions . . . Lumber . . . Measurements . . . Remodeling . . . Remodeling, exterior

Next, full-thick, foil-face insulation was installed between rafters and the ceiling was skinned with ½-in. plasterboard. Simulated rafters were added (to divide the ceiling) at 6½-ft. intervals. Finally, for acoustical reasons, the plasterboard ceiling was sprayed with textured cement-type paint.

Floor. It was necessary to remove the existing concrete floor along three sides of the outside perimeter in order to dig a trench to contain the heat ducts. To minimize heat loss, 1-in. Styrofoam was placed along the footings. Next, the concrete was leveled to match the existing floor and 6-mil polyethylene was placed over the floor to cut down any chance of moisture damage to carpeting from below.

In this home, the original heating plant was large enough to take on the added room. In many homes this may not hold true. If you have any doubt about the B.T.U. output of your furnace, consult a heating expert. Whether you have to add heating or can utilize your existing plant, the room should be controlled by its own thermostat for greatest comfort.

Fireplace. Though admittedly its size makes it a luxury, the owner decided to install an oversize fireplace. (The opening is approximately 4½ ft. wide by 3 ft. high.) Because of these dimensions, extra footings were installed to support the structure. For textural contrast with the paneled walls, the hearth was constructed of smooth-cut stone while the fireplace face was skinned with a lightweight volcanic stone. Built-ins which flank the fireplace are a matter of personal taste. If your budget is limited, they can always be added later.

Walls. Framing, as shown in the drawing, is the conventional stud-wall. In the garage-door opening, holes were bored in the slab, and after some concrete was slushed in, anchor bolts for holding the sole plate were dropped in place.

From this point on, all construction was standard with the exception of the recessed paneled walls. Like the ceiling, the walls were insulated with full-thick batts and covered with ½-in. plasterboard. To insure against drafts, joints were taped and spackled as were all countersunk nailheads.

use prefinished paneling

Next, if you're duplicating the room, apply ¼-in. prefinished paneling over the drywall using mastic and nails. Then carefully measure the four walls for height and length to determine exact placement of the 1 x 6 vertical and horizontal framing members. Once these are up, it is simply a matter of mitering and placing the base-cap molding which surrounds each recessed panel. Bear in mind when selecting the paneling that you will have to match and stain those 1 x 6 members and moldings. How much of a job this will be depends in part on the type of paneling you choose.

The look of old-world craftsmanship that this room boasts is actually achieved mostly through the use of stock moldings. (Even the dentil is available at lumber-yards.)

Lighting. At the angle between roof and wall, a decorative alcove was installed to conceal fluorescent fixtures, controlled by a switch within the room.

Cost for a garage conversion will vary considerably, depending on how much work you will do yourself, and to what extent you will contract work.

The experienced handyman can probably handle most of the job himself—including the fireplace, which can be a relatively simple chore if you install one of the many factory-built versions that are self-insulating and require no footings.

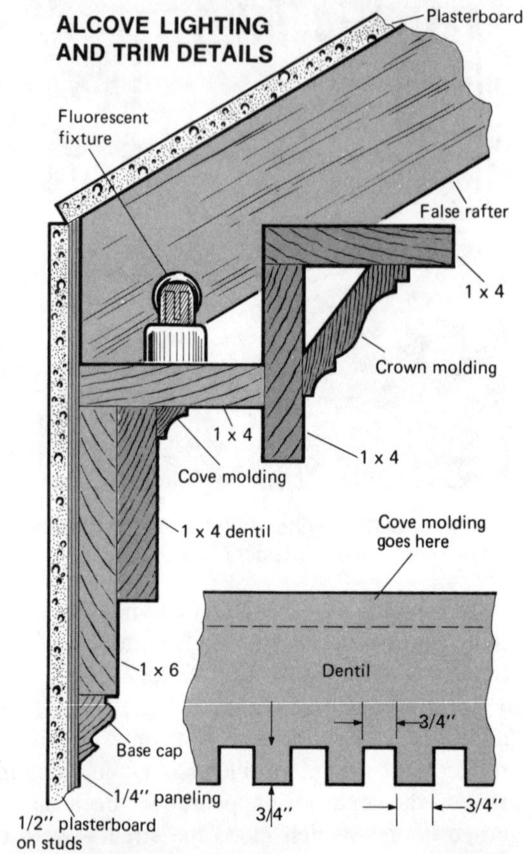

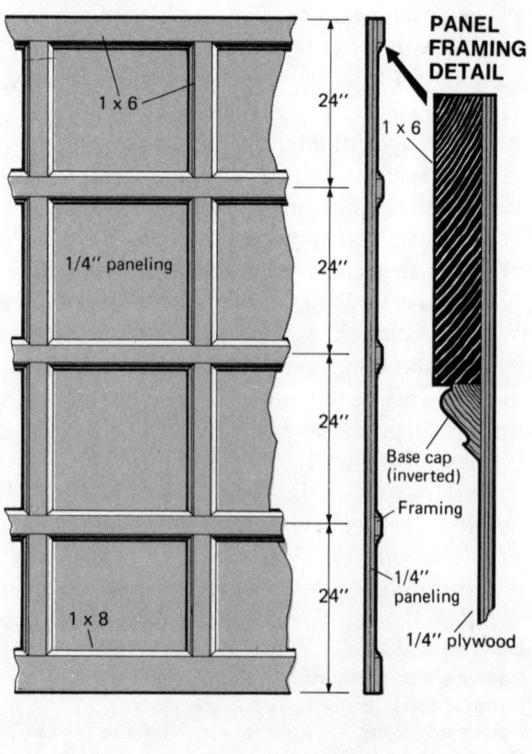

SECTION OF FALSE BEAM

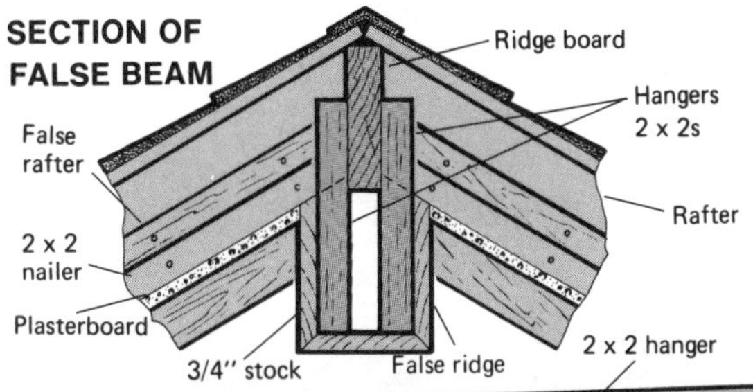

FALSE RAFTER

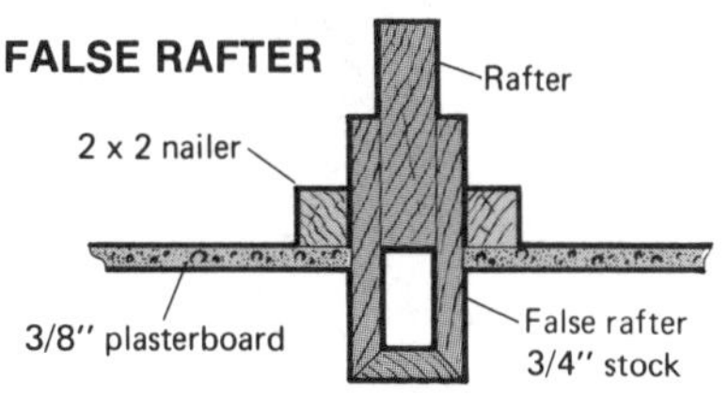

Wall-and-Ceiling Framing

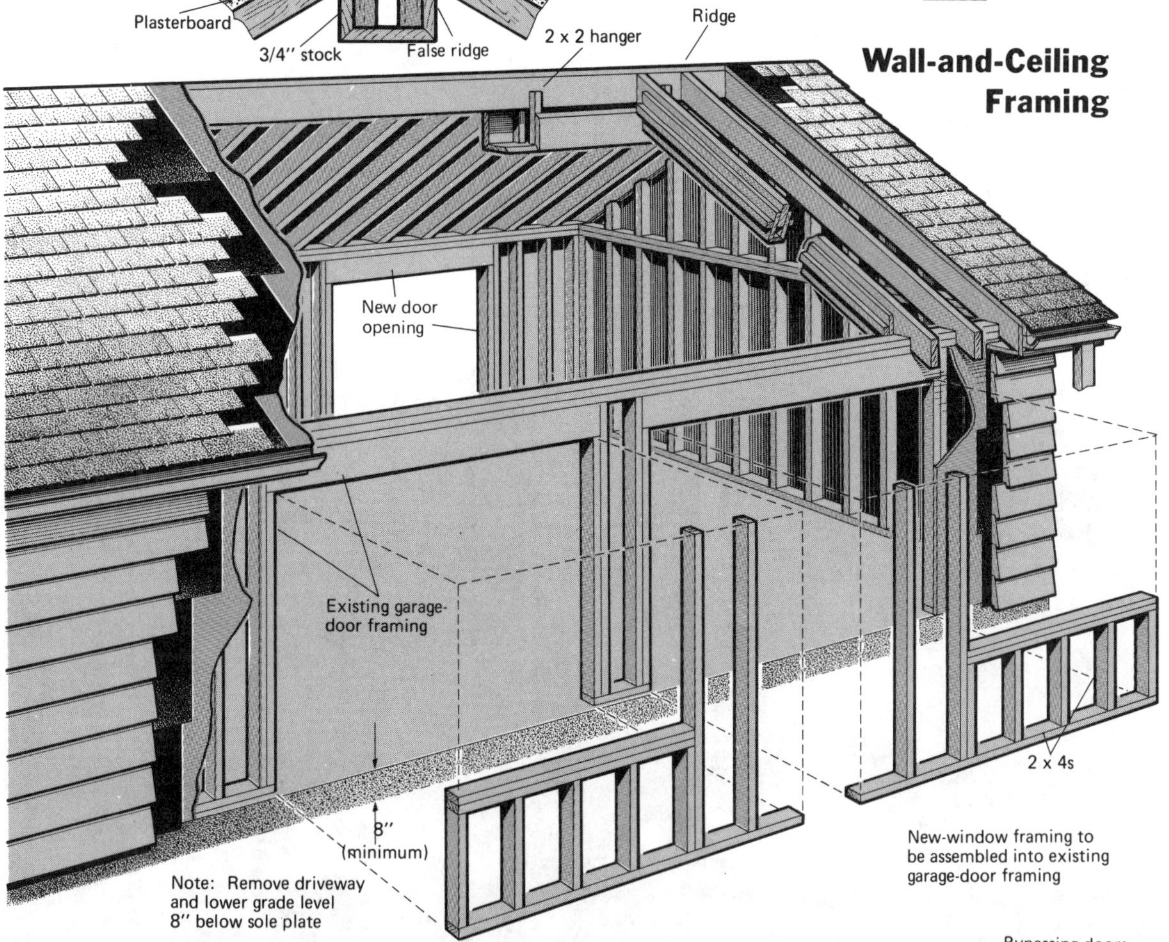

FLOOR PLAN

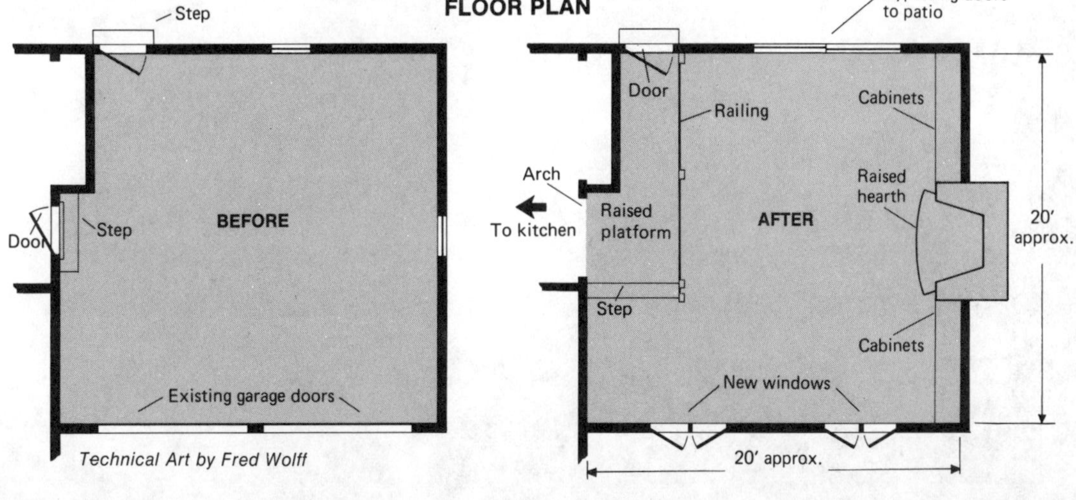

Technical Art by Fred Wolff

This was once a detached garage

By HARRY WICKS

A LARGE PART of the fun of having a second home in the country is that you can have friends and relatives out for visits. However, extended visits often crowd the hosts as well as their guests. Weary of this inconvenience, an enterprising couple recently looked about their property on the eastern tip of Long Island to see what they could do about getting the room they often needed.

They first considered an addition to the main house. Contractor cost estimates, and the news that their year-old heating plant would have to be replaced because it could not warm additional

BEFORE: Three-car garage offered 560 sq. ft.

AFTER: Same building, a comfortable guest house.

SEE ALSO

Basement remodeling . . . Cabanas . . .
Contractors . . . Garage doors . . .
House additions . . . Lumber . . . Measurements . . .
Remodeling . . . Remodeling, exterior . . .
Screened summer rooms . . . Windows

WICKER FURNITURE comfortably seats six or seven without crowding the room.

KITCHEN-DINING AREA. All needed appliances are in the King unit next to the half-wall.

BEDROOM NO. 2 has ample space for two beds, roomy dresser and a nightstand.

THE HIGH-RISER used in the bedroom is a sofa by day, converts to a pair of beds by night.

space, quickly discouraged them. Next, they looked at the usually vacant three-car garage located 150 feet from the house proper. This, they decided, would be their guest house.

Such a conversion is logical for several reasons:

1. Because the structure (shell) is already there, cost of building is sharply reduced.

2. A "guest room" set apart would assure guests and hosts complete privacy.

3. If they chose, the little house could be rented to help defray the cost.

Alterations were kept simple; no unusual or custom-built features were planned or incorporated. The biggest job on the shell was to close up the wall where the garage doors originally were located, and to install a 9-ft.-wide, sliding-door unit. The sliding-door unit selected is easy

Fitting paneling around the windows is done by holding the panel in place and marking directly from window

to assemble and install. Two men did this job in one day.

Perhaps the hardest part of the job was selecting the material to use for the interior. The small rooms demanded crisp, clean decorating which would create an illusion of spaciousness. At the same time, the man of the house wanted an in-

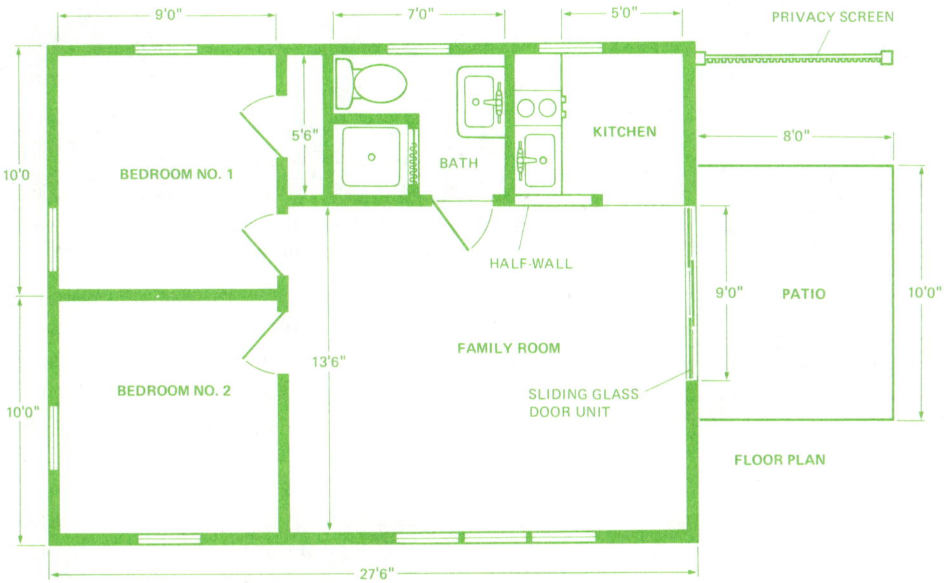

FLOOR PLAN

WINDOW CUTOUT in panel is made from the back side, using a circular saw. To start, use a vertical plunge.

PANELING is secured in place by driving precolored nails that match the panel color.

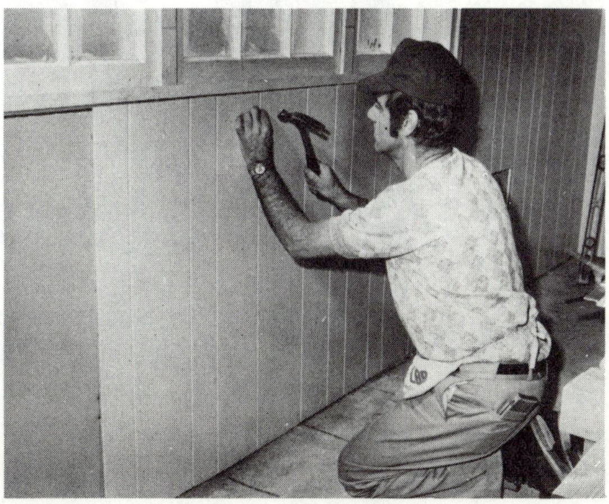

SOUTH WALL OF GARAGE prior to conversion. Peachtree aluminum sliding doors were installed.

WALL SECTION comes down fast. Because wall was first framed, there is no need for temporary support.

TWO MEN PUSH FRAME into the opening. After plumbing frame with level, it is fastened to studs.

LAST STEP is to install the door itself. Door shown is fully weatherstripped.

TRIPLE-WINDOW MULLION was installed in the wall which replaced garage doors on the original front.

terior that would require minimum maintenance. Both problems were solved by covering all walls and ceilings with a slightly off-white paneling, the textured look of Ranchero Nevada (by U.S. Plywood). Its finish is tough, and care consists of nothing more than an occasional wiping.

The owners felt that their guests needed a small kitchen primarily for preparing breakfast. What makes it possible to have a kitchen in such small space is the All-In-One-Kitchen Center made by the King Refrigerator Corp. In the 24x 36x39-in. cabinet there is a small sink, two cooktops and a mini-refrigerator.

While limited space did not permit a bathtub, the 5½x7-ft. bathroom does have a full-size shower. Also, because of its size, the house had to be carefully decorated. Old wicker furniture was resurrected, scrubbed down and painted white, and fabrics were then selected to complete the light, spacious feeling of the rooms. The attractive bedroom furniture groupings and the shutters were selected from the Montgomery Ward catalog.

Floors in the family room and bedrooms were covered with Armstrong's shag carpeting over a polyethylene vapor barrier, while kitchen and bath were treated with seamless vinyl covering.

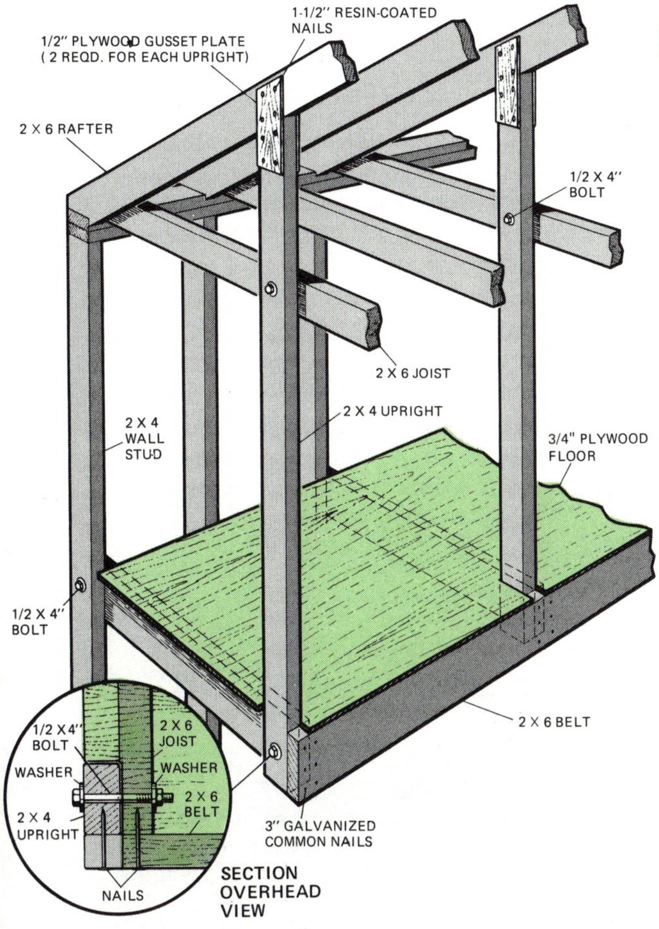

Garage space-saver

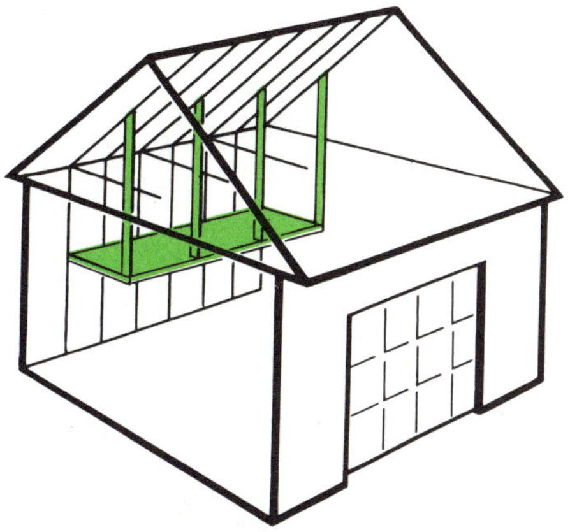

PUT AN END to clutter in your garage with this strong storage platform. You can build it level with the top of the wall or a few feet down for extra storage. Either is a low-cost way to add "floor space."

■ HAS YOUR GARAGE gradually turned into just a storage barn? Well, here's an easy way to add enough storage space so you can clear an area to park the car. This project requires only minimal carpentry experience, no special tools, and all materials are stock items.

plan for materials

Count the studs along the wall where your platform will be located. For every two studs you'll need one length of 2 x 6 for the floor joist, one 2 x 4 upright to connect the joist to the rafter, two ½-in. plywood gusset plates (figure about 3½ x 10 in. for each) to attach the upright to the rafter, and 5/16 x 4-in. bolts with washers.

Once you've picked the location, mark a level line across the wall studs where the 2 x 6s connect. Then measure 4 ft. along each sidewall to allow for the plywood platform. Using a level, carry this mark up the wall until you reach the rafter. **Tip:** If you make careful measurements along the outside walls, you can mark all the rafters and studs accurately by snapping a chalkline held between your measured marks.

Here's how to figure the right lengths for the joists and uprights. For the joists you have to allow 3½ in. for bolting to the wall stud, plus 4-ft. under the plywood platform, less 1½ in. under the platform for the run of the 2 x 6 belt. Total length: 50 in. The length of the uprights will depend on where you mount the platform. Measure from your mark on the rafter to the bottom of the 2 x 6 joist and remember to allow for the angle cut where the upright and the rafter meet. The only other piece of framing you'll need is a single length of 2 x 6 for the belt. It stiffens the assembly and supports the outside edge of the plywood between the joists.

building the platform

After cutting your materials to the proper lengths, attach the joists to the wall studs. **Tip:** Tack the joist in position and clamp it. Then drill through both pieces (the hole alignment is automatically correct) and install the bolt. This procedure can be used at every bolted joint.

Make the angle cut on your uprights and then nail the gusset plates to them. Spot a few nails on the free ends of the plates. This way, as you raise the upright to your mark, the plates sandwich the rafter and you can lock the joint easily. A coat of a preservative like Woodlife will help keep the platform in good shape.

SEE ALSO
**Additions, house . . . Fasteners . . .
Garage remodeling . . . Home improvement . . .
House additions . . . Lumber . . . Shelves . . .
Small-parts storage . . . Storage ideas . . .**

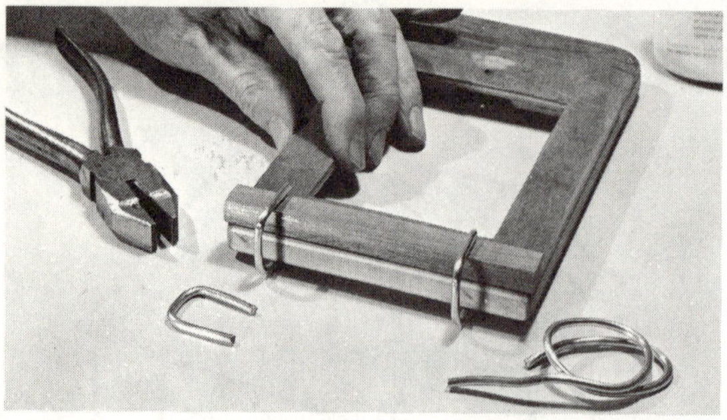

LIGHT PRESSURE CLAMPS can be made quickly from solid wire solder. The little C-clamps shown were bent so their ends were closer together than the thickness to be spanned, then carefully forced into position. After use, such clamps always can be returned to their original purpose—that of soldering metal.—*E. B. Walters, Chicago.*

DISPOSABLE BRUSHES or applicators for applying lacquer and other finishing materials are easily made from felt salvaged from old hats. For a typical brush, cut a felt strip 2½ in. long and ¾ in. wide. Fold it crosswise at the center and push it into a ⅝-in.-long slot in a ⅜-in. hardwood dowel "handle."—*Wm. T. Mayor, Philadelphia.*

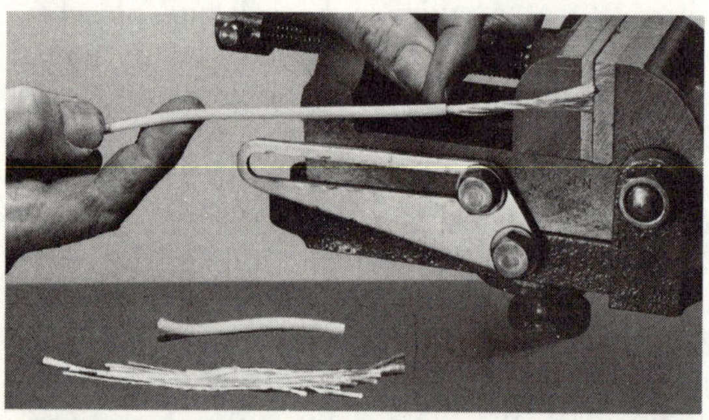

AN EMERGENCY SOURCE of small-diameter flexible tubing can be plastic-covered clothesline. A half inch or so of the cover is peeled from one end so the rayon core can be clamped between vise jaws. Then the tubular cover (usually vinyl) is pulled off. Pressing the tubing end back with a finger helps loosen it.—*Henry Jones, Houston.*

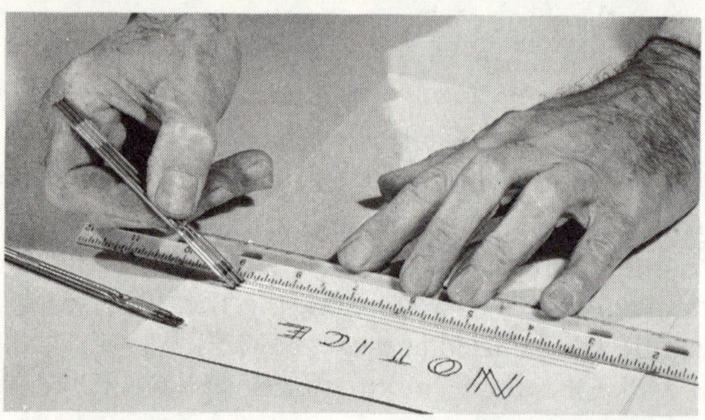

WHEN TAPED TOGETHER side by side, two or more ballpoint refills make handy instruments for drawing parallel lines. Novel signs can be made by using such a setup as a lettering pen. After the letters have been roughed out, lines can be strengthened, shading added or other modifications made with a single ballpoint.—*Walter E. Burton, Akron, OH.*

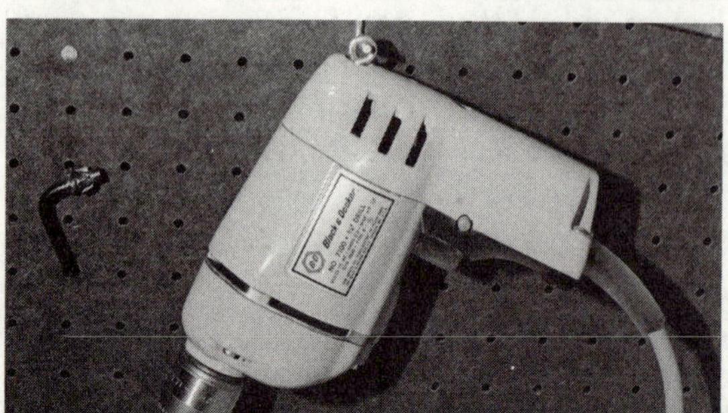

BY REPLACING ONE BOLT with an eyebolt, I made my drill easy to hang. To keep the chuck key handy, I have mine fastened to a length of monofilament fishline fed through a hole in the perforated board. A sinker—heavier than the key—is tied to the other end of the line to hold the key against the board.—*Don Anderson, Sunnyvale, CA.*

You can install a garbage disposer yourself

By WAYNE C. LECKEY

IF YOU HAVE SHIED AWAY from installing your own food-waste disposer because you figured it was too difficult, you're in for a surprise. Outside of the back-breaking position you have to assume in the cramped quarters under a sink, the job of connecting it to the drain-pipe actually requires little or no previous plumbing experience. It doesn't even involve the water lines.

As for special tools, I installed the Norge continuous-feed disposer shown here with a pipe wrench, an adjustable wrench and a screwdriver. To wire it, you won't need any more tools than you have in your toolbox.

There are two types of disposers: continuous and batch feed. The first lets you deposit food waste into the unit while it's running, and is operated by a separate switch. A batch feed unit does one load of food waste at a time. It runs only when a cover is locked over its opening, which triggers a built-in switch.

Study the before and after installation drawings and photos. Your particular hookup should look much like that in the before photo. If you

SEE ALSO
Drains . . . Kitchens . . . Plastic pipe . . . Plumbing . . . Sewage systems

IF THE DISPOSER is shipped with the drain ell detached, you must install it with the mounting plate and screws furnished.

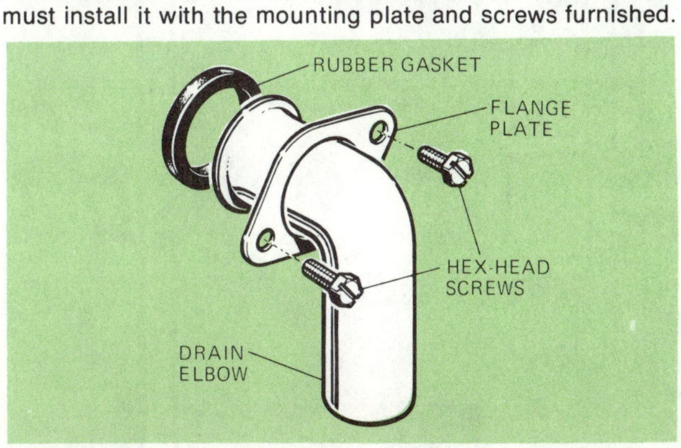

THE SINK FLANGE IS ATTACHED by turning slot-head screws in the tapped holes.

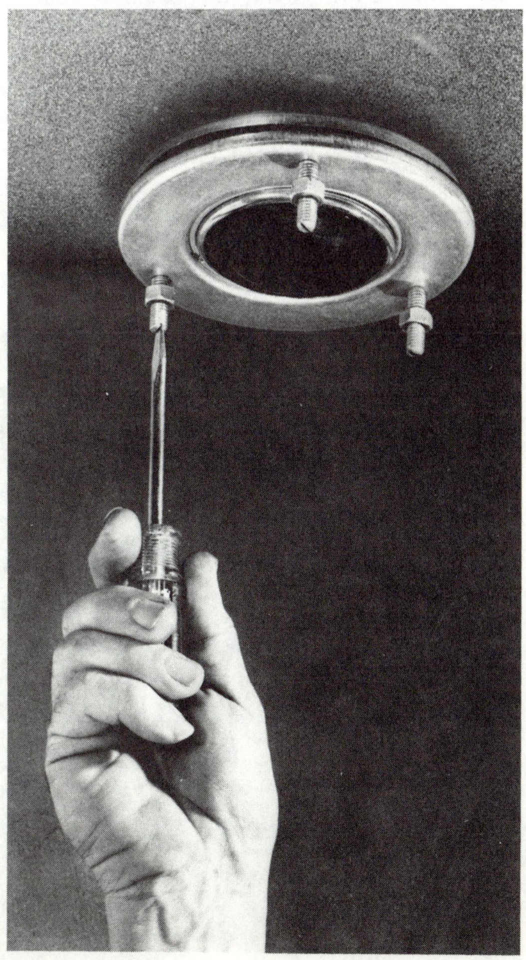

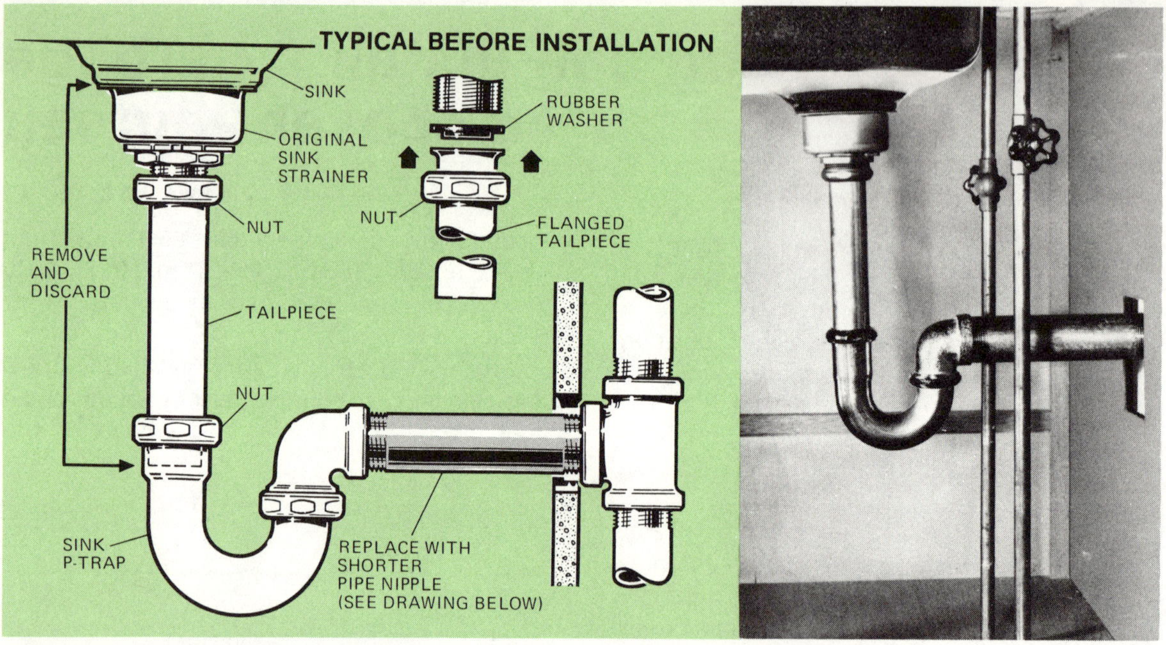

THE PHOTO ABOVE SHOWS typical installation of the waste pipe for a single-basin sink.

have a two-basin sink, you'll have twin drains which could either go out the back of the cabinet or through the floor.

Since the disposer replaces the original sink-strainer assembly and tailpiece, these parts are removed (as indicated) and discarded. You simply back off the two nuts that hold the tailpiece to the strainer body and P-trap, and then the nut which holds the P-trap to the waste pipe. Use a flat-jaw adjustable wrench. To remove the strainer body, just back off the flat nut which holds it.

Because the disposer requires a shorter waste pipe than the original, you then unscrew the old nipple from the drainpipe in the wall, using a good-size pipe wrench—if the nipple is rusted or corroded, it may take muscle to break it loose. Sometimes a length of pipe slipped over the wrench handle gives the extra leverage needed. Now you are ready to install the disposer.

THIS PHOTO SHOWS DISPOSER installed in the above set up. Notice that the same trap is used but pipe is shorter.

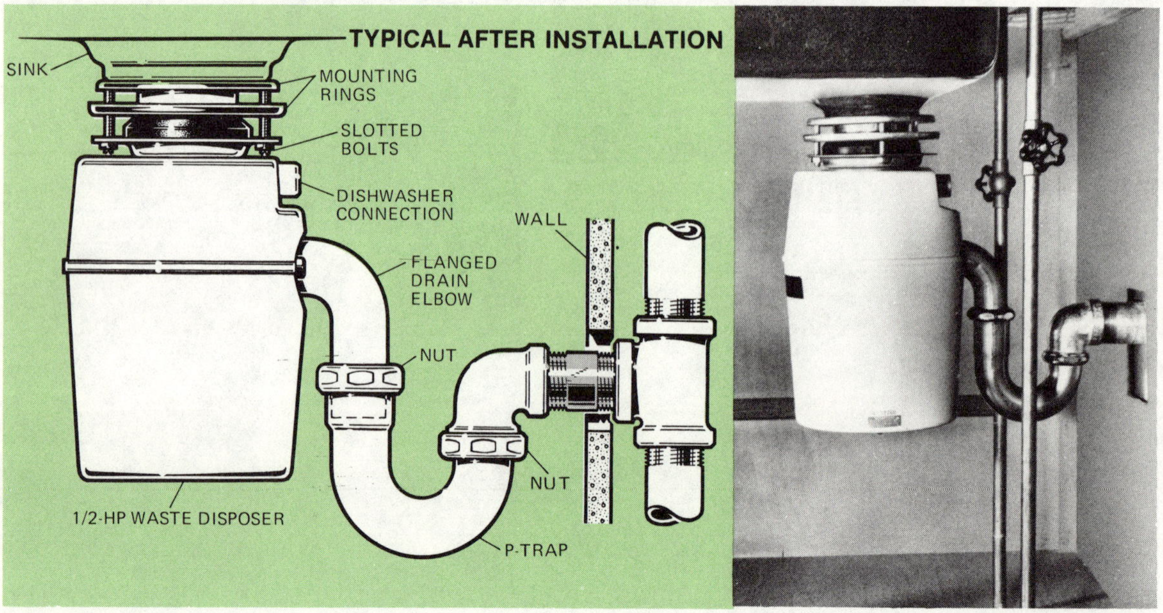

TYPICAL OFFSET WASTE CONNECTIONS

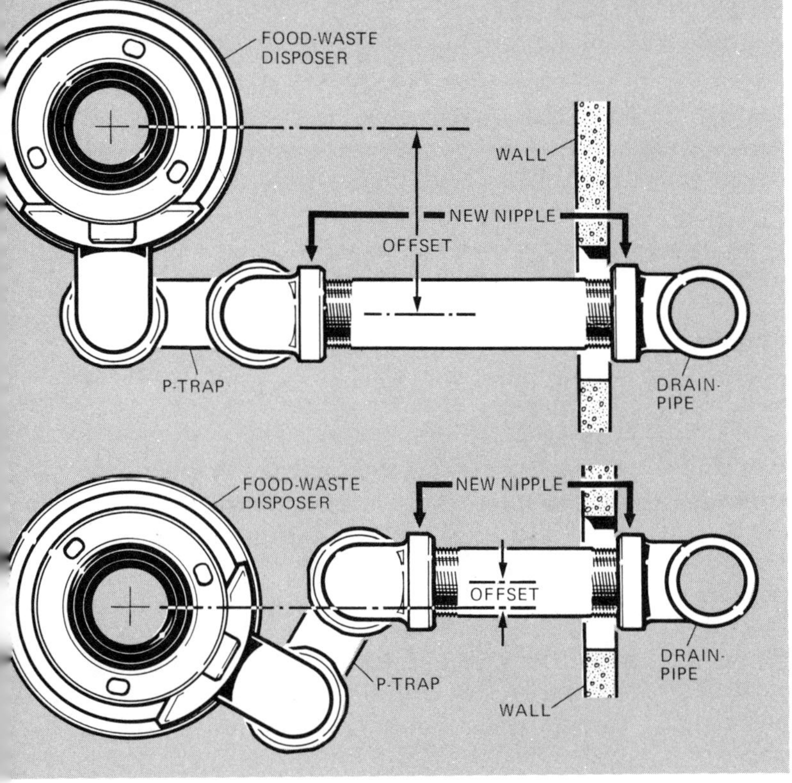

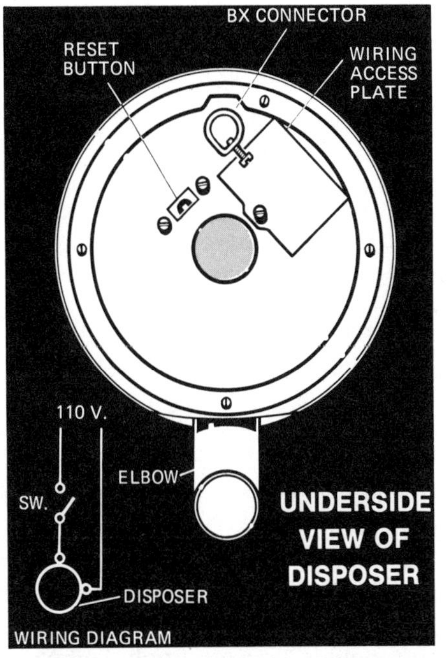

UNDERSIDE VIEW OF DISPOSER

Your particular disposer dictates the way it attaches to the sink. In the case of the Norge (Fedders Corp., Edison, N.J. 08817) that I installed, a separate mounting ring with slotted screws locks the sink flange in place. Before it can be installed in the sink, a snap ring has to be pried off and later replaced. Then place plumber's putty under the sink flange to prevent leaking, tighten screws evenly from below and trim away excess putty. (If the flanged drain elbow is not already attached to the disposer when you get it, attach it and the rubber gasket with two hex-head bolts furnished.)

You're now ready to lift and attach the disposer to the mounting ring. Holes in a mating ring at the top of the disposer are aligned with the slotted screws and hex nuts are applied and tightened with an open-end wrench. It might help to support the heavy disposer (if you have room) with a 2x4 prop until the three nuts are in place. Elongated holes in the ring let you turn the disposer slightly to align the drain elbow with the waste pipe.

With the disposer mounted you can determine the length of the new nipple needed. Where the disposer center might not be in direct line with the waste pipe, you may have to swing the disposer for joining the trap. Examples of offset waste pipes are shown in the drawings above. Note that the P-trap is positioned accordingly. Steel pipe nipples (1½ in. o.d.) come in 2, 3, 4, 6, 8, 10 and 12-in. lengths. You should be able to reuse the original P-trap and elbow; you need only replace the nipple. When screwing the latter in the drain fitting, coat the threads with joint compound and turn the pipe as tightly as you can with your pipe wrench. Add the elbow to the outer end and finally remount the P-trap.

Since it is difficult to determine the exact length of pipe nipple your installation will require, it will pay to have several different lengths on hand. Nipples you don't use can be returned.

To wire the disposer, just run a length of BX cable from a nearby 110-v. outlet box to an access plate on the bottom of the disposer for hookup to the disposer wires. If you have a continuous-feed disposer, you will have to locate a separate wall switch near the sink and wire it into the line.

Naturally, plumbing and electrical connections should conform to local codes. If you have a septic tank, the U.S. Public Health Service advises that you can safely use a waste disposer if your septic system meets the following standards:

House occupants	Minimum Tank Capacity
4	750 gallons
6	900 gallons
8	1000 gallons
10	1250 gallons

A disposer will not cause the absorption field of a septic system to flood.

How to repair a garbage disposer

Garbage disposers are tough appliances and seldom need repair. But you do need to know how to clear up jams, how to load them, and how to clean them

YOUR GARBAGE DISPOSER is a simple, reliable unit which should seldom give you any trouble unless you ask it to do things which it wasn't designed for. The first rule in maintaining your unit is to know exactly what should and should not be put into it. The instructions which came with it will tell you what you need to know.

Basically, there are two types of garbage disposers. The chief difference between the two types is the kind of motor each has. Less expensive models have a split-phase motor, while the costlier units have capacitor-start motors.

BATCH-TYPE garbage disposers have a removable stopper, which must be inserted in the sink opening and turned to start the grinding action.

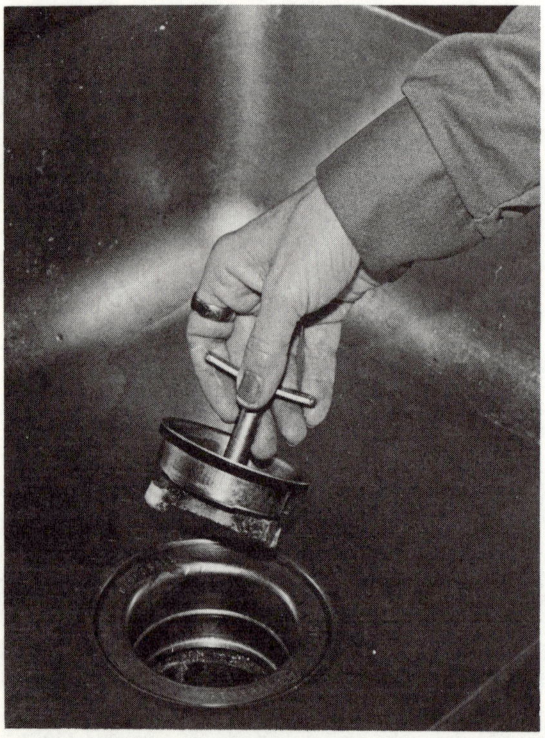

These motors are similar in most respects, but the capacitor-start motor has a capacitor which gives it an assist in starting—a substantial starting torque which allows it to handle heavier loads.

All garbage disposers will grind and get rid of soft food wastes—meat particles, bread scraps, soft vegetable leftovers—but only those with capacitor-start motors have the muscle to grind seafood shells, bones, corncobs and other heavy food matter.

No garbage disposer is designed to handle non-food wastes. Don't try to grind glass, pottery, broken dishes, bottle caps, rubber, bits of metal or plastic. And keep silverware, paper, cardboard and even bits of string out of the unit. All of these items can damage the disposer and clog your drain.

SOME DISPOSERS have a small wrench which can be inserted in the bottom to help free jam-ups. The wrench is used to turn the mechanism backwards.

SEE ALSO
Appliance repair . . . Dishwashers . . . Drains . . . Kitchens . . . Plumbing

If you have heard those stories about grinding pop bottles in your disposer as a way of cleaning it, forget them. Broken bottles are bad, not good, for your unit.

Here are some good rules for getting the best and most trouble-free service from your disposer:

1. Grind only food wastes.
2. Follow the instructions which came with your unit as to what you should and should not put into it. The manufacturer knows the limitations of his unit and passes his knowledge to you through those instructions.
3. Never use hot water when using the disposer. Always use cold water. Hot water melts fat and allows it to flow through the drain pipes. As the fat cools during this trip, it may cling to the sidewalls of the pipe and solidify. Eventually this will cause a blockage in the pipes. Cold water, on the other hand, solidifies the fat. The disposer then grinds it into solid bits which can be carried easily through the drain pipes.
4. Before doing any work on a disposer, shut off the current in the disposer circuit. Do this by removing the circuit fuse or by tripping the circuit breaker to OFF. In some cases, disposers are plugged into wall outlets, and you cut off the current by unplugging the unit. Power must be cut off to guarantee that no one accidentally starts the disposer while you are working on it. Such an accidental start can cause severe injury.

how it works

Each disposer has an upper and a lower chamber. Garbage is stuffed down the throat of the disposer into the upper chamber, where it falls on a rotating table or flywheel. The flywheel has on it two or more small pivoted hammers, which lie flat when the flywheel is at rest, but which fly outward and revolve when the flywheel is spinning. They toss the garbage against the sidewall of the upper chamber.

A metal ring with teeth in it, called a shredder, is built into this wall. The shredder rips the garbage into tiny bits. These bits are washed down the drain by a flow of cold water.

Some disposers are continuous-feed, and others are batch-feed. The continuous-feed type has a rubber baffle plate over its mouth, through which garbage is fed. It is controlled by a wall switch. Once you turn this on, you continuously feed garbage into the unit until the job is done. Great care must be taken to see that you don't allow your fingers to go down through the rubber baffle while the unit is operating.

THE FIRST THING to do when your disposer fails to start after a jam or an overload is to locate the overload switch. Wait several minutes, then press it to reset the safety circuit. Some disposers have an automatic resetter and no button. Others have buttons on the side of the unit.

The batch-feed models have a cover which must be in place before the unit will operate. In this type, you feed a batch of garbage into the unit, fit the cover into the mouth and turn it. The cover activates a switch which turns on the unit. When the first batch has been disposed of, you remove the cover and feed in the next batch. This unit is safer because there is no way to get your fingers into the upper chamber while the unit is in operation.

what can go wrong

There really isn't much that can go wrong with the average garbage disposer. It is ruggedly built and has only a few moving parts. The biggest source of trouble is jamming—the result of overloading the unit or putting material into it which it wasn't designed to take. Once you remove the jam, the unit operates once again.

It is possible that there will be failures in the motor. Experience has shown that the life of the average unit is from five to ten years, and that if the motor wears out or burns out, it is usually more economical to buy a new disposer than repair the old one.

There are several switches in each disposer, and switches are subject to wear. Therefore the switches are sometimes a source of trouble. As a rule, you can buy a replacement switch, remove the old switch, and install the new one. However, it is important to get an exact replacement. When ordering a new switch, take the model number and the part number to the dealer.

The switches include the on-off switch mounted on the counter or wall near the unit for continuous-feed models, and the on-off switch mounted in the neck of batch-feed models. Some units have another on-off switch in the cold water line that works in conjunction with the other on-off switch. Its function is to assure that the disposer won't operate until cold water is flowing. Check your owner's manual to learn which switches your unit has and where they are located.

the overload switch

Many garbage disposers have an overload switch which shuts off the current when too heavy a load is imposed on the motor. This switch usually trips to OFF when the unit becomes jammed, and thus saves the motor from burning out. If your unit has an overload switch, know about it and know where it is located. Otherwise, you may not be able to start the unit after clearing a jam, and may assume that the motor has burned out when it has not. Many a service man has made a repair call only to discover that the only problem is an overload switch in the OFF position.

On some later models, the overload switch automatically resets itself after about five minutes, during which time the switch cools off. With switches which must be reset manually, wait five minutes before pressing the reset.

clearing jammed units

When a disposer jams, it stops grinding. In most jams, you can hear the motor humming as it attempts to drive the unit. What you hear, of course, is the motor being overloaded—a situation which is relieved when the overload switch shuts off the power after about 30 seconds.

Important: Remember to cut off the current to the disposer circuit before starting to work on the jam. It is not enough to depend on the overload switch to keep the disposer turned off. When you have finished working out the jam, remember both to reset the overload switch *and* restore current to the disposer circuit.

clearing a jam

A disposer jams when some type of material prevents the flywheel from returning. To clear the jam, it is necessary to remove the material. Some units have an automatic reverse-action switch which kicks in automatically after a jam. Very frequently, the reverse action will loosen the clogging object. Other units have a manual reverse-action switch. With these units, the first step to take following a jam is to flip this switch.

If the reverse-action, either manual or automatic, does not clear the jam, then you must fish out the jamming object. *Do not attempt to do this until you are absolutely certain the current in the disposer circuit is off.* With the current off, use long-handled tongs to fish the jamming object out. It may be necessary to use a long screwdriver as a pry bar to move the flywheel backward a bit to free the jamming object.

Remember that when you have cleared the jam, you must return power to the circuit and reset the overload switch. When the jam has been cleared, the disposer should work without difficulty. Jams seldom damage the disposer.

maintenance

Garbage disposers are self-cleaning because they are flushed with water as they operate.

Problem	Causes	Procedure
Motor hums, but disposer doesn't operate	1. Garbage is jamming the unit	1. If your unit has a reversing switch that switches flywheel direction, causing the unit to spin in an opposite direction and dislodge particles, use it. If not, reach into the hopper and try to turn the flywheel counterclockwise by grasping an impeller and using it as a handle. If you have a special wrench that some manufacturers supply to help clear jams, use it. If nothing works, unscrew the bottom housing from the upper housing, but be careful not to let the bottom half drop. It is heavy. Remove obstructing particles from below.
	2. Bearings are frozen	2. Remove the bottom housing and try to turn the flywheel. If it binds (not because of jamming waste), replace the flywheel and motor bearings if they are accessible. If they aren't accessible, you will have to take apart the entire unit, including the motor, to reach them.
Motor shows no life	1. Tripped overload	1. Relieve the heavy load and press the overload reset relay.
	2. On-off switch of batch-feed model has shifted	2. See that the stopper engages the switch when it is locked. If it doesn't, reposition the switch so it is in its proper place.
	3. Burned-out switch	3. Check all switches for continuity with the switch turned on, but make sure the disposer is not connected.
	4. Burned-out motor	4. Direct-test motor with a line cord. If it doesn't show life when the cord is connected to its terminals and plugged in, dispose of the disposer.
Disposer won't shut off	1. On-off or cold-water switch is stuck	1. Replace the switch.
Disposer shuts itself off	1. Tripped overload switch	1. Relieve the heavy load and press the overload reset relay.
	2. Defective overload switch	2. Remove the lower housing to get at the motor and replace the switch.
Lengthy grinding time	1. Impeller is stuck	1. Reach into the hopper and try to move the impellers. If one doesn't move, pry it up with a small screwdriver.
	2. Shredder is worn	2. Replace the shredder if it is replaceable and if a replacement part is available. If not, consider replacing the disposer.
Disposer leaks	1. Worn bearings and seals	1. Disposer requires a complete overhaul. It will probably be more economical to buy a new unit.
Offensive odors		Fill the disposer with ice cubes and run it for 15-30 seconds while keeping the unit shut off unless there is a cold-water switch. Follow with a good flushing of the unit with cold water—then give it a minute. Now, put two lemon halves down the tube and run the unit for 30-60 seconds with the water off, if possible. Follow with a water flush for another 30 seconds. With the disposer turned off, fill the sink with cold water. Turn the disposer on, force-flushing the water through the disposer.

However, bits of garbage may lodge in the system from time to time. To flush these out, fill the sink with cold water about once a month, then open the stopper and allow the water to drain through the disposer. This should flush away garbage bits and any detergent scum.

Do not use chemical drain cleaners in any drain equipped with a disposer. The chemicals may damage the unit. If your kitchen has a double bowl, remember that both bowls empty through the same drain system. Therefore, chemicals should not be put into either side of the sink.

It is a good idea to process all scraps through the disposer immediately, and not allow them to stand in the unit for long—because they will produce a bad odor in a short time. But even with good operation, a disposer may begin to smell. To eliminate this smell, fill the chamber with ice cubes, then run the disposer for about 15 or 20 seconds with the water turned off. Then turn on the water and flush out the unit.

Next, turn off the water again, and drop a lemon which you have cut in half into it. Operate the disposer without water for 20 to 30 seconds, then turn on the water and run for another 15 seconds. Finally, fill the sink with water, then turn on the disposer and lift the sink drain plug. This will allow the water in the sink to drain through the unit which then pumps it under pressure into the drain. The result of this treatment is a neutralizing and forced cleaning of the fat and garbage bits which have been causing the bad odor.

Two attractive garden shelters

Both these shelters seem to bid you welcome from a distance

A GRACEFUL GARDEN shelter offers much more than escape from burning sun, chilling shower or gusting winds—it's an enticing nook where soothing solitude or suave sociality can be savored and enjoyed. The physical structure itself can be a rewarding expression of your own individuality, for shelters like these offer unlimited freedom of design.

This freedom is mainly due to the availability, attractiveness and sound durability of redwood; especially attractive when complemented by brick, concrete, bamboo or plastic.

Don't trouble yourself with the thought of rot or finishing problems, either, for the natural chemicals in California redwood make it impervious to decay and termites. And yet, redwood holds finishes well—you can paint it, stain it, bleach it, or just let it weather to a soft gray. As a matter of fact, redwood becomes more attractive as it ages.

SEE ALSO

Cabanas . . . Cookout bars . . . Decks . . .
Fences . . . Gazebos . . . Grills . . . Patios . . .
Playhouses . . . Poolhouses . . . Privacy screens . . .
Screened summer rooms . . . Summer houses . . .
Vacation homes . . . Yard lighting

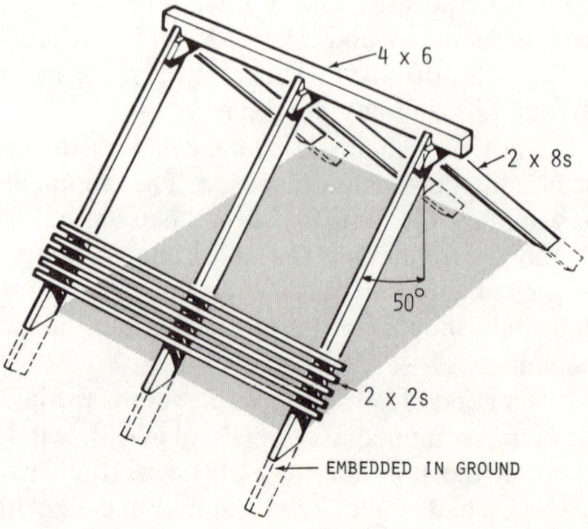

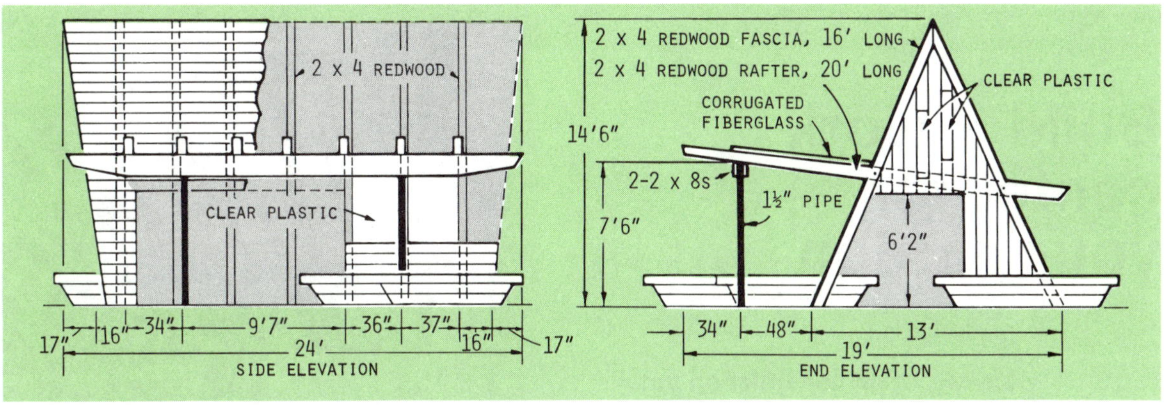

CLEAR PLASTIC PANELS pass sunlight to interior of shelter while the fiberglass panels filter sun's rays.

LEFT: The geometric A-frame shelter is a simple, surefire way to add to your enjoyment of outdoor living. The frame consists of 2x8-in. redwood legs and a single 4x6 notched into the apex of the legs. The 2x2-in. strips are spaced about 2 in. apart.

ABOVE: Plastic panels offset an extensive array of redwood for a pleasing blend of dissimilar materials. As seen below, the shelter seems to invite passersby in for a few quiet moments. Colorful concrete discs and Japanese lanterns add to the pleasing effect.

SETTING FOR midsummer night's dream is also appropriate for afternoon baskings and evening buffets.

Build a work center for your garden

Here are basic construction details for building potting benches, storage bins and the structure itself

■ USING A LITTLE imagination—and the construction know-how given on these pages—you can create a garden center as handsome as the one shown on the opposite page. Designed by the California Redwood Assn., it solves storage problems, gives a comfortable work area for gardening chores and adds beauty to your back yard.

Whether you stick close to the one pictured or design your own, there are three things to remember when selecting a garden center site: 1. Locate the center so that materials can be conveniently hauled to it from the car; 2. Study shade and sun patterns (and prevailing winds) at the exact location; 3. If you plan to erect a greenhouse adjacent to the center, locate it so that the greenhouse will face south and east (to avoid excessive solar heat).

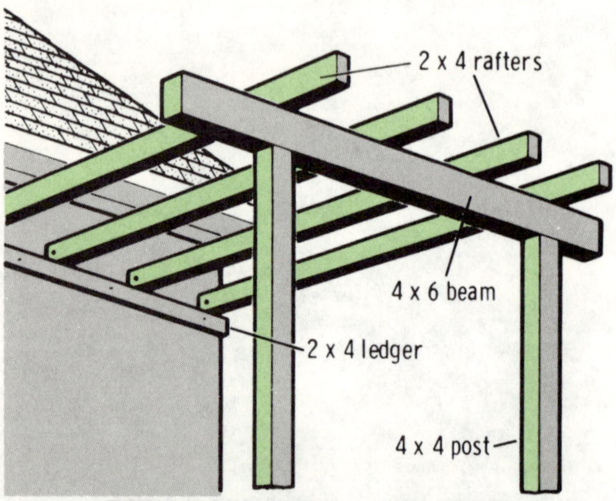

BASIC STRUCTURAL ELEMENTS

The basic elements of a functional garden center are a bench for potting, transplanting, labeling and other gardening jobs and, a weatherproof storage locker for protection of garden tools and equipment. If you have the space, add storage bins for bulk planting materials such as peat moss, sand, loam and fertilizer. A convenient water supply is a necessity and the structure should be built with a minimum 8-ft. headroom.

The center itself can be attached to an existing structure or built freestanding. Depth to which the 4x4-in. posts should be set can vary with soil and weather conditions but generally, 36 in. is adequate. The simplest method is to set the post directly into the ground. However, if the soil is sandy or unstable, posts should be anchored in concrete.

SEE ALSO
Cabanas . . . Decks . . . Fences . . . Gardening . . . Gazebos . . . Playhouses . . . Poolhouses . . . Screened summer rooms . . . Summer houses

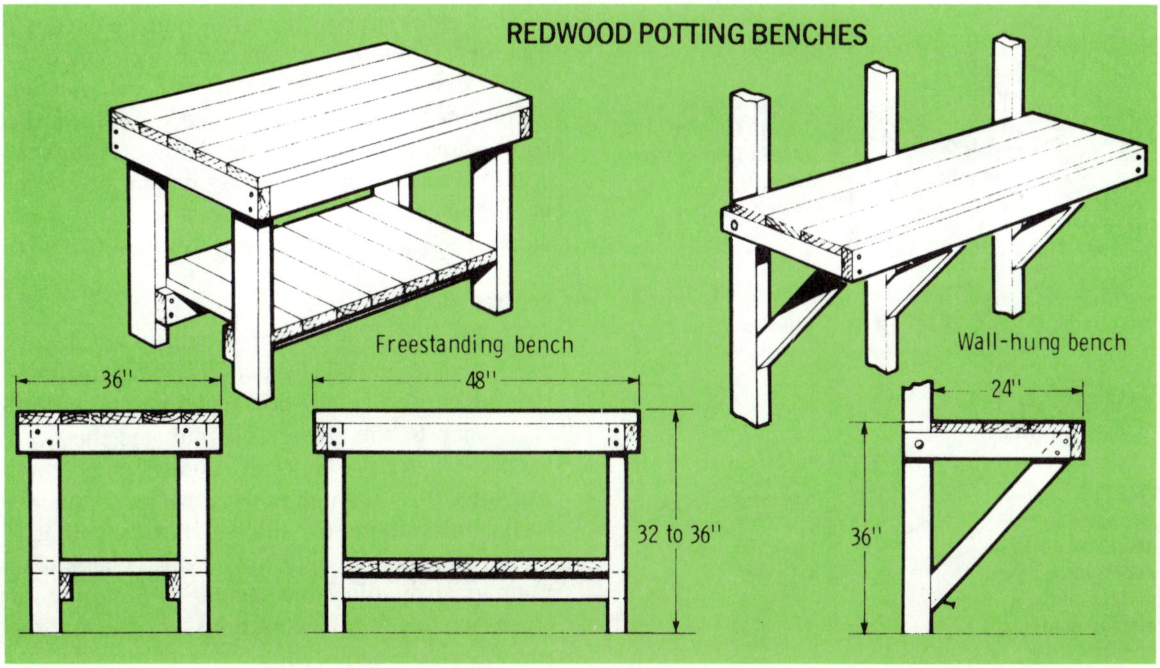
REDWOOD POTTING BENCHES
Freestanding bench
Wall-hung bench
36"
48"
32 to 36"
24"
36"

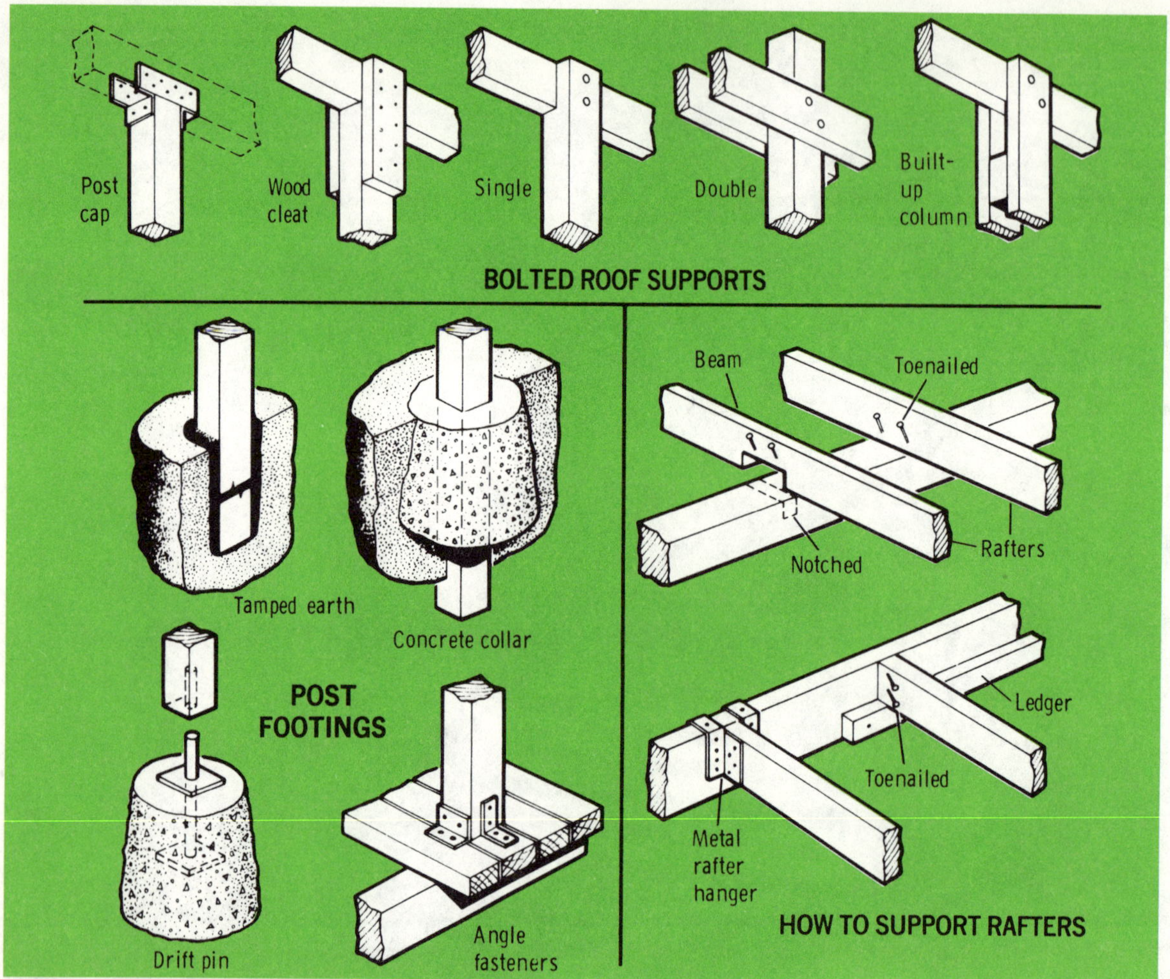

ALTERNATE METHODS for construction shown here give you a choice as to how you build your garden center. Accessories (below) make gardening tasks pleasant.

STORAGE BIN

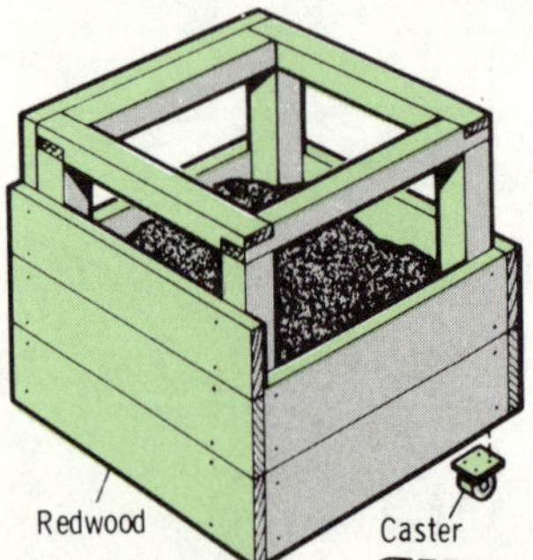

A BIN built of all-heart redwood stores fertilizer or other bulk garden materials. For greater mobility, the bin can be set on casters.

CAN CRADLE

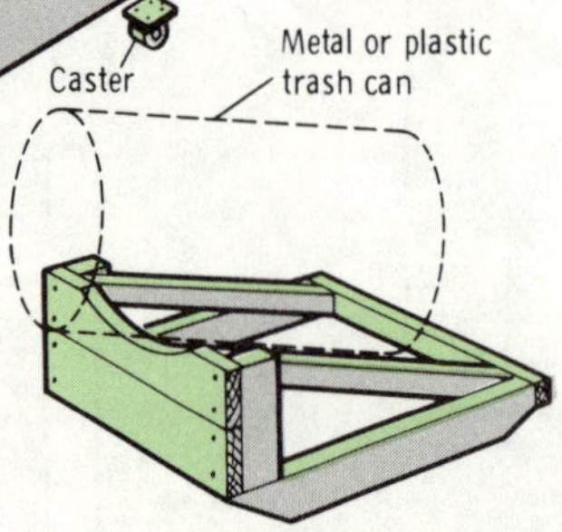

A METAL or plastic garbage can resting on a framed cradle under the bench makes removal of material an easy chore.

The beams support the rafters and tie the posts together. Though the roof can be left open, in many areas this would be impractical. A wide variety of materials can be used to close-in the roof: shingles, reed fencing, bamboo, canvas, window screening, lath, glass or plastic are all good choices. If you decide to close in the roof, slope it to provide positive water runoff.

construction tips

Highly resistant to both weather and decay-producing organisms, redwood is a logical material for garden center construction. Its natural resistance to the elements eliminates the need for preservatives which can be harmful to plants. For maximum holding power, use only noncorroding aluminum or quality, hot-dipped galvanized fastenings. Before you start, check with your local building department to determine if there are any legal restrictions or if a building permit will be required.

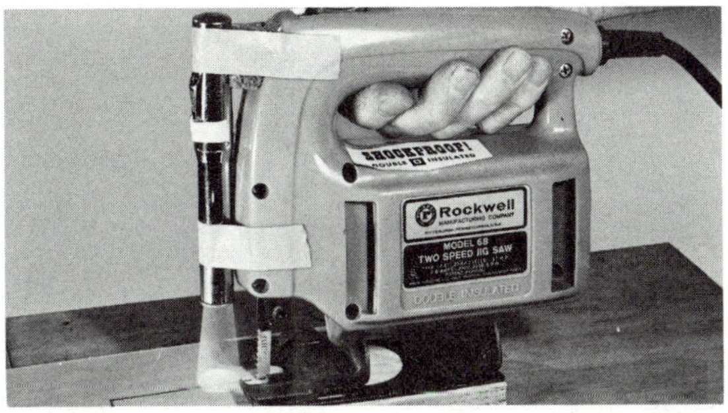

WHEN YOU MAKE a scroll cut, it is often necessary to cut in the shadow of the sabre saw. To eliminate eyestrain and the chance of cutting off the line, I temporarily attach my penlight to the saw with a wide strip of tape. Make certain the tape doesn't cover the saw's vent holes.—*Andrew Vena, Philadelphia.*

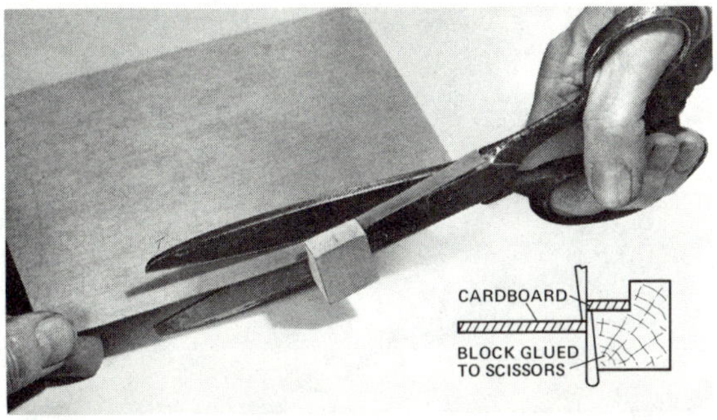

RECENTLY, WHEN I had to cut a lot of like strips from cardboard, I did it without drawing repeat guidelines. A block of wood of the same thickness as the width of the strips was glued on the outside of the blade with household cement. After the gauge block had done its work, I pried it loose and cleaned the blade with solvent.—*Walter E. Burton, Akron, OH.*

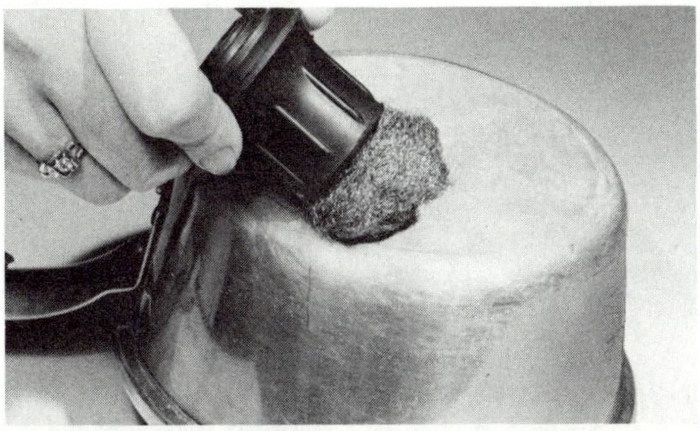

AN EXCELLENT HOLDER for steel-wool can be made from a large crutch tip. It provides a good grip, and when you desire to work with a small portion only, you can pack most of the wool inside the tip. If desired, two or three tips can be color-coded and kept for various grades of steel wool.—*William Swallow, Brooklyn, NY.*

A HAND "CHUCK" for turning drills or taps in a cramped space where a power drill will not fit can be made by threading a faucet handle to fit the stud on the chuck of your power drill. Lacking an old faucet in your junk box, you can probably find one at a fix-it shop.—*Marshall Lincoln, Wickenburg, AZ.*

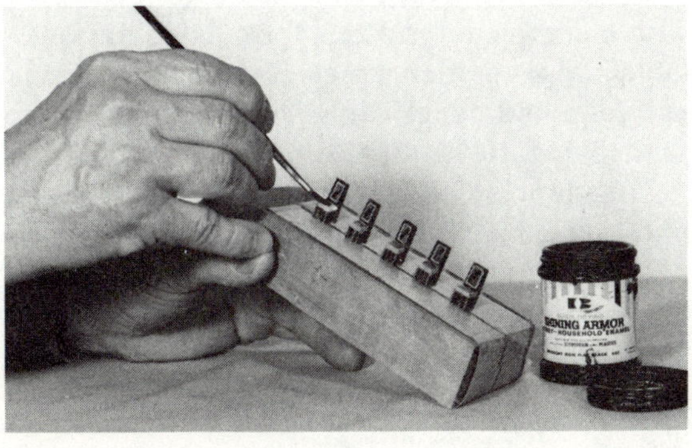

FRAGILE ITEMS like these five tiny chairs can be safely painted using this setup. Simply wrap masking tape, sticky side out, around a wood block. Lightly press the pieces into place, paint the miniatures, and when they're dry, shift and reposition the pieces to expose the unpainted areas.—*Harold T. Bodkin, Jr., Wyandotte, MI.*

Grow a vegetable bonanza in a small plot

Not only can a home garden help ease the food budget, but your own produce will have a lot more freshness and flavor than anything you're likely to buy at the supermarket. Here's how to make sure it's healthy

By JAMES DWYER and JOHN ALBERT

IN GARDENING, the magic words are *sunlight* and *nutrients*. Your first step is to pick a spot for the garden in full day-long sun, where the roots of large trees are not consuming the lion's share of the soil's nutrients and moisture. A plot of only 6 by 15 feet—basic size discussed in this article—can produce plenty of food for your table. If you have more area, better still.

SEE ALSO

Benches, potting . . . Cold frames . . . Dryers, food . . . Garden shelters . . . House plants . . . Strawberry barrels . . . Tractor lifts . . . Tractor trailers . . . Transplanting . . . Vegetable gardening

fertilizers

Today's vegetables, hybridized for rapid growth and high yield, need help in the form of extra nutrients. You give them the needed boost with a complete fertilizer, formulated for vegetables. Most garden stores have such fertilizers in five-pound boxes carrying designations such as 5-10-5, 5-10-10, 10-15-10.

The numbers denote percentages of nitrogen, phosphate and potash (in that order). Normally, before planting you'll want to work into the soil about five pounds of 5-10-5 per 100 square feet after each four weeks of growth. Use smaller amounts if you're working with a fertilizer of higher concentration.

In the growing season, never let fertilizer remain on leaves or within an inch of plant stems. It's wise to rake the soil lightly after each application and then give the whole garden a good watering.

Fertilizers that are completely soluble in water are excellent for use during the growing season. Used as directed, they will not burn leaves.

compact soil

Soil too tightly packed inhibits root development. During rainy periods it will waterlog, cutting off normal aeration both to the roots and to beneficial microorganisms. In dry periods, it will cake on top so that water from the hose runs off or forms puddles while the soil beneath remains dry. Eventually, the soil may crack under the hot sun and cause damage to tender root growth.

The remedy is to work into the soil (up to one-third the volume of the soil in your garden) compost mixed with sand or perlite. This will allow drainage.

FENCING CAN be used to support cucumbers and melons, and let them climb (above). Tomatoes (right) should be staked when planted to avoid root injury later. Stakes up to seven feet high are recommended. Inverted paper cup at base of the plant will hold off hungry cutworms. Hoe handle (below) pressed into ground makes trench for planting seeds half-inch-deep. Cold frame (below, left) for protection and propagation of plants should be placed against a south wall or tight fence. Since frame usually is without bottom, drainage must be good. A good way to start seeds is in peat pellets (lower, right). When sprouts are ready to be put out, you plant the entire pellet. Peat breaks down after it has been in the ground for a period of time.

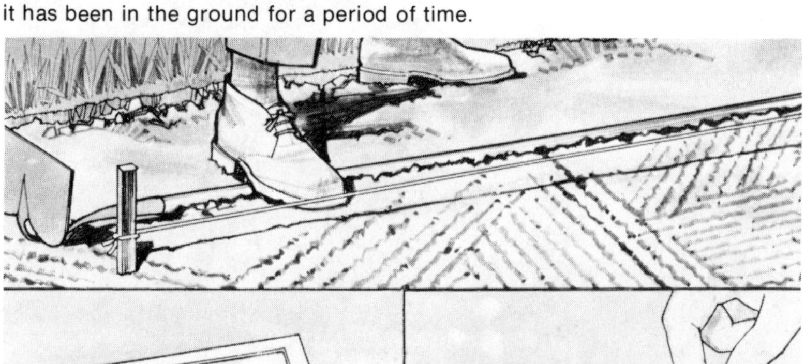

loose soil

Sandy soil is structurally the best for good root development, but if it is too sandy, it doesn't retain much moisture or nutrients. Solve the problem with compost or manure (again, one-third of the volume) along with peat moss. Since compost and manure break down to provide nourishment for plants, they should be replaced each year. Peat moss, while of no direct nutritive value, will remain in the soil for a long time, serving as a storehouse of water and fertilizer.

acid or alkaline?

Soil pH is the measure of hydrogen ion concentration in the soil, which is, in turn, a measure of soil acidity. It can be determined to a fair degree of accuracy with a simple soil-test kit, obtainable for less than $5 at a garden-supply store.

A pH reading of 1 is acid to the extreme, a pH 14 is as alkaline as your can get, and pH 7 is neutral soil. Most vegetables grow in slightly acid soil (pH 6 to 6.5). Much more acidity can be toxic to many plants, while very alkaline soil makes many trace elements unavailable to them.

The usual problem is acidity. If pH is below 5, add 10 pounds of ground limestone for each 100 square feet of garden. If it's only slightly low, make it 5 pounds. You can add it in the fall as a top dressing, giving you the chance to double check the reading in the spring, or put it on in the spring after having worked in the fertilizer. Rake it gently into the top inch of earth. Recheck the pH each year as lime is slowly leached out by rain.

If you live in an area rich in limestone, your soil problem is probably alkalinity. Fork in compost, manure, or peat moss to acidify. If the imbalance is extreme, say pH 8 or 9, add finely ground sulphur or aluminum sulfate.

designing the plot

Maximum use of space is the keynote. Remember that space is three-dimensional, and that sun in the northern hemisphere comes from the south, particularly in early spring and late fall. This means that plants should be arranged

1

2

3

4

1. WHEN SEEDLINGS of root vegetables appear, thin out the weaker ones until there are but three or four plants to the inch. This allows remaining plants to grow to a good size. 2. Though the best defense against disease and pests is to maintain strong growth in plants, you may have to resort to sprays. There is a wide variety of chemical agents on the market. 3. A good "instant" mulch is provided by plastic covering. It holds in heat, discourages weeds. Plants grow through cutouts; slits provide ample drainage. 4. If you have planted crops in straight rows, cultivating with hoe is easy. A good time to weed is when the ground is moist from rain or soon after watering.

SPRING

In spring, seedlings must be "hardened off"—gradually acclimated to outside temperatures — before planting in ground. Crops shown here can be planted well before the last frost of spring, just about the time ground is workable. Care must be taken with cabbage. If a cold spell hits and plants are subjected to a week or more of daytime temperatures below 50°F., heads will begin to form prematurely

1 Spinach
2 Beets
3 Broccoli or cauliflower
4 Onions
5 Spinach
6 Early cabbage
7 Radishes
8 Early head lettuce
9 Peas

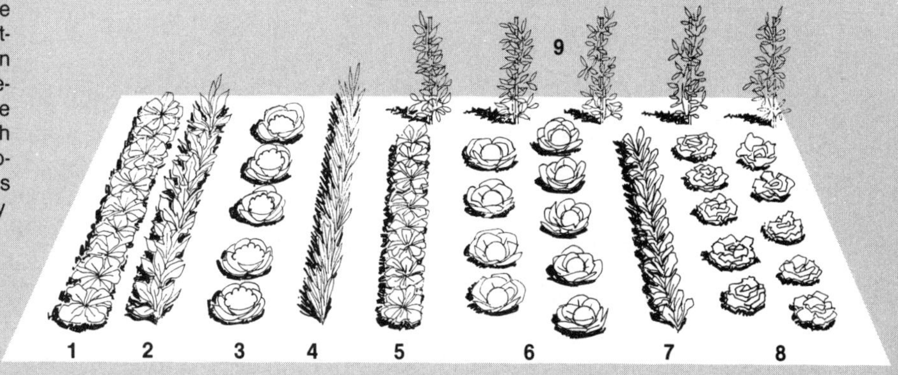

SUMMER

To give beans head start—and avoid possible frost injury—soak seeds indoors until almost germinated before planting in garden during a mild spell. Put in tomatoes, peppers and eggplant seedlings after all danger of frost is past. Follow in about a week with seed plantings of cucumbers, melons, pumpkins and squash.

1 Leaf lettuce
2 Carrots or parsley
3 Beets or kohlrabi
4 String beans
5 Onions (from spring planting harvest July)
6 Sweet pepper
7 Zucchini
8 Bush pumpkins
9 Eggplant
10 Tomatoes
11 Cucumbers

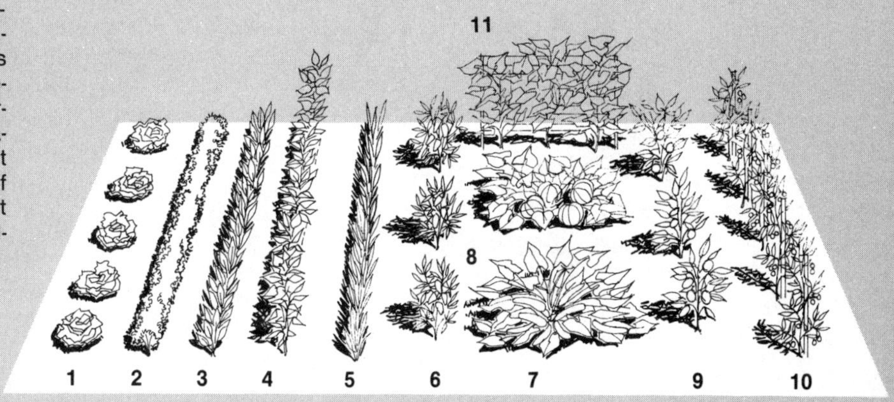

FALL

Lettuce, cabbage, beets, radishes, carrots, spinach and peas can all be planted in August or even September, depending on your area's climate. Again, planting seedlings will mean more of a harvest before winter. In all but the coldest climates, you can plant leaf lettuce, beets, carrots, onions and spinach in the fall and allow them to winter over for an exceedingly early harvest next spring. During the coldest of winter weather, you should cover crops with good mulch.

1 Radishes
2 Parsley
3 Spinach
4 Radishes
5 Cabbage
6 Head lettuce seedlings
7 Peas

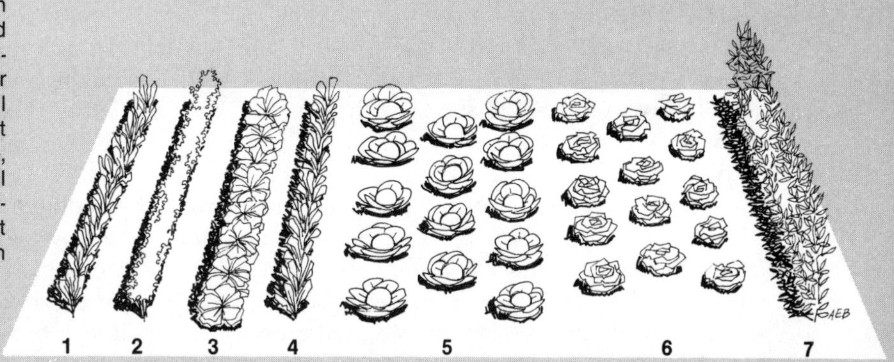

BEFORE FALL frost hits, cut off tomato vines at base and hang the plants upside-down to force ripening of the remaining fruit. You will find that onions will store well if they are hung in a dark, cool place.

not only as closely together as their well-being permits, but with the taller ones to the north so they won't shade the others.

Plant tomatoes in a line along the northern edge, about a foot apart and tied up on stakes or cattle fencing. Pinch off side shoots during early growth. Today's varieties are very fruitful, so it doesn't take many plants for a good crop.

Cucumbers and melons should also be allowed to climb, but no staking for them—they need cattle fencing or chicken wire. Cucumber vines easily support their fruit this way, but you may have to rig cloth slings to support canteloupe and other melons as they get fully ripe.

Sweet peppers may need staking. The branches are quite brittle and crack easily under the weight of today's large peppers.

harvest alternate plants

Plant cabbage and lettuce in twos or threes at close spacings. Head sizes won't be as large as they could be, but overall yield will be greater and be spread over a longer period. Harvest by pulling up an alternate plant every two or three days, as soon as the heads are developed enough to be edible. By the time you get back to the beginning of the row, the remaining plants should have nearly filled in the spaces. Don't let your lettuce harvest go into hot weather, as the heads will "bolt"—grow into stalks.

Beets, radishes, all the root vegetables, will benefit from the same alternating harvest principle, but practiced more extremely. Sprinkle seeds generously into a very straight, half-inch-deep trench—straightness will prove important when you're weeding the garden later—and let nature take its course. When the seedlings have appeared, thin out the weaker ones until you're left with three or four plants to the inch.

Allow plants to grow to a point where fruit formation is evident. Now thin out sparingly. Though fruit may not be large, it certainly will be edible. From then on, you'll be able to gather a small bunch of vegetables every week or two, taking them alternately from the row.

Onions are particularly good to grow in abundance. They can be stored by hanging them on a string in a dark, cool place, and will last all winter. You can buy onion "sets" (bulbs) at some garden shops for spring planting.

starting seedlings

You can extend the productive life of much of your garden by starting seedlings in flats or pots. Tomatoes, eggplants and peppers will begin producing earlier and thus will last longer. Head lettuce will have time to head completely before the heat of summer causes bolting (growing into stalks). For the cabbage family, transplanted seedlings mean an earlier harvest.

Sow seeds near the surface in flats containing about two inches of loose, well-drained soil, six to eight weeks before you plan to put plants in the ground. Maintain a temperature of 70° to 75° F. until the seeds germinate. When the young sprouts have produced their first set of real leaves, they are ready to be transplanted to small pots, to other flats or to a cold frame. In frame or flat, allow two inches between plants.

Seedlings should be sprayed with Maneb to prevent "damping off"—a fungus that attacks the stems. Also, give the seedlings as much light as possible and guard against extreme humidity.

A simpler propagation method is to use peat pellets, sowing several seeds in each pellet and letting the strongest sprout remain. At the proper time, plant them in the ground, pellet and all. Easiest way is to buy seedlings ready for planting.

when to plant

The sample plot designs presented with this article allow for consecutive spring, summer and fall plantings, making the small garden as productive as possible. Harvest times of each season's plants roughly coincide with the times of planting of new crops.

The timetable reflects conditions of the lower New York State area, a moderate climate typical of much of continental U.S.A. Of course, growing seasons are shorter farther north and longer in the South. The fall planting schedule presented here applies only to areas where the first frost comes no earlier than the latter part of October or the fall season continues to be relatively mild even after a frost.

"harden off" seedlings

Remember that all seedlings must be "hardened off"—they must have a week's exposure to gradually lower temperatures in making the transition from greenhouse warmth (or the sunny southern window where they've been kept) to outdoor temperatures.

Extra care should be taken with some crops. Cabbage, for example, should not go through a 7-to-10-day period of daytime temperatures consistently below 50° F. or heads will form permaturely.

choosing varieties

Another result of the sophisticated hybrids developed is that there is a variety of every vegetable especially suited to nearly every specific locality. This is particularly true of tomatoes, eggplant, peppers and lettuce—in some cases a difference of 50 miles can call for two varieties. Most state agricultural colleges publish annual lists of recommended varieties by locality. These are available by mail. Your local agricultural agent will also have this information.

diseases and pests

The best defense against disease and pests in the small garden is prevention. Maintain the plants in vigorous growth, remove all weeds from the plot and the close surroundings, and choose resistant strains of vegetables adapted to your region. To prevent cutworms from decapitating young seedlings, protect them with paper cups, the bottoms of which have been removed, when you put them in the ground.

Beyond this, weekly sprays or dustings of a pyrethrum-rotenone mixture can be very effective against a wide range of pests. Both substances are natural derivatives of plants and have a low toxicity to mammals. Caterpillars can be discouraged quite effectively with bacillus thuringlensis (sold under the trade names Dipel WP, Biotrol XK, an Thuricide HPC), which is nontoxic to mammals and other insects. This will prevent most of the damage done to members of the cabbage family.

Cabbages, brussels sprouts, cauliflower and kale also may suffer from maggots attacking their root stems. Onions and radishes may also be maggot victims. Use Malathion, a systemic spray that enters the plant's tissues. Malathion is also effective against leaf miners, a real problem in beets, turnips and leafy vegetables. These insects enter the leaf, leaving a telltale line of dead tissue to mark their paths as they eat it away. Malathion is one of the least toxic of the systemics, but that's not saying a lot.

Corn will almost certainly be attacked by many pests. Two of the worst, corn borer and earworm, can be prevented by applications of Sevin. This has a low toxicity to mammals, but is deadly to bees and many beneficial insects, so don't use it on anything in flower.

fighting fungus diseases

Most fungus diseases can be controlled by selecting resistant strains of vegetables and maintaining the garden properly. In case of "club root," a fungus that greatly enlarges parts of the roots of cabbage, raising the pH of the soil to neutral is a good preventive.

Other likely fungus victims are the leaves of cucumbers and melons. Use Maneb, as directed, but only if you have to. Difolatan, Phaltan and Bravo are also very effective.

Probably the best preventive is also the simplest: Water in the morning rather than late in the day. Fungus likes it best when the soil is dark and damp at the same time.

Well, there you have it—a down-to-earth approach to the home vegetable garden. But before you begin, make sure there's room in the freezer for those late crops of beans, squash and other goodies. It is often surprising how many vegetables you end up with at the end of the season from a small garden plot.

How to replace gaskets and seals

By MORT SCHULTZ

■ NOT EVERYONE is equipped to replace a head gasket. But a head gasket is only one of many gaskets and oil and grease seals in a car.

The gaskets and seals you will get involved with most often include the carburetor air-cleaner gasket, carburetor-mounting gasket, manifold gaskets, water-pump gasket, exhaust-pipe flange gasket, rocker-arm (valve) cover gasket, thermostat-housing gasket, fuel-pump mounting gasket, oil-pan gasket, oil-filter gasket, automatic-transmission pan gasket, and front- or rear-wheel seals (front-wheel seals if car has rear differential and rear-wheel seals if car has front transaxle).

A gasket is a thin sheet of compressible, fibrous material which makes a seal between two

WHEEL-SEAL care may require special seating tool (below). Gently tap tool until seal is fully seated. Before installing, lightly coat surfaces with grease.

SEE ALSO

**Airconditioners, auto . . . Autos, maintenance . . .
Autos, ramps . . . Differentials, auto . . .
Distributors, auto . . . Engines, auto . . .
Fuel systems, auto . . . Lubrication, auto . . .
Ramps, auto repair . . . Tune-up, auto**

CYLINDER-HEAD gasket of your engine must be handled carefully to avoid damaging it. After gasket installation, tighten cylinder-head bolts following proper sequence (see the specifications of the manufacturer).

BEFORE REPLACING carburetor make sure its mounting surface is free of old gasket material and spotlessly clean.

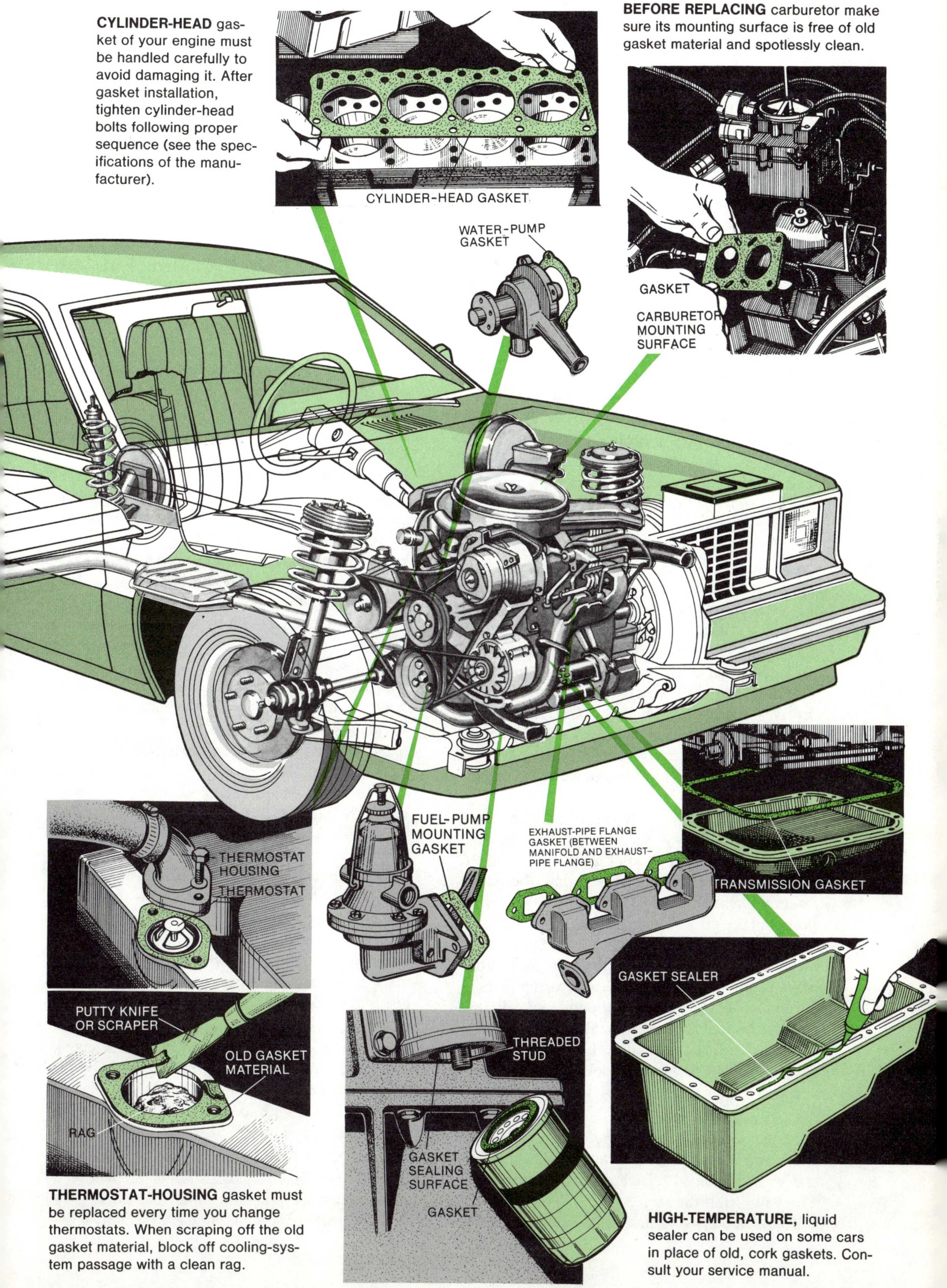

THERMOSTAT-HOUSING gasket must be replaced every time you change thermostats. When scraping off the old gasket material, block off cooling-system passage with a clean rag.

HIGH-TEMPERATURE, liquid sealer can be used on some cars in place of old, cork gaskets. Consult your service manual.

metal surfaces to prevent fluid and/or pressure leaks.

The main job of oil and grease seals is different. In practically every instance, it is to protect bearings by preventing loss of lubricant and contamination of the bearing by dirt and water.

In addition to front and rear wheels, seals are found at the front and rear of the crankshaft, in the transmissions, at the differential pinion and in the steering system. You will come in contact with gaskets more often than with seals. However, the one seal you encounter in doing maintenance, the wheel seal, is extremely important, since it has a bearing on safety.

working on front-wheel seals

According to CR Industries, a leading manufacturer of oil and grease seals, safety requires greasing front-wheel bearings (rear bearings in the case of a front transaxle) and installing new seals every 10,000 miles. This interval provides an ideal time for brake inspection.

After removing the outer wheel bearing, lay the wheel (drum brake) or rotor (disc brake) on the floor. Use a drift pin or piece of broomstick and a rubber or rawhide mallet to gently tap out the old seal and inner wheel bearing.

After servicing bearings and the wheel, install a new seal. Don't reuse the old seal. It usually is damaged when being removed.

A damaged seal causes loss of grease, which deprives bearings of lubricant. Grease can run onto brake linings, causing brakes to grab, which may in turn cause loss of control in a panic stop. A damaged seal also lets dirt and water reach and ruin bearings.

Get the correct seal for the wheel. The part number, embossed on the old seal, may be discernible. It can be used to order the new seal. If the part number is obliterated, tell the parts dealer the make and model of your car. As a precaution, take the old seal with you for matching.

After placing the inner wheel bearing back in the hub, lightly coat the sealing lip and outer edges of the new seal with wheel-bearing grease. If you have a wheel-seal installation tool, slip the seal on the tool so that the sealing lip faces the bearing. The side of the seal with the larger opening should be over the tool.

Hold the tool firmly in a straight line and place the seal over the wheel hub. Tap the tool gently until the seal seats. A change in sound as the mallet strikes the tool lets you know when the seal was "bottomed." Don't pound on the tool. You will distort the seal.

To avoid damaging the seal, it's best to use an installation tool. If you don't have one, use a block of hardwood that is large enough to cover the seal. Hand-place the seal over the bearing. Make sure it's straight. Lay the wood block over the seal and gently tap in place.

How can you tell when a gasket is shot? That depends on the gasket.

With a water pump, for example, coolant will leak past a bad gasket. A consistently low coolant level tips you off even if you overlook wet spots beneath the car. With an oil-pan or oil-filter gasket, you will be aware of oil puddles on the floor beneath the engine or notice the need to add oil frequently.

Different gaskets require different installation procedures. However, some procedures apply to most gaskets, as follows:

■ Be sure you have thoroughly clean mating surfaces. According to Daniel E. Zernik, chief product engineer of Fel-Pro Inc., a manufacturer of gaskets, "No operation is more important in gasketing than thorough cleaning. Even the best gasket will have trouble sealing a dirty installation." Use a putty knife to scrape away old gasket material, dirt, carbon and rust.

■ Don't re-use an old gasket even if it isn't destroyed during disassembly. Compressibility and resiliency are not the same. A cork gasket can be compressed up to 50 percent of its thickness, but it doesn't have sufficient resiliency to return to its original thickness. Re-using the compressed gasket may well result in leakage.

■ Depending on the area, inspect mating surfaces for irregularities and warping. Lay a flat straight-edge lengthwise and then crosswise across the surface. If the straight-edge doesn't lie flat, the surface is distorted. Replace the part or, if practical, have it machined.

Incidentally, if you ever need a cylinder head(s) or block of a V-type engine machined, the intake manifold may also have to be machined. The heads will be positioned inward and downward in relation to where they were before machining, causing misalignment between the heads and manifold.

■ Be sure to get the right gasket. The wrong one won't fit. Be aware, too, that many gaskets have a right and wrong side, and they have to be installed right-side up. Gaskets are often marked with some designation, such as "this side up" to guide you.

■ You may have a choice of gasket materials. For instance, oil-pan gaskets are made of cork, a combination of vegetable fiber and cork, or a synthetic-rubber compound. Cork is highly compressible, but must be handled carefully because it is easily torn.

A gasket that is made of vegetable fiber and cork is also highly compressible, can withstand rougher handling than cork and is less subject to shrinking. Gaskets made of synthetic-rubber compounds, the latest innovation, are tough, they won't shrink, they are compressible and they are not affected by oils and greases.

■ Be careful how you tighten an assembly following the installation of a new gasket. First, install all bolts finger-tight. Then, following the bolt-tightening sequence recommended by the car manufacturer (if there is one), use a torque wrench to tighten to manufacturer specification. (Consult the service manual.) Do not apply full pressure at once. Instead, first tighten each bolt part way. Then, repeat the process until recommended torque value is reached to assure even compression of the gasket.

■ After completing installation, run the engine for a few minutes. Check around the sealing surface for leaks. If there is a leak, snug up bolts. If this fails, disassemble and check for dirt, an irregular surface or gasket damage.

■ In the case of head gaskets, the head(s) should be retightened after the car is driven 300 to 500 miles. Heat expansion and contraction sometimes alter torque.

oil-filter gasket

After cleaning the oil-filter seat on the engine, apply a light coating of engine oil to the gasket of the new filter and to the seating surface on the engine. Start the filter on to its seat, being careful not to cross or strip threads.

Hand-tighten the filter until the gasket touches the seating surface. Now, hand-tighten another one-half to three-quarter turn. This is sufficient to compress the gasket and form a secure seat. Do not tighten an oil filter with a wrench. After filling the crankcase with oil, start the engine and check for leaks around the filter.

thermostat gasket

Before cleaning the old gasket and sealer from the thermostat gasket seat, stuff a clean rag into the hole in which the thermostat goes. This is done to prevent debris from falling in the engine.

Install the thermostat and coat both sides of the new gasket with gasket sealer. Put the gasket in place, carefully lay the thermostat housing into position and tighten the bolts finger-tight. Using a wrench, secure the bolts. Start the engine and check around the housing for a coolant leak.

fuel-pump gasket

After cleaning the fuel-pump mounting pad at the engine block or timing-gear cover, apply an oil-resistant sealer to both sides of the new gasket. Place the gasket on the fuel-pump flange and carefully position the pump against the mounting pad.

Holding the pump tightly to the pad, install mounting bolts. Tighten bolts alternately until they are torqued to specification.

oil-pan gasket

If an oil pan has been sealed with a cork gasket, the gasket may, in time, deteriorate and allow oil to leak. After draining oil, remove the pan and clean the pan flange and engine.

Apply a drop of silicone-rubber, adhesive gasket sealer to each corner of the gasket. The sealer holds the gasket in place during the installation. Place the gasket on the oil-pan flange.

Put the pan back in position, hand-tighten bolts, and then tighten them to specification. You could easily distort the oil pan if the tightening procedure is not done carefully. Torque bolts in steps evenly around the pan to avoid warping the pan.

Some late-model cars use a chemical rather than a material gasket. These are silicones, called RTV sealants, applied to the oil-pan flange. The pan is bolted in place while the chemical gasket is wet.

In using an RTV sealant, apply a 3/16-inch-wide bead evenly around the oil-pan flange, inboard of the bolt holes. Don't allow the liquid to block the holes, and don't leave a gap in the flow, since the seal will not be complete.

rocker arm (valve) cover

After cleaning the surfaces, apply a thin coat of gasket adhesive to the valve-cover flange. The purpose of the adhesive is to keep the gasket in place—not to help seal the area. Do not apply adhesive to the gasket.

Lay the gasket on the valve-cover flange and allow adhesive to dry. You can tell when it is dry by applying light finger pressure to the gasket. If the gasket slides away from the flange, the adhesive is not dry. Premature installation of the valve cover on the engine will destroy the fit and cause leakage.

Tighten the cover to manufacturer specification. Do not overtighten. You will distort the cover.

A thing of beauty, this distinctive entertainment center will add excitement to your outdoor living. It's an attractive back-yard gazebo with its own built-in grill

Build this handsome cookout gazebo

By WAYNE C. LECKEY

IF IT DID NOTHING MORE than just stand there, this charming back-yard gazebo would make your yard the prettiest one in the block.

No longer need you worry about a cookout being rained out. The chef and his steaks are high and dry under the protection of a big umbrella roof. Wooden benches around three sides make the covered deck a natural eating place when a sudden shower tries to ruin everything.

The built-in grill occupies the center of the open deck and sits under a central flue which carries heat, smoke and cooking fumes out through the roof. Hanging from the sides, the grill has boxlike counters fitted with hinged lids to provide convenient storage for charcoal, barbecue tools and the like.

The gazebo you see here was adapted from an original plan developed by the Western Wood Products Assn. We modified it to simplify construction and cut down its roof from 18 ft. square to 12 ft. square to fit the yard.

The supporting framework consists of heavy timbers, the posts being 4x8s, the deck beams, roof plates and hip rafters 4x6s. The deck is covered with 2x4s, the roof framed with 2x6 common rafters, the three benches assembled from 2x12s, 4x4s and 4x12s. All members are standard, nominal-size timbers which most lumberyards stock in Douglas fir, ponderosa pine, western hemlock, spruce or western larch.

In studying the floor plan, notice that the crisscrossed deck beams are supported by eight 8-in.-dia. piers, while the four corner posts are supported by 10-in-dia. poured footings. The holes for these are dug below the frost line and located from a center point of the structure. We found that regular clay flue tile made neat ready-made forms for the eight piers and forms which remain as part of the pier. All forms must be leveled in both directions, which can be done with a long straightedge and level or, more professionally, with a builder's transit.

You have a choice of setting the four corner posts right in the footings or bolting them to steel anchor plates embedded in the concrete. The former method will make a more sturdy structure, but poses a replacement problem if a post should ever rot off at the footing. However, if first treated with a wood preservative, the posts could last 20 years or more. If the posts are to stand in the footings, they must be plumbed and braced prior to pouring the concrete and be longer than otherwise.

You'll save a lot of time and aching muscles by ordering premixed concrete. The depth of the holes will determine how much concrete is required. We used 1½ cu. yds. of 1/2/4 mix. Strike off the concrete flush with the tops of the tile forms and then place a ½ x 10-in. bolt in the center of each one.

Notch the supporting deck beams to form a 30-in.-sq. opening in the center when the four members are half lapped. The grill box later sits inside this opening. Holes are bored in the timbers so they will sit down over the bolts. Before drawing up the nuts, check the beams with a level. You may have to shim them. Draw the nuts only moderately tight.

The four posts are joined at the top with 4x6

text continued on page 1350

SEE ALSO

**Barbecues . . . Benches, deck . . . Cabanas . . .
Cookout bars . . . Decks . . . Firepits . . .
Garden shelters . . . Grills . . . Insect traps . . .
Patios . . . Planters . . .
Screened summer rooms . . . Yard lighting**

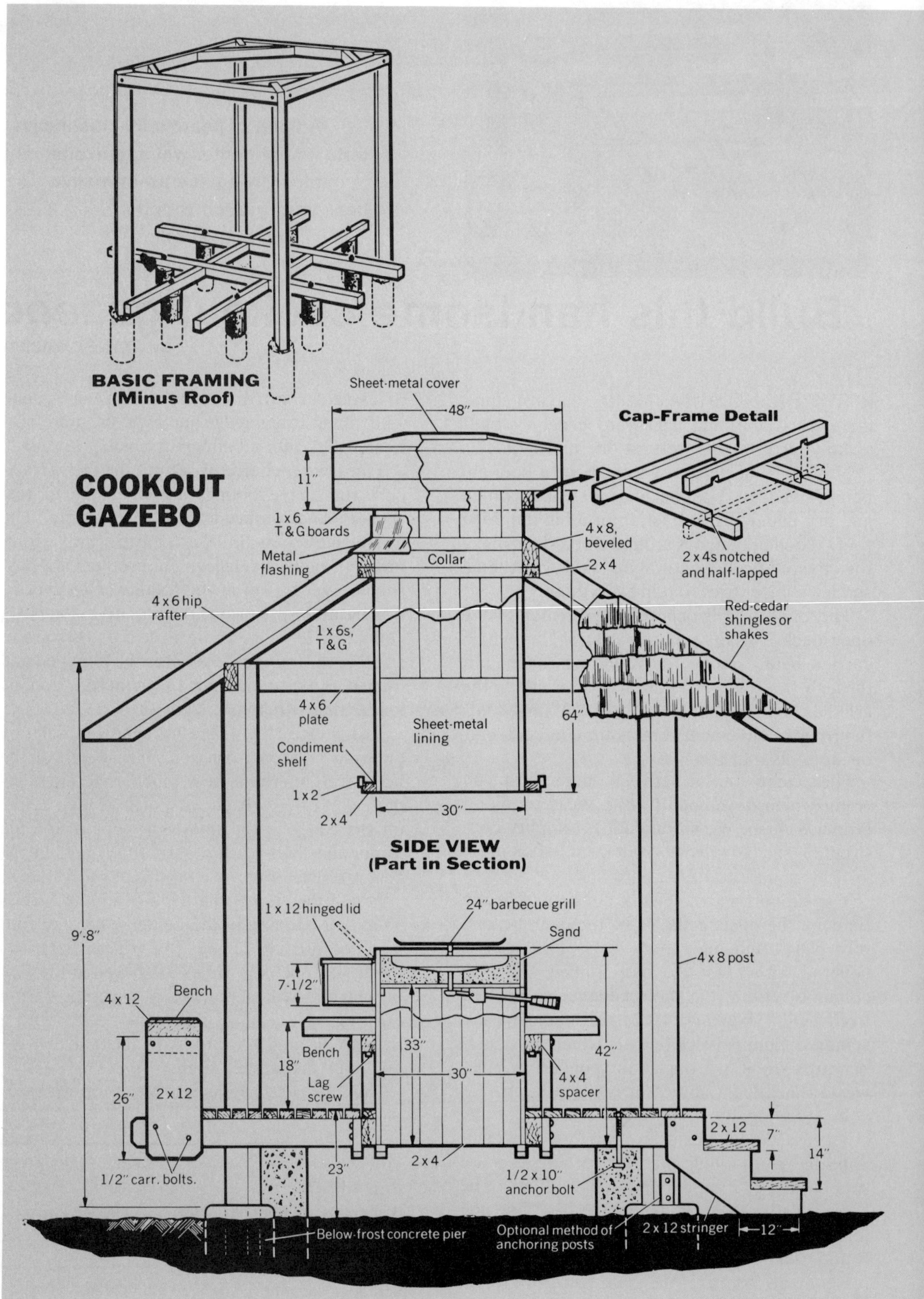

BASIC FRAMING
(Minus Roof)
COOKOUT
GAZEBO
Sheet-metal cover
48"
Cap-Frame Detail
11"
1 x 6
T & G boards
4 x 8,
beveled
2 x 4s notched
and half-lapped
Metal
flashing
Collar
2 x 4
4 x 6 hip
rafter
Red-cedar
shingles or
shakes
1 x 6s,
T & G
4 x 6
plate
Sheet-metal
lining
64"
Condiment
shelf
1 x 2
2 x 4
30"
SIDE VIEW
(Part in Section)
1 x 12 hinged lid
24" barbecue grill
Sand
9'-8"
4 x 8 post
7-1/2"
4 x 12
Bench
Bench
33"
42"
18"
Lag
screw
30"
4 x 4
spacer
26"
2 x 12
2 x 12
7"
14"
1/2" carr. bolts.
23"
2 x 4
1/2 x 10"
anchor bolt
Below-frost concrete pier
Optional method of
anchoring posts
2 x 12 stringer
12"

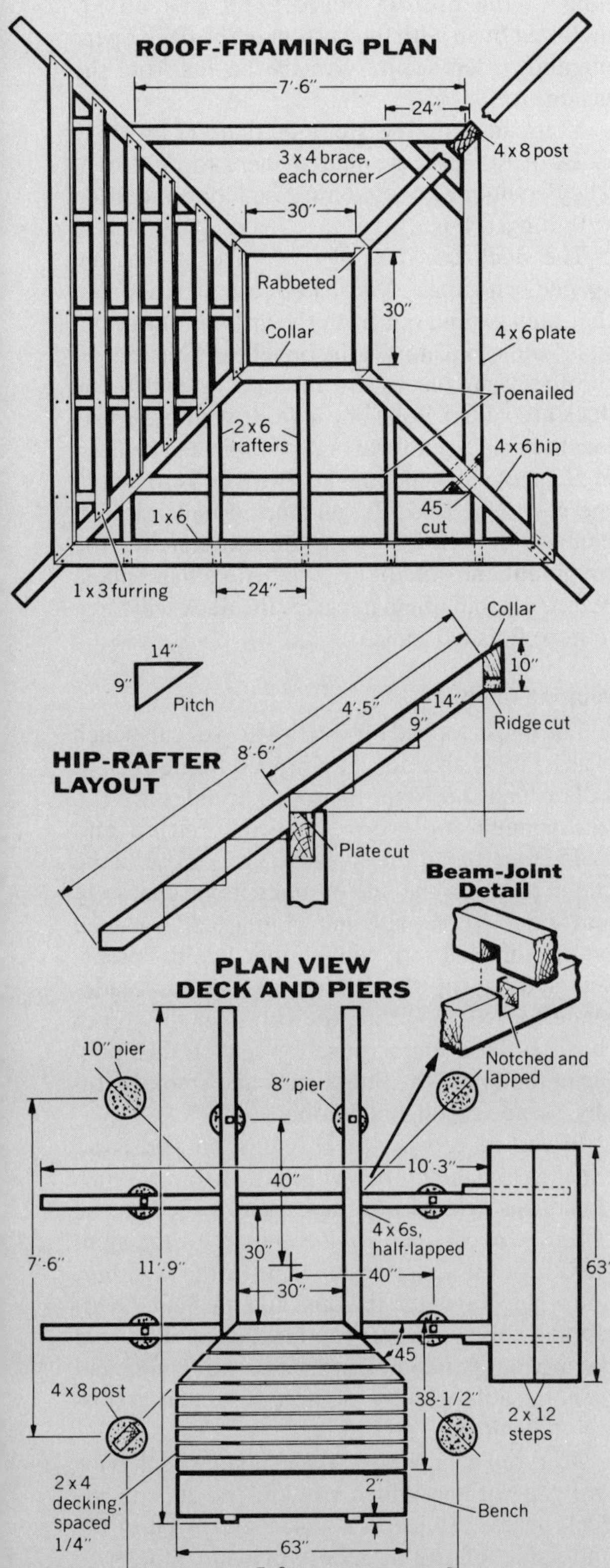

Technical Art by Stanley Cohen

U-SHAPED LEGS of the benches straddle outboard ends of the 4x6 deck beams and are bolted to them.

PIER-SUPPORTED BEAMS are decked with 2x4s placed flat and ¼ in. apart. Fasten with 12d nails.

A BOX-LIKE FLUE is made with 1x6 V-groove boards, shoved up through the roof collar and nailed.

members (plates) kept even with the tops of the posts and flush with the front edges. Ends of the plates are mitered 45° and tied to the faces of the posts with long bolts. These pass through holes bored through both post and plates, one bolt for each post. Inside corner braces (3x4s) are required when the corner posts are bolted to the footings.

Make the supporting collar for the flue next. In studying the rafter plan, note that its inside opening is 30 in. sq. and that the members are rabbeted at the corners. The corners of the collar are trimmed 45° to provide a flat face against which the hip rafters butt and toenail. Also, you'll see that 2x4s are added to the bottom of the 4x6s to increase their width. Finally, the top edges of the collar are beveled to match the roof pitch.

cutting the hip rafters

The hip rafters are laid out to a 9 and 14 pitch. To determine their length and the location of the plate cut, you step off the 9-in. rise in a 14-in. run with a framing square. Here you first mark the ridge cut which butts against the corner of the collar, and then pace off the required number of steps as indicated. The hip rafters actually rest on top of the posts to which they are toenailed.

You'll need help to lift these heavy rafters and set them in position. Long supports nailed to the deck beams will temporarily elevate the collar at the right height so you can toenail the hips to it. Once you have the hips nailed, it's less of a job to continue to fill the space between with common rafters which are spaced 24 in. on centers. For laying out the 2x6 common rafters, use 9 and 12 in. on the framing square.

Both the grill and the flue are built up of 1x6 vee, tongue-and-groove boards. They are nothing more than square, open-end boxes having an outside dimension of 30 in. The flue box is shoved up through the collar from inside the gazebo. It projects 10 in. and is nailed securely to the collar from inside. A 2x4 shelf circles the bottom of the flue to provide a place to keep salt and pepper handy. Four pieces of sheet metal line the flue for a height of 24 in.

The grill box has a loose, wood bottom which rests on cleats placed 6 in. down from the top. We made use of the bowl of an inexpensive 24-in. patio grill (brazier) and brought the raising and lowering handle out through a slot in the side of the box. This works fine when the original center post is replaced with a longer one of ½-in. copper tubing. The grill we used was made by Crestline, Division of Federal Steel Corp., Raritan, NJ. It's placed in a bed of sand, and a tunafish can, minus its bottom, is used as a ring to keep the sand from sifting through the center hole in the bottom board. The grill box is mounted flush with the bottom of the deck opening and nailed securely to the beams from the inside.

You can hang the storage counters on three sides of the grill; we added them to only two. They're simple boxes about 29 in. long and fitted with hinged lids.

The deck consists of 2x4s placed flat and spaced ¼ in. apart. You'll notice in the floor plan that they extend out from the grill in four directions and run as far as the benches. The ends of the first four pieces are mitered. Steps to the deck are added along one side. If your gazebo is located near a pool like ours, a ramp can be used in place of steps and decked with 2x4s to match the rest. Use two 12d galvanized nails at each nailing point. If you take time to chamfer the rough-cut ends of all the 2x4s with a hand plane before you nail them in place, the deck will have a more finished look.

capping the flue

The flue is topped off with a 4-ft.-sq. cap which is assembled around a half-lapped framework of 2x4s which slips over the top. The sides are 1x6 vee tongue-and-groove boards, butted and nailed together at the corners. You can build the cap in place on the flue or make it up separately and add it as complete unit. A long ladder placed on the shingled roof will let you slide the preassembled cap up the ladder rails and give adequate footing for lifting the cap over the top of the flue. Sheet metal is used to seal off the opening in the top of the flue; fumes and smoke actually escape through side openings.

We used red cedar shingles on the roof. (Shakes look better but will cost you more.) Furring strips spaced 6 in. apart and nailed to the rafters support and provide nailing for the shingles. Lay the latter about 5 in. to the weather, and when you reach the flue, add flashing. Overlapping shingles cover the hip ridges. To avoid having nail points poke through the furring and be noticeable, pick ¾-in. large-head nails to fasten the shingles.

All three benches are made alike, each having two pairs of legs which straddle the ends of the deck beams. Spacers of 4x4, lagscrewed to the underside of the benches, provide blocks to which the legs are cross-bolted. Bolts are used to fasten the benches to the beams.

'You-haul' kiddie car

By C. L. WIDDICOMBE

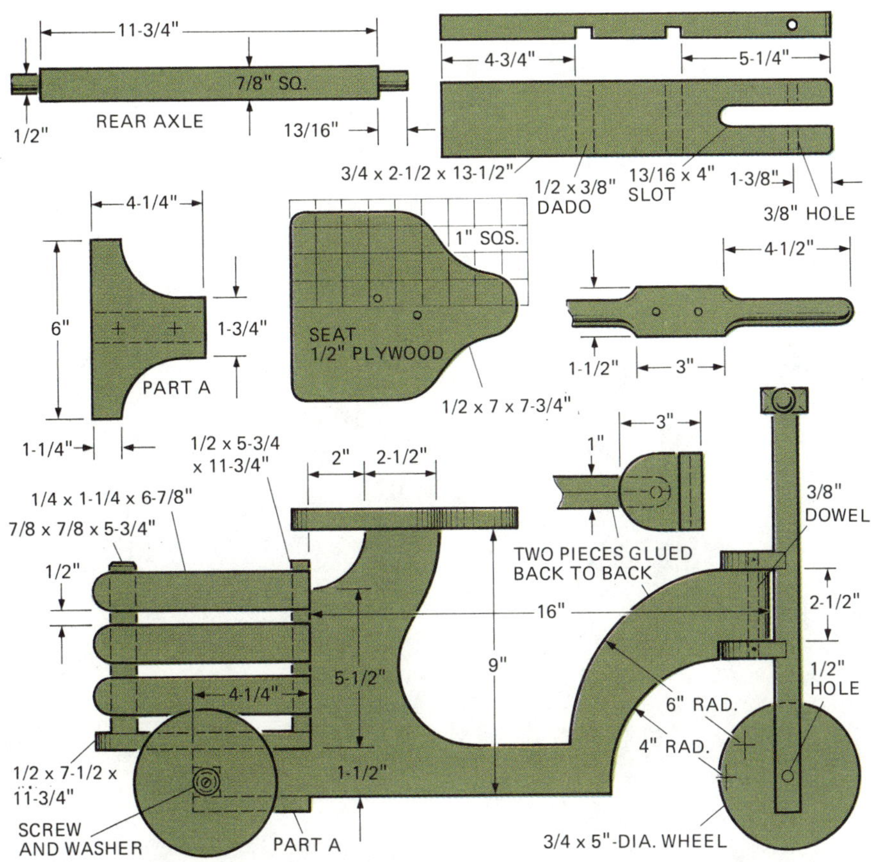

SAND all parts thoroughly, round all sharp edges. Paint with a non-toxic finish. Wheels, seat and handle can be red, the rest kept natural and given a coat of clear urethane. If you find that the seat needs extra support, a small wood bracket can be glued to each side and fastened to the seat with FH wood screws.

THIS "YOU HAUL" VERSION of the popular three-wheel kiddie car is a toy young truckers will like to find under the tree Christmas morning. The 1-in.-thick center frame consists of two pieces of ½-in. plywood. Bandsaw both pieces together, then glue and clamp them face to face and sand the edges. Make the 5-in. wheels, seat, floor and front of the stake body from plywood also. Cut the rest of the parts from hardwood such as birch.

If you don't have a wood lathe, the turned tenons on the ends of the rear axle can be formed by drilling the ends for 3-in. lengths of ½-in. dowel. The turned steering handle can be made in a similar way. Slot the steering post for the front wheel and pivot the post to the center frame with two wood brackets and a loose-fitting dowel. Both brackets are glued and nailed in ⅜-in.-deep dadoes. Part A supports the rear axle in its ⅞-in. square notch, and a screw and washer are used to hold each wheel to the tenon. Make the holes in the wheels a bit larger than the tenons. A ⅜-in. dowel is the front axle, glued to the post. Drill a ½-in. hole in the wheel to make it turn freely and apply paste wax to tenons.

SEE ALSO

Children's furniture . . . Dump trucks, toy . . . Kites . . . Pull toys . . . Toys

Gifts to make for Christmas

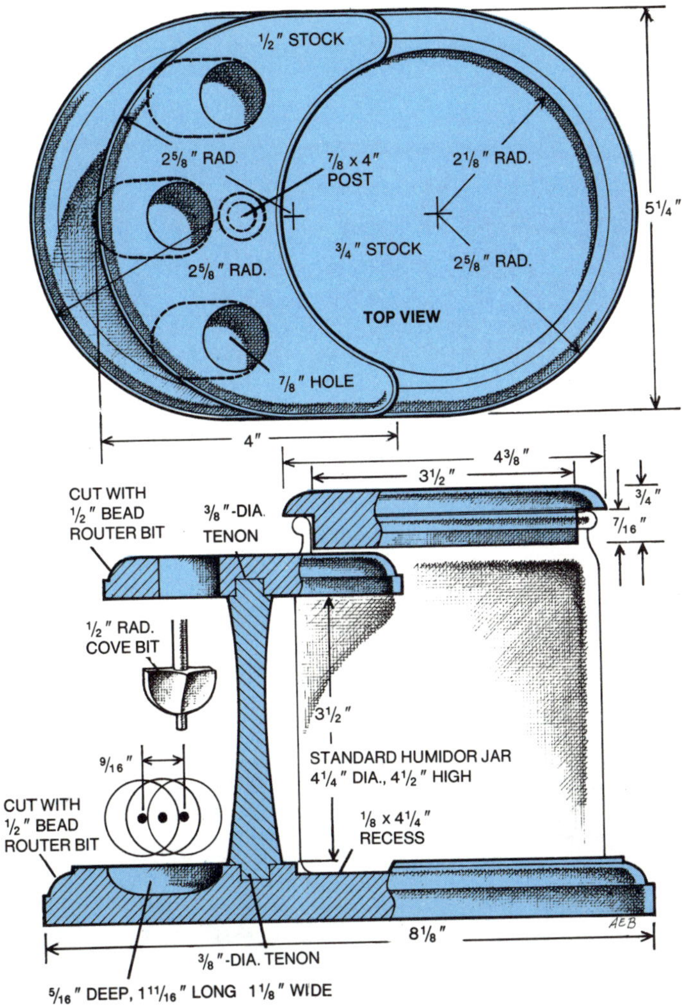

Pipe rack and humidor

A PIPE SMOKER'S DREAM, this pipe rack and humidor set makes a great gift for a pipe lover. It's a lathe, router and drill-press project holding three pipes and a tobacco jar you can buy at any pipe shop. The jar rests in a 1/8-in.-deep recess you make with a circle cutter, then a router and a straight bit. The three oval wells for pipe bowls are made with a 1/2-in.-radius cove router bit chucked in the drill press. The bit is guided by three holes the same size as its pilot and lowered 3/8 in. into the work. Overlapping depressions are evened up with a wood chisel and holes filled with wood putty. If you wish, you can line wells with modelmaker's grass sprinkled in wet glue. The jar cover is faceplate-turned to fit, and a spindle made to support the rack 3½ in. above the pipe wells. Edges of rack and base are shaped with a 1/2-in.-bead bit. Green felt is glued to the bottom for a finishing touch.

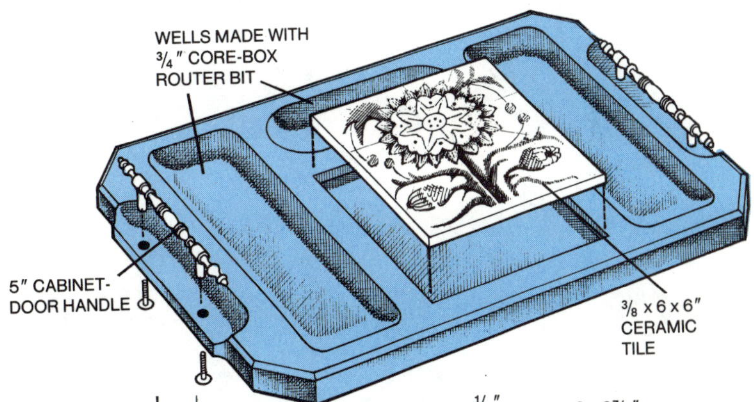

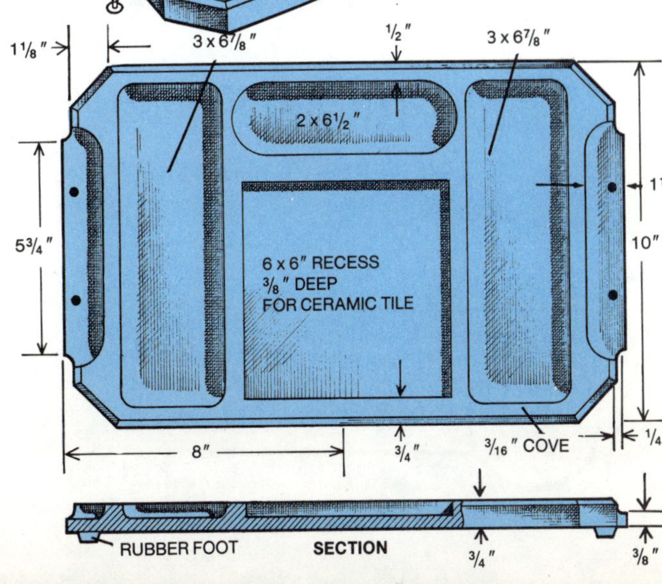

Cheese tray

A DECORATIVE 6x6-in. ceramic tile is used for the cutting surface of this handsome cheese tray. The three olive and cracker depressions, and the tile recess, are made with a router and a hardboard template that's used to guide the cutter. Openings in the template are made 3/16 in. less all around than overall sizes of the recesses to accommodate a shouldered guide ring that fits the base of the router. Short brads driven through ends of template hold it in place. A 3/4-in.-dia. core-box cutter is used to scoop out the olive and cracker "trays" and a straight bit to cut the tile recess. Routed areas at handle ends of the tray are made last with the core-box bit.

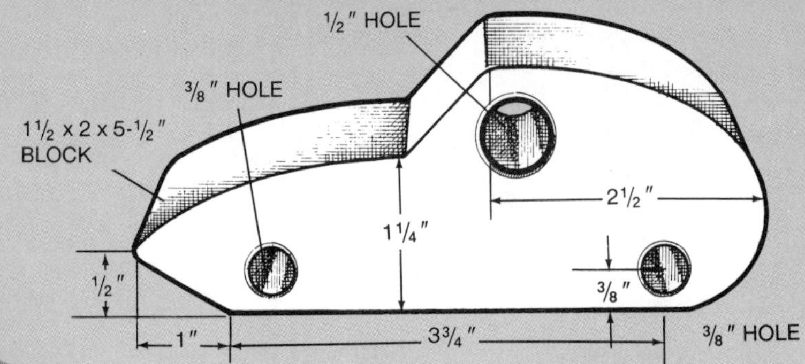

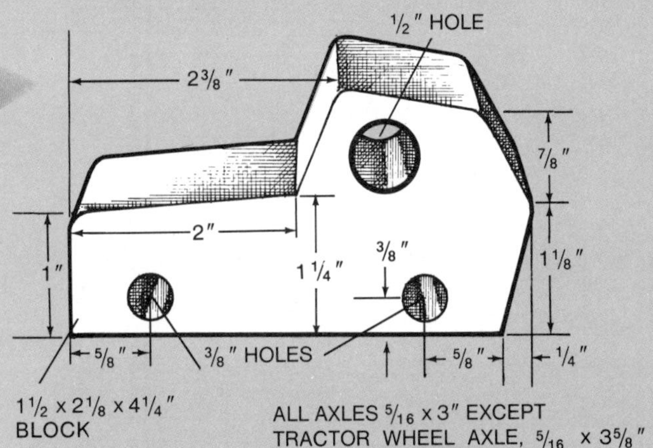

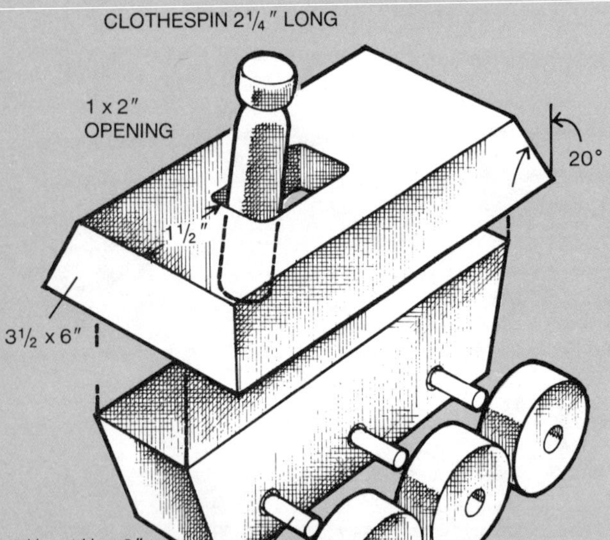

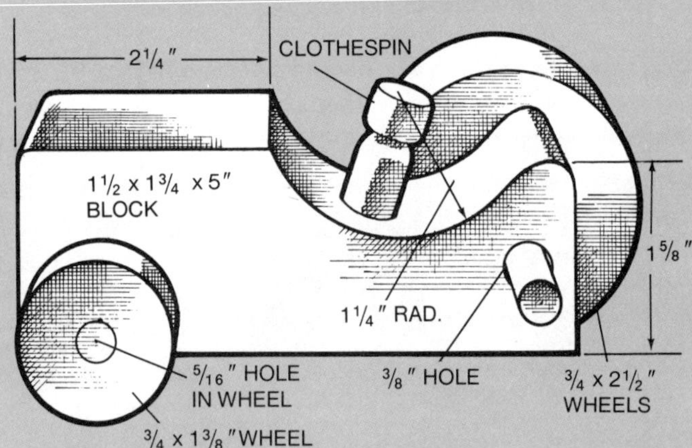

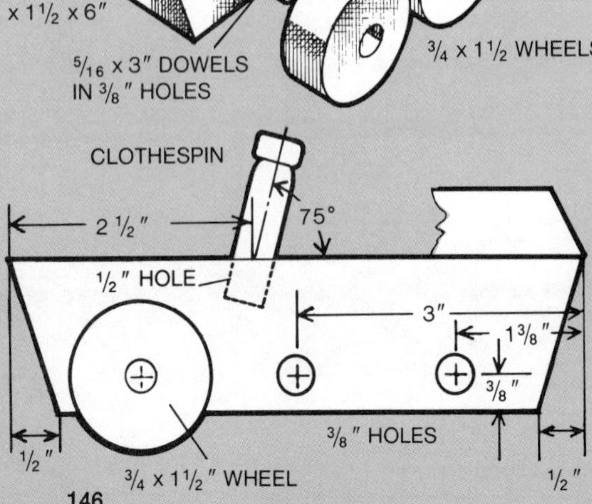

Block cars

BLOCK TOYS ARE always favorites with little folks, and the four vehicles you see here can be turned out by the dozen from scrap wood for the most part. A quick way to mass-produce the wheels in quantity is to buy a length of wooden closet pole, slice it up in a miterbox and drill holes in the centers. The wheels fit tightly on 5/16-in. dowel axles which turn freely in 3/8-in. holes. Wood clothespins are used for the drivers. All sharp edges including wheels should be rounded and surfaces sanded smoothly. Cars can be left unpainted; it you paint and varnish them, use nontoxic finishes.

Treasure chest

IT'S LITTLE MORE than a plain wooden box, but add solid-brass hardware and a tiny padlock after giving it a hand-rubbed finish, and it takes on the look of a handsome miniature treasure chest. It's a gift most anyone can use to keep trinkets and other personal possessions under lock and key. Make it from pine or walnut, ¼ to ½ in. thick, and glue it together as a complete box. Sand it well and, with your table-saw blade projecting a bit more than the thickness of the wood, carefully saw around the four sides, as shown at the right, to form the lid. Some screws must be filed flush when the box is made of ¼-in. wood. Stanley sells the brass hardware—two hinges, four corners, four feet, a hasp and padlock. Red velvet lining adds the finishing touch.

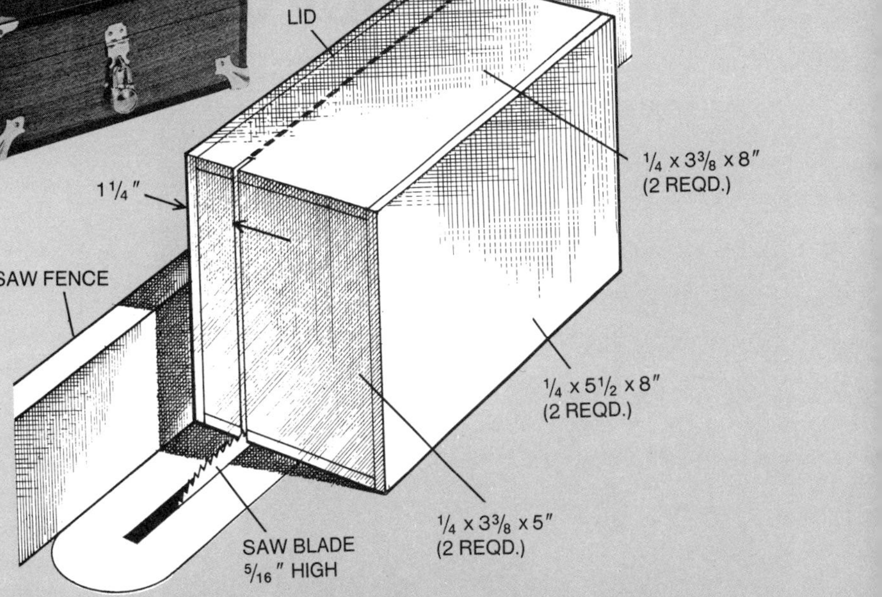

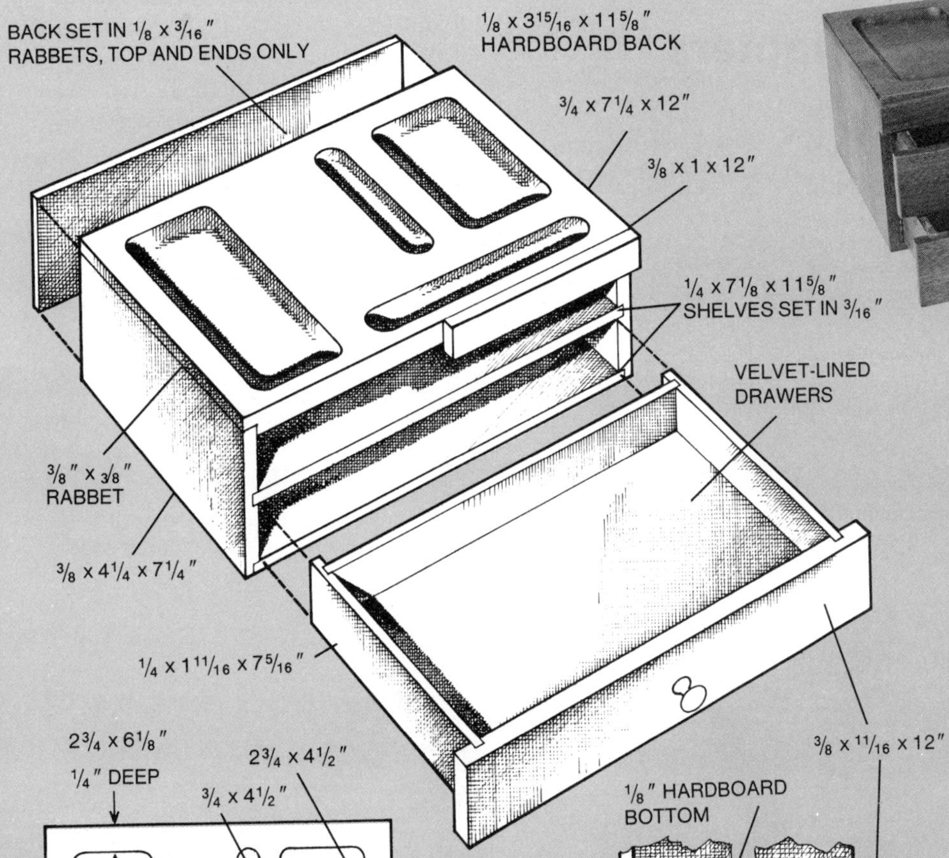

Dresser-top valet

HANDY FOR overnight parking of wallet, watch, lighter and loose change, here's a gift a dad or son will appreciate. Its two velvet-lined drawers will keep tie clips, rings and cuff links in one handy place. The recessed top is dished out in the same way as that of the cheese tray—with router, template and a shouldered guide. You start with a longer board than needed, and cut it to length when recessed. The two shallow drawers lap the openings on three sides, (bottom and ends). Use walnut or other fine cabinet wood and finish it with two coats of a self-rubbing polyurethane.

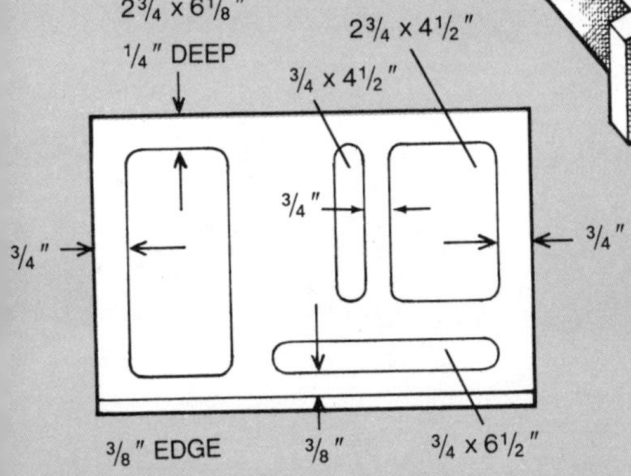

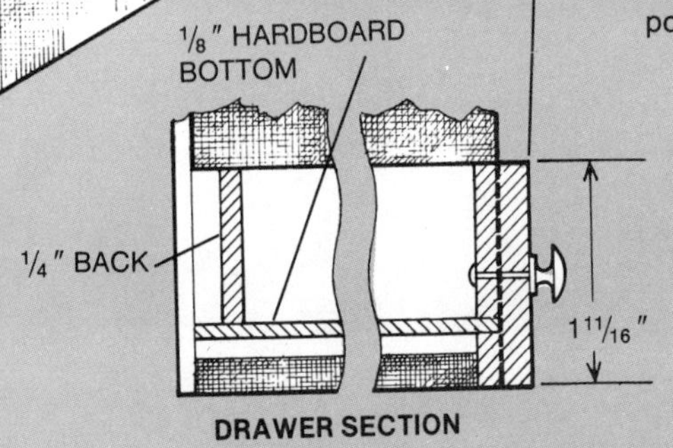

DRAWER SECTION

More gifts for Christmas

■ BECAUSE THEY FIT into almost any decor, these simple planters might be the ideal gift for many of your "green-thumb" friends. The basic design consists of two redwood end pieces cut from 1x6 stock and 21 lengths of ½-in. half-round molding. The planters shown are approximately 1 ft. long, but the length, like the decorative touches, is strictly a matter of personal taste.

There's really no need to varnish or stain the planter, since unfinished wood is most-effective in achieving the desired rustic appearance.

After cutting and sanding the end pieces, stand them on their flat edges the proper distance apart and connect them by nailing one length of molding down the center. This should project about ½ in. beyond the outside faces. To hold the end pieces square, temporarily nail a second length of molding 90° from the first, being careful to maintain the same distance between the ends. Then it's simply a matter of nailing the rest of the molding in position, ten pieces on each side.

Adhesive-backed metallic trim tape may be used to dress up the appearance. If you want to add legs, nail spools in position from the inside. To make a hanging version, all you need are two screw eyes and some fine brass chain.

Choice of rustic planters

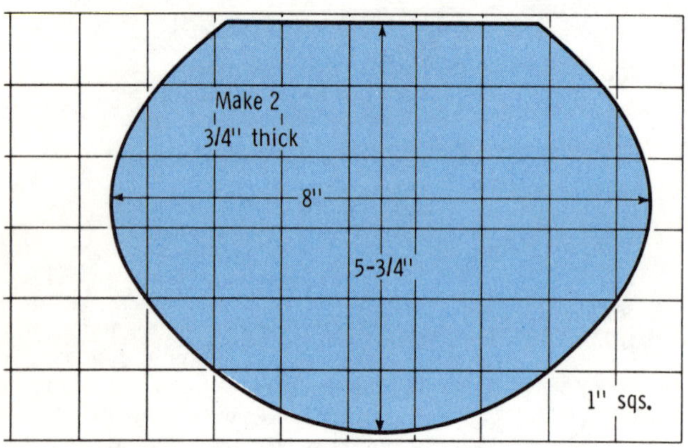

TO BRACE ends square, connect them with two pieces of molding 90° apart. The ends must be parallel.

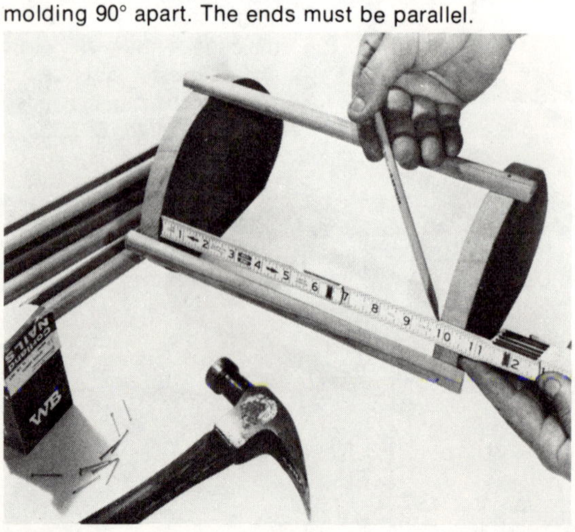

START IN MIDDLE when nailing the other lengths of half round in place. Use one small nail at each of the ends.

Colonial bell shelf

■ IN DAYS GONE BY, the farmer's wife used a small bell to call the family together for meals. When not in use, it was kept in a decorative bracket or shelf near the kitchen door.

Such a shelf—equipped with a bell, of course—makes the perfect gift for anyone who appreciates a touch of Americana. While it probably won't be used to "ring in" the family at meal time, the bell and shelf make a pleasing plus in any informal kitchen.

You can make it from any kind of lumber available. Even plywood can be used. The choice of stain and finish will depend on the decor in the room in which the shelf will probably be hung.

Cut out the pieces and sand each one well. Since no great loads are involved, the shelf can be assembled with glue without any nails or screws.

SEE ALSO
Christmas cards . . . Christmas decorations . . . Kitchen accessories . . . Planters . . . Weekend projects . . . Wood sculpture

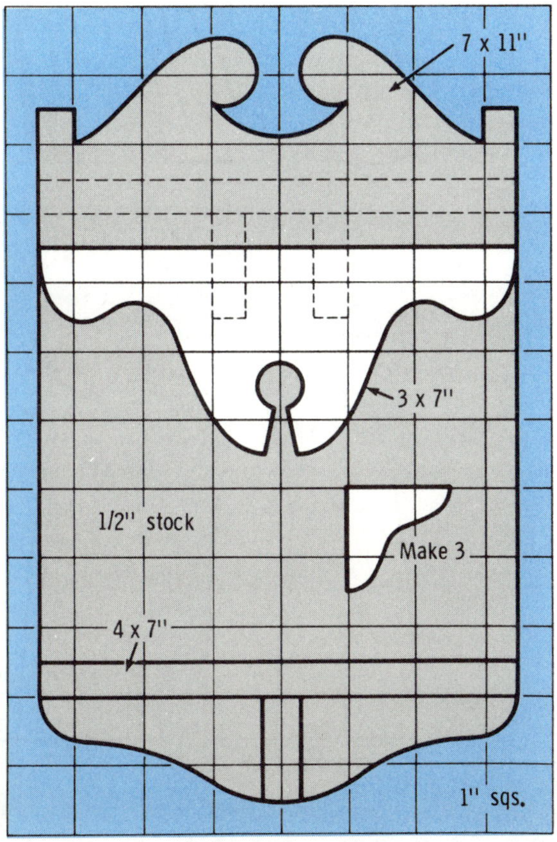

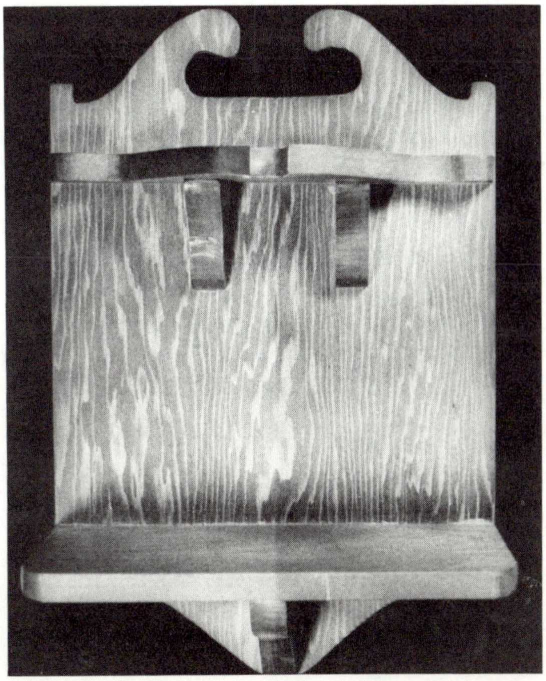

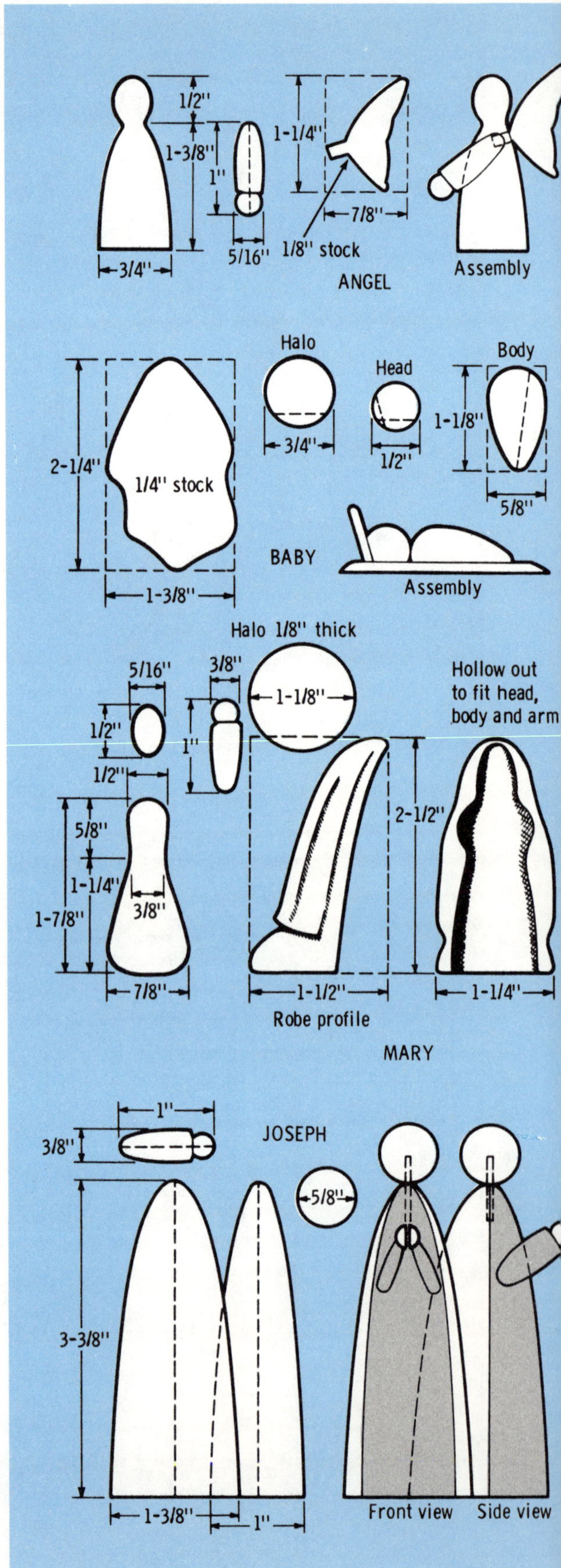

Artisan's musical crèche

THIS CLASSIC Christmas Nativity scene takes on an unusual and thoroughly modern look when imaginatively made as an abstract.

Both the figures and the shelter require some hand carving to bring out some of the finer details but a beginner's talent here lends a realistic and authentic touch. As detailed in the patterns at right, the lathe-turned figures are quite presentable without the carving, however, should you so desire.

Another option is the inclusion of a music works that fits neatly in the small boxlike structure on the right of the crèche. In this case, an 18-note *Silent Night* movement is used and is available from Walters Modern Hobby Shop, 207 French Rd., Utica, NY 13502.

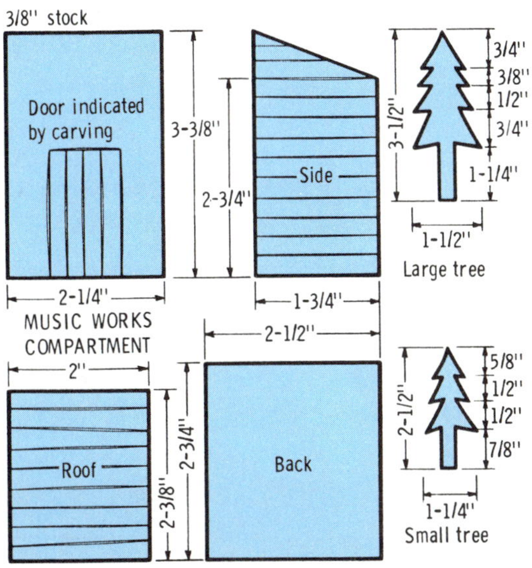

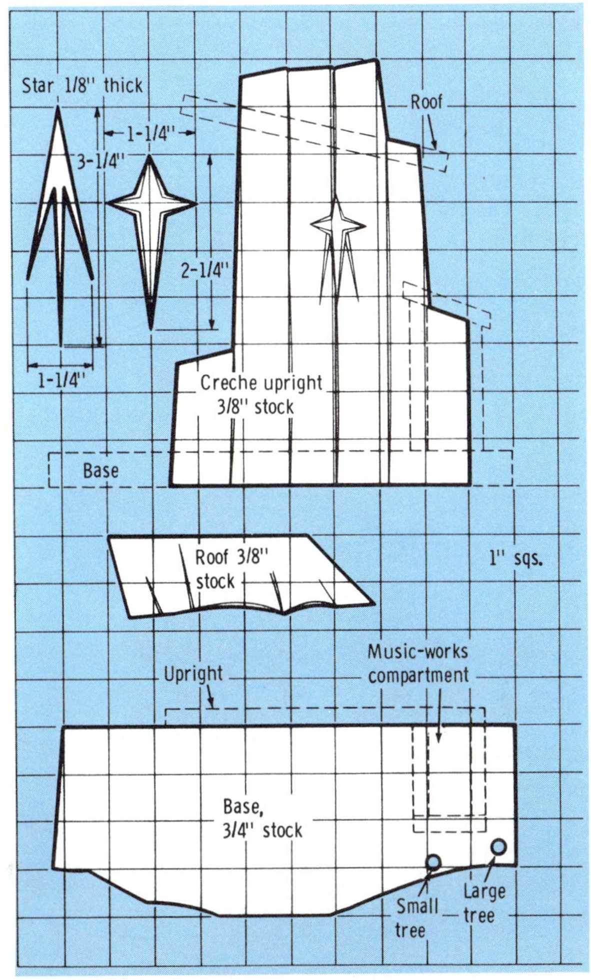

FIGURES ARE made up of different wood species as listed, then finished to suit your preference (below left). Trees (below right) also need some rough carving.

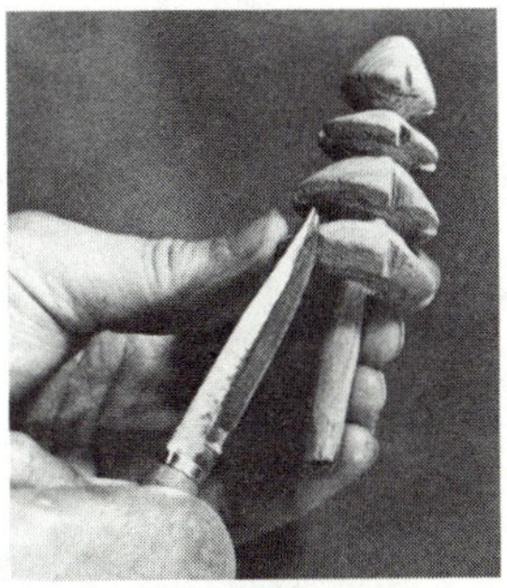

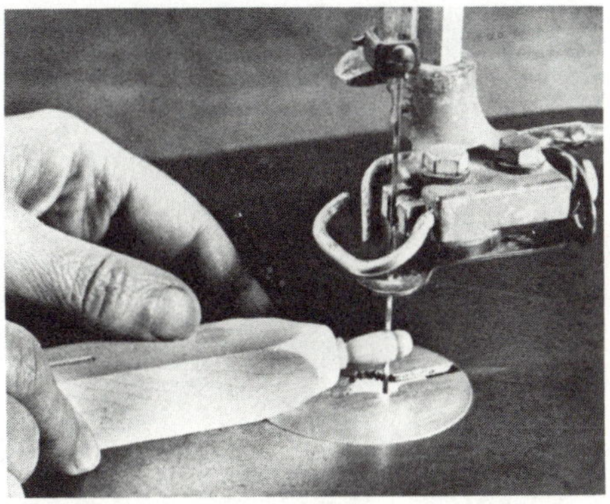

COMPACT MUSIC movement fits tidily into neat structure on right side of crèche. Jigsaw is required as is some carving (left).

1 Frame for tilting heart-shaped mirror is constructed of ½-in. plywood. The tilt action is made possible by force fit.

2 Our attractive ring caddy keeps rings, small jewelry convenient on a vanity. A felt cuff holds earrings in full view for easy selection.

3 Solid-wood, linked hearts bored with many holes become a handy crayon holder for your youngest valentine.

4 Layered-pine jewel box can be painted in stripes or solid as shown. A circular cutout is affixed to top's underside to assure alignment when the box is closed.

Valentines from your shop

By HARRY WICKS

■ BY SPENDING A COUPLE of Saturdays in your workshop building these delightful items you are sure to create the most pleasant Valentine's Day your family has ever enjoyed. We asked designer C. J. Castelberry to come up with some Valentine gifts that our woodworking readers could create for their wives and daughters. Her successful results are shown on the facing page.

Construction is easy

Happily, we were able to retain the boutique-like look that the designer wanted—even though the goal was to create the prototypes in wood with the least amount of effort. The result is that all of the projects can be easily reproduced by anyone with a typical home workshop. The mirror project requires the greatest carpentry skill—and certain tools—(you will need handscrews to hold vertical legs and mirror in alignment when boring the dowel hinge holes).

General instructions

■ To minimize the time needed for sanding and/or planing, use a hollow ground planer (or finer) blade to cut out all parts on the table saw.

■ For cuts made with jigsaw or bandsaw, use the finest-possible blade that won't break when turning a sharp radius.

■ Sanding of scrolls (heart shapes) goes very quickly if you use a flap-type sander (such as Merit Abrasive's Sand-O-Flex) in either portable drill or drill press.

■ Seal all parts before painting with a thinned coat of shellac; thin 3-lb.-cut shellac one part shellac to three parts denatured alcohol. A pigmented shellac, such as Bin or Enamelac, is an even better primer. These can go on full strength as they come from the can.

■ For the multicolored items—mirror and varicolor jewelry box—our designer used acrylic paints which are available in artists' supply stores. The acrylic paints are water soluble. When completely dry they should be protected with several coats of a clear, compatible sealer. I used Krylon's No. 1301 clear spray on the projects shown.

■ For projects where a high gloss is desired, use enamel. For the red jewelry box and the crayon holder I opted for an aerosol paint called LeSpray. Though the paint produces a very high gloss finish, it is a water-soluble coating. Thus, cleanup is fast and easy. The same product is also available in a brush-on form called LeBrush, if you prefer brushing on to aerosol cans. (Available at hardware and paint stores, both versions of this paint are manufactured by Sensico Inc., Oakland, CA. 94608.)

No complicated hardware is used to hold the mirror in a tilt position. Our version is designed with dowel "hinges" which are merely a force fit.

The mirror pretty much stays at the angle to which it is tilted. It will not, however, stand out at extreme angles (i.e., parallel to the base). The force-fit design works perfectly for any of the typical dresser-top mirror uses.

Beginning work on the mirror

Start by laying out the heart shape on either cardboard or ⅛-in. hardboard. Cut out the template and transfer the design to one of the pieces of plywood. Tack this piece to the second piece of plywood and then cut out both of them at one time, using either a scroll saw or a bandsaw.

MATERIALS LIST—MIRROR

Key	Pcs.	Size and description (use)
A	2	1 x 1 x 8-1/2" pine (uprights)
B	1	1 x 1 x 10-3/4" pine (sub-base)
C	1	1 x 2 x 11-3/4" pine (base)
D	2	7/16 x 1-3/4" dowel (hinges)
E	2	3/4 x 3/4" dowel (hinge caps)
F	2	1/2 x 8 x 8" plywood (heart)
G	2	Custom-cut heart 1/8" mirrors

Misc: 4d finishing nails, shellac, sandpaper, acrylic paints, Krylon clear spray (No. 1301).

While the pieces are still tacked together, use a rabbet cutter in your router to cut the mirror-holding rabbet. Once you've gone this far, you can bring the cutouts to your local glazier and order the ⅛-in. mirror hearts. The glazier can't cut a perfect heart—as you can with wood—but he should cut it close enough so all rounded spots will be hidden in the rabbet when the halves are joined. Remember to sand all of the edges before you separate the hearts.

Cut the remaining parts for the stand and assemble, using glue and nails. Separate the tacked-together heart pieces and temporarily reassemble them as they will be when they hold the mirror. Using a pair of hand screws, clamp the heart in position with the stand. With the setup held rigid in a vise, bore the holes for the hinge dowels. Then make a test assembly and, when satisfied, permanently assemble the mirror.

Seal all parts and paint with acrylic paints using the color photo on page 1360 as a guide. Seal with Krylon No. 1301 spray.

Ring caddy

Start by gluing up wood for the base (unless you have a suitably sized hardwood block in your scrap box). *Do* use hardwood for the base because you need its weight for stability.

MATERIALS LIST—RING CADDY

No.	Size and description (use)
1	1/4 x 6 x 10" plywood (hand)
1	1-3/4 x 2-3/4 x 5-1/2" hardwood block (base)

Misc: Felt, 1/4" brass cup hooks, sandpaper, acrylic paints, clear sealing spray.

Shape the block on the table saw, locate and bore cup-hook holes, sand, set aside. Lay out the hand on the ¼-in. plywood and cut it out with a coping saw, scroll saw, sabre- or bandsaw. Sand all of the edges and surfaces and then seal them with shellac.

After checking parts for fit—remember that the hand should be "sloppy" in the kerf to allow for the flannel cuff—paint all parts, using the color photo on page 1360 as a guide. When dry, assemble the caddy using glue.

Crayon holder

To get the desired thickness, I created a laminated block by gluing up four layers of ¾-in. pine. Use carpenter's glue and clamps—no nails are needed—and allow the block to dry for at least 24 hours.

MATERIALS LIST—CRAYON HOLDER

No.	Size and description
1	3 × 5 × 9" pine (or glue up blocks of thinner stock to desired thickness)

Misc.: Sandpaper, paint.

It is easiest to do a neat job if you bore the crayon-holding holes and cut the slanting front *before* cutting the hearts to shape. You can do the first on the drill press and the second

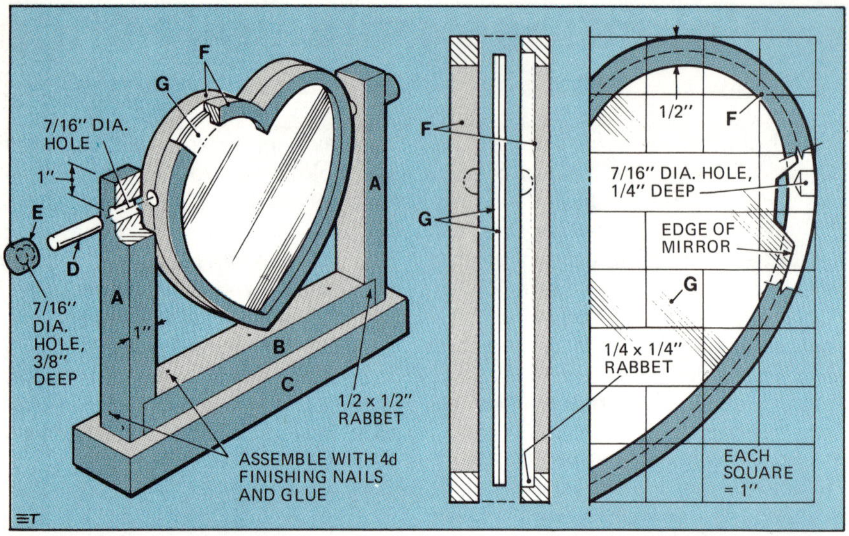

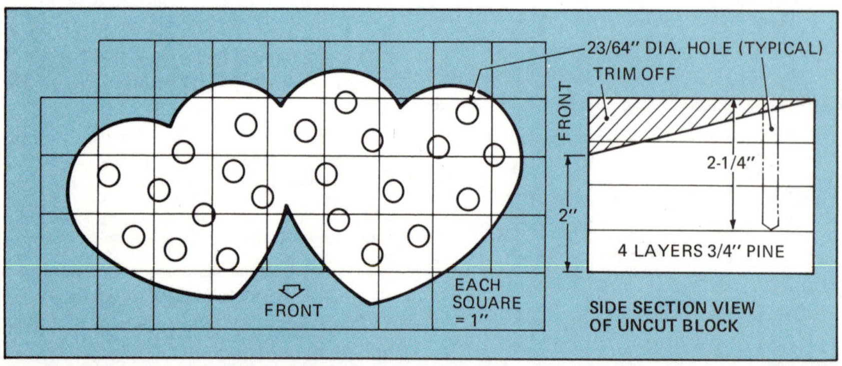

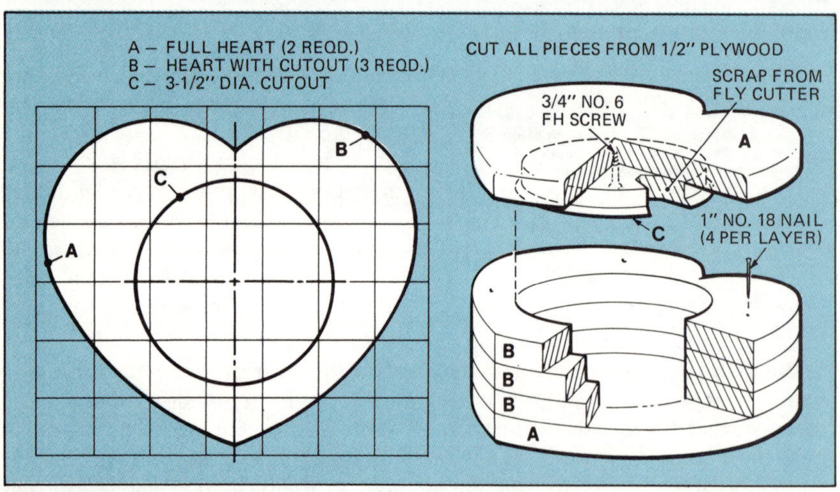

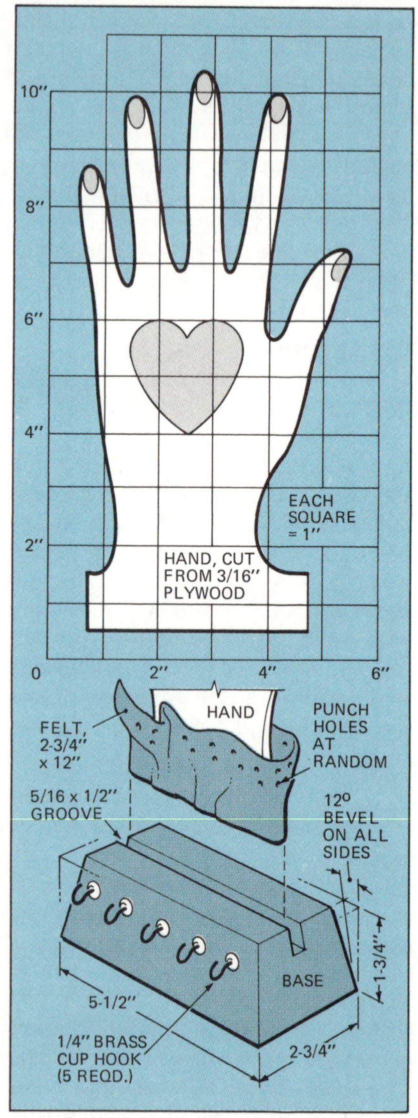

on either a radial or table saw using conventional cutting techniques.

In case you should forget to cut the angle first, use a belt sander and coarse-grit paper to shape the slanted front.

Sand the holder smooth, dust and apply spray paint. Some paint will fill the crayon holes a bit; you may have to use a rattail file to bring them back to easy-fit crayon-holding capacity.

Jewelry box

You can use either ½-in. pine or plywood to make the heart layers. The former takes the paint better but the latter is stronger.

If you should decide to go with pine, you can increase its stability by alternating the grain direction of the hearts so each successive layer will have its grain at 90° to the one below it.

The three middle layers are cut out using a circle cutter (often called fly cutter) in the drill press. The cutter should be used with drill press at a slow speed and the workpiece must be clamped rigidly for safety. Set one of the circular cutouts aside for use as the cover's guide. This is simply glued and screw-fastened, using a single flathead screw.

Sand the box well, dust it off and then finish as per general instructions.

MATERIALS LIST—JEWELRY BOX

No.	Size and description
5	½ × 6 × 6" clear pine (or A-D grade plywood)

Misc.: Sandpaper, shellac, assorted spray paints, white glue.

Short course in glass cutting

By PHILIP HERMANN

Glass cutting can be an exercise in frustration. Here's how to do it right

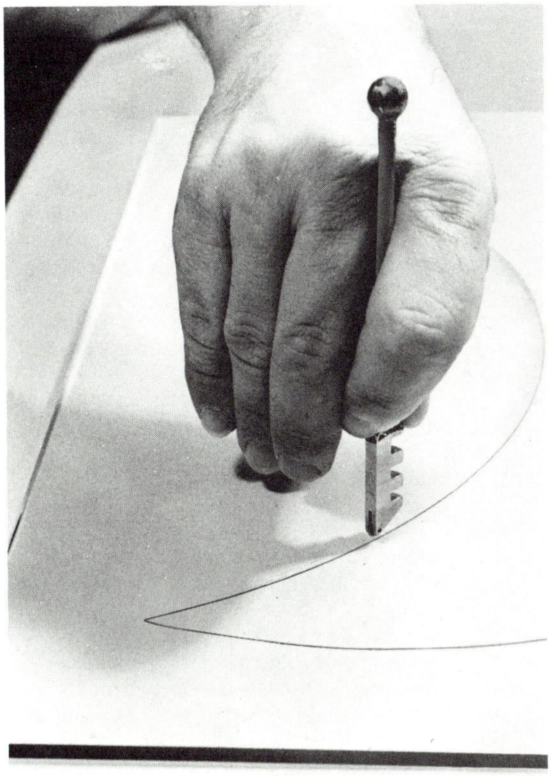

TRACING a contoured pattern on glass is possible if the cutter is kept well oiled and sharp.

TWO BASIC TOOLS—plate pliers and a glass cutter—were the only ones used to complete this quarter-moon design in glass. For such work, the benchtop must be covered with a scrap piece of short-pile rug.

■ MOST OF US have lived through at least one exasperating work session in which a couple of sheets of glass were shattered by clumsy glass-cutting efforts. Usually, the aggravation is compounded later when you stand in the glazier's shop and watch him make the cuts while hardly looking at the material. With the tips listed here, plus the right tools and some careful practice, you should come close to duplicating his expertise.

A good glass cutter can be purchased at your hardware store. If you plan to do any pattern cutting, you'll also need plate pliers. For most work, straight pliers—with the jaws ground *so the tips meet first*—will suffice. The only other

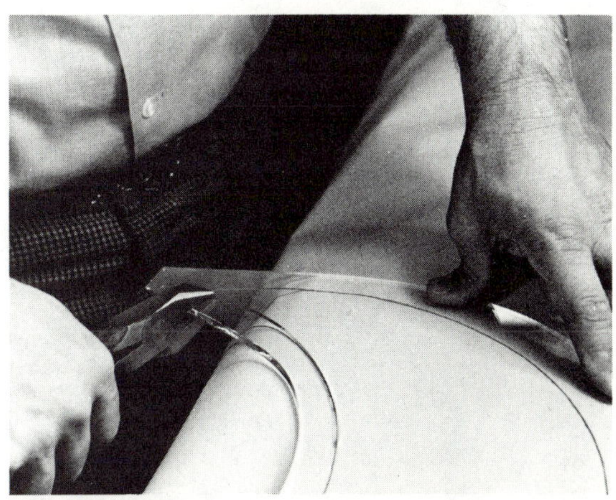

THE PATTERN to be cut from glass is traced onto paper. The paper is placed under glass and the glass scored, following the pattern. After the excess glass is removed, the score line is "run" (above) with plate pliers.

SEE ALSO

Cutting boards . . . Frames, picture . . . Stained glass . . . Storm doors and windows . . . Windows

tools needed are tape measure, straightedge and a square. Finally, your worktable cutting surface should be covered with a piece of short-pile rug.

When making a straight cut on either sheet or plate glass, similar techniques are used, but there is a slight variation in cutter pressure. As a rule, sheet glass requires roughly twice the pressure that plate glass does due to its harder surface. Never apply excessive pressure because the glass will fracture on the surface, and the cut will run erratically.

Because of the cutting wheel's shape, a straightedge should be placed $^{1}/_{16}$ in. away from and parallel to the intended cut. Before scoring, dip the cutter wheel in a lightweight motor oil.

Score with one movement—no stops. The cut should sound smooth and be free of skips. After scoring, the cut can be run (removed). If the cutoff is 1 in. or less, remove it with plate pliers. Let the glass hang over the cutting-surface edge. Then place the flat end of the pliers on the score line and apply a downward twist to peel off the glass in one piece. If the cutoff piece is more than 1 in. wide, the glass can be snapped off.

In pattern cutting, place the paper pattern under the glass. With cutter in normal position, follow the pattern on the glass. Before breaking, remove all excess material to within 1 in. of the score line, then run the original cut.

ABOUT GLASS

Contemporary glass terminology isn't complicated, but you may still hear some outdated expressions. The term "plate" is still sometimes used to suggest quality, but true, ground and polished plate glass is no longer made. "Sheet glass," too, is virtually extinct. Nearly all flat glass is now made by the float process. A wide belt of soft but solidifying glass is pulled across a pool of molten metal. Often such glass is even flatter than the old ground and polished plate was.

This annealed float glass has strength proportional to its thickness. Hardware stores usually stock $^{1}/_{8}$-in. to $^{3}/_{16}$-in. thicknesses. For $^{1}/_{4}$-in. glass—for a big picture window, for example—go to a glass shop instead of a hardware store.

Since a glass cutter is a seldom-used tool, make some practice cuts on scrap if possible. Though you can hold the cutter as if it were a pencil and apply pressure with your index finger, most pros prefer the more stable grip between first and second finger shown below. Here, the ball end of cutter rests on your knuckles and, by placing the first finger on top and your thumb directly underneath—and the notches facing down—you will be able to master this handy—but sometimes ornery—tool.

Making straight cuts

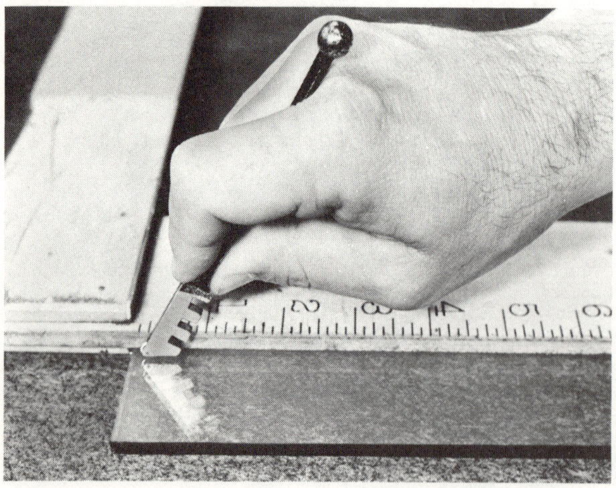

A PROPER GRIP on the cutter is important when moving it along a straightedge. The grip shown above is the best method. A small strip of glass (top right) is snapped by placing the flat edge of the pliers on the score line and applying a downward twist. To break off a large piece (right) the straightedge is carefully placed squarely under the score, then the glass is snapped off by applying a quick, definite pressure. Notice that all glass-cutting steps are done on carpet to avoid breakage by impact.

An early American gossip bench

By WAYNE C. LECKEY

IF YOU LIKE FURNITURE with a past, you'll like this authentic Early American gossip bench. Crafted in solid cherry in our own cabinet shop, this handsome piece is something you'll cherish for years to come. It has a shelf for the phone and a place below for directories.

To make it you'll need a wood lathe to turn the 4 legs and 13 spindles. The legs are turned from 1¾-in. turning squares, 16 in. long. When mounting the blanks between centers, place the unturned end of the leg at the headstock end of the lathe. Turn the first leg by following the pattern given, then use it as a sample in turning the others. Notice that the tops of the legs require a compound cut to provide the proper leg splay. This is done by tilting both the blade and the miter gauge on your table saw. A similar bevel is made at the opposite end of each leg but this is done after the base is completed.

Each of the 13 spindles is turned from 1-in.-sq. stock, approximately 12 in. long. Finish-sand each spindle while in the lathe and turn a ½-in. tenon at each end. Use the first turning as a sample for the others.

The ¾-in. seat aprons are ripped 2⅝ in. wide. Notice that the top edges are beveled and that the ends are cut at an 84° angle. The end aprons are 11¾ in. long, the side rails 29½ in.

The aprons are attached to the legs with ⅜-in. dowels and are set in ⅛ in. Assemble the legs and end aprons in pairs, then add the side aprons. Check for squareness and hold it squarely with a temporary cross brace.

The seat is 1⅛-in. solid cherry. If you wish, you can simulate this thickness by adding ¼ x 1⅛-in. strips to the edges of a 16¾ x 34¾-in. panel of veneer-face, lumber-core plywood and mitering the corners. Use your router to round

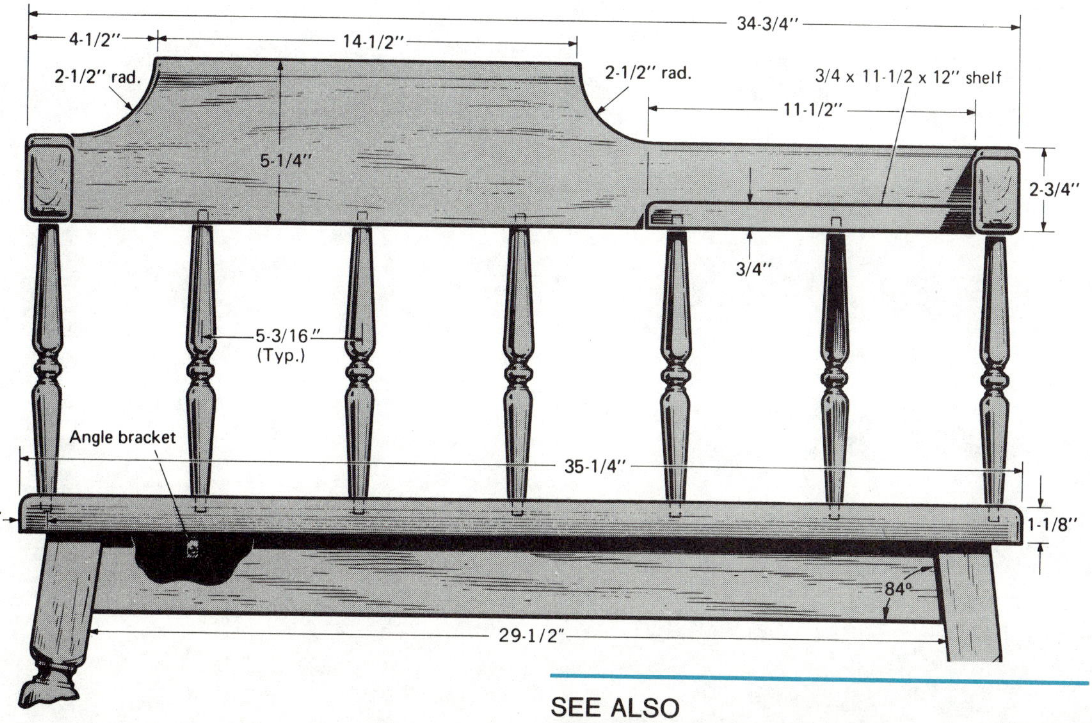

SEE ALSO

Cupboards, china . . . Dry sinks . . .
Finishes, wood . . . Legs, furniture . . . Servers . . .
Shaving cabinets . . . Wood lathes . . .
Wood lathe techniques

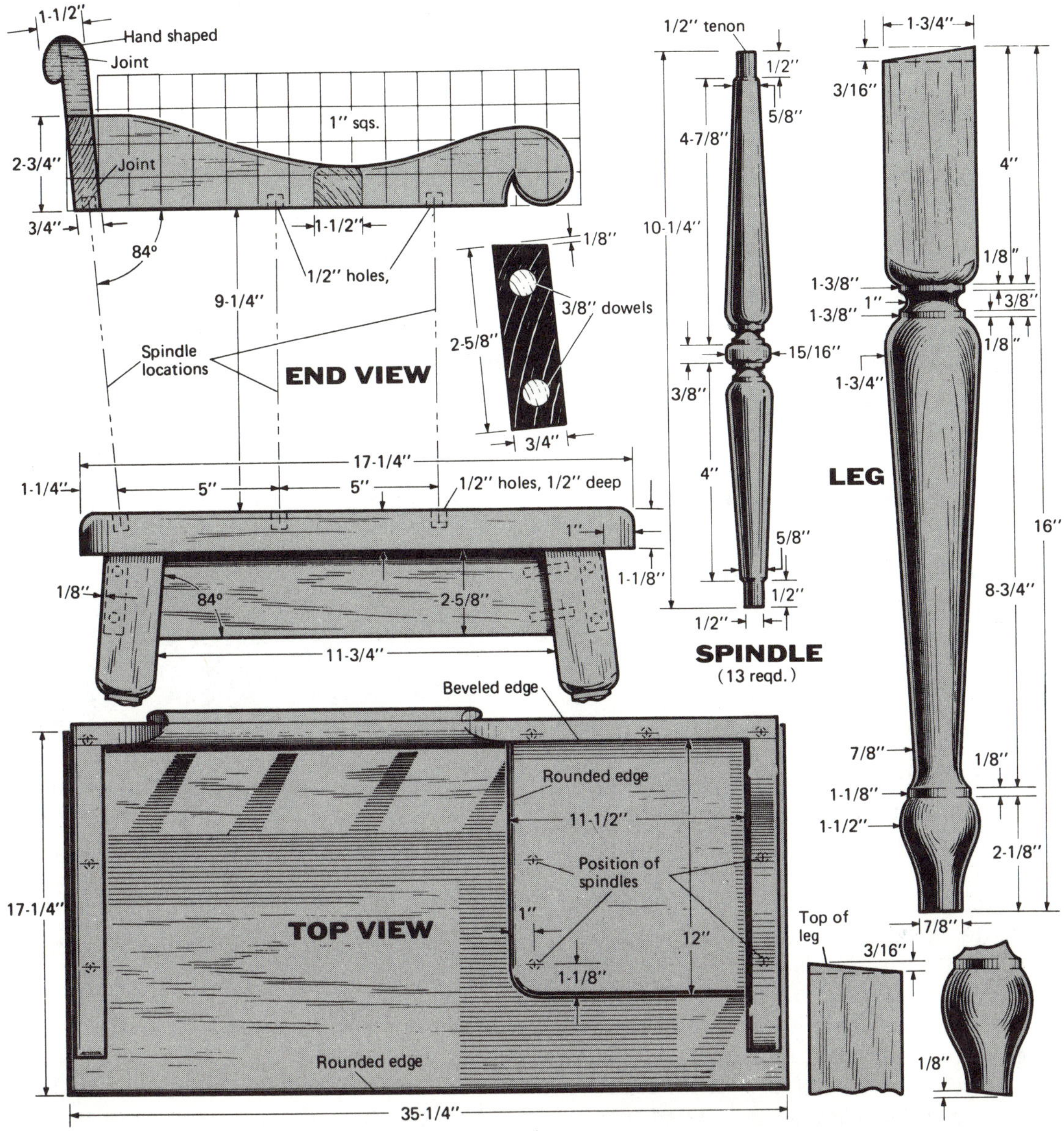

gossip bench, continued

the top edges of the seat, then lay out and bore the ½-in. holes for the 13 spindles. Notice that all are bored at a 90° angle except those along the back. Here the holes are bored at an 84° angle.

Next, cut out the back rail according to the dimensions given in the front and end views. You'll notice that the decorative "curl" along the top of the rail is hand-shaped after you double the thickness with a second ¾-in. strip.

Seven ½-in. spindle holes are required in the back rail. These are aligned with the ones in the seat, centered in the rail thickness and bored at right angles.

The pattern for the two arms is traced on 1½-in. stock, bandsawed and then the top edges rounded. From the top view drawing you'll see that the arms butt against the back rail. Two spindle holes are bored in each arm.

This leaves the 11½ x 12-in. telephone shelf which is beveled along the rear edge to meet the slanting back rail. It's glued to both the rail and arm and is supported by two spindles.

Now go over your bench and sand it glass-smooth. After a coat of maple NGR (nongrain raising) stain, apply two coats of Wood Lore (a self-rubbing, clear, satin finish) and sand lightly between coats with a type-4 finishing paper.

What to do in fall for healthy summer grass

Fall is the ideal time to get your lawn in shape. It will last longer into winter and green up earlier next spring. Here's how to seed, fertilize and control weeds

■ WHILE YOU'RE TRIMMING and getting your shrubs ready for winter, why not do the same for your lawn? Fall is the best time to revitalize it. The time is right for three things:

1. Seeding: Those warm days and cool nights provide the best growing conditions. As long as the days stay warm, there's time.

2. Fertilizing: Feeding the lawn with a slow-release fertilizer will help it stay green later and turn green sooner in the spring.

3. Controlling weeds: Now, while weeds are still growing, is the time to spread a weed control (if you're not seeding this fall), or a product that will fertilize *and* weed.

seeding

Seeds need protective grooves in which to lodge, so slice the soil ¼ in. deep with a sharp-tined rake or a rented power rake.

Next, put down seed and fertilizer separately. Use of a spreader will assure even and economical results. Both can be put down the same day.

SEE ALSO

Hand mowers . . . Landscaping . . . Lawns . . . Mowers . . . Paths, garden . . . Patios . . . Retaining walls . . . Shears, gardening . . . Stepping stones . . . Transplanting . . . Trees

Buy top quality seed—it will determine the kind of lawn you have for years. The fertilizer should be one specially made for new seeding.

If you seed on bare ground, lightly mix the seed into the soil with the back of a lawn rake. Light mulching with straw so you can still see the ground helps hold moisture.

Once the seed has germinated, keep the top inch of ground moist until the seedlings are established.

For an even healthier lawn feed it again after about six weeks with a slow-release type of fertilizer that's high in nitrogen—the first number of three listed on the bag.

fertilizing

Grass needs help to replenish itself after the hot, often dry summer. In the fall more than at any other time of year, grass plants will multiply themselves when fertilized, producing new leaves and new off-shoot plants (called rhizomes) to thicken and strengthen the lawn. Fall-fed grass plants also produce and store carbohydrates over the winter, which the plants use in the spring. This late fall feeding speeds green-up in spring.

Select a long-acting fertilizer that nourishes for six to eight weeks. You can cover a 5000-sq.-ft. lawn in an easy half-hour walk with a lawn spreader. Start by fertilizing a strip at each end of a lawn section. To prevent fertilizer oversatura-

FALL LAWN CARE TIPS

1. When the weather cools and your grass is slowing its growth, mow the lawn about ½ in. lower than its usual height. Letting it go into winter short cuts down on the possibility of its becoming diseased.

2. Both your shrubs and lawn need plenty of moisture to help them survive the winter. If nature doesn't cooperate, give your grass 1 to 1½ in. of water a week. You can tell how long you need to leave the sprinkler on by setting out three or four tin cans at varying distances from it. After a set period of time—say, a half hour—find the average of the water depths in the cans. If it's ¼-in., for example, one hour's sprinkling will give the lawn ½ in. of water.

3. Rake up the fall leaves and debris so they don't mat the grass. But it *is* wise to pile leaves around shrubs. It gives them added winter protection.

4. Sprinkle a little fertilizer on the compost pile between layers of grass clippings and garden debris. You'll get quicker, richer compost in the spring to use for your early garden.

5. Don't bother trying to rake up the late-season crabgrass. The frost will kill it permanently. Crabgrass comes up new each year from seed. You can stop it from cropping up next spring by putting down a crabgrass preventer, which you can buy combined with fertilizer. Even if you need to re-seed this fall, you can leave the dead crabgrass in the ground. The new grass will sprout up through it.

FERTILIZER can make a difference. Right side was fertilized; other wasn't.

A NEWLY seeded area is patchy with weeds; many will die when mowed.

COMPARE untreated lawn and one treated with weed control and fertilizer.

tion, shut off the spreader as you reach each strip and turn around.

controlling broadleaf weeds

To be an instant expert on controlling dandelions and other broadleaf weeds, you need to know two things:

■ The control should be put on the weeds during their active growing season, since its effectiveness depends on being absorbed by the plant;

■ The control particles need to stick to the leaves for at least 24 hours, so the leaves should be moist when the control is spread. Water the lawn before spreading on weed control or do it when the grass is moist from early morning dew.

You can get additional help from a magazine like *Lawn Care.* It's available free on request to Scotts, Marysville, OH 43040. Regional editions contain seasonal tips and instructions.

CUTAWAY (left) shows dandelion with long taproot before weed control treatment. Two weeks later dandelion (center) is failing; a month later (right) it's absorbed.

Build a portable electric grill

By WAYNE C. LECKEY

Get out of the hot kitchen and cook where the fun is with this portable grill. It can be used in your family room or living room as it has a 'porthole' in the outside wall that vents cooking odors outdoors

HIDDEN UNDER fold-over top, the grill masquerades as a handsome piece of furniture when not in use.

WHEN YOUR GUESTS are having a ball and you're slaving over a hot stove in the kitchen, entertaining friends is not all fun. With this electric grill-on-wheels the host can join the fun from the start and charbroil mouth-watering steaks right in the center of the party.

You install the drop-in grill in a smart roll-about cabinet (which we show you how to build) rather than in a kitchen counter so you can be with your friends right where the action is.

To enjoy this modern indoor cooking, you roll the cabinet up to a "porthole" in an outside wall, connect the grill to it with a 24-in. flexible duct and plug the cord into a 240-v. outlet. In seconds you have 2800 watts of clean radiant heat which will charbroil steaks, hamburgers, hot dogs, fish or fowl faster than an outdoor grill. A powerful below-the-surface fan pulls smoke and fumes directly into the exhaust system without a trace in the room.

The grill is made by Jenn-Air Corp., 3035 Shadeland Ave., Indianapolis, IN 46226. Besides including a cast-aluminum nonstick griddle, the grill features a lighted fan switch and grill pilot light, a built-in timer and a convenience outlet.

There are several gourmet accessories you can add, including a rotisserie, shish kebab and french fryer. A kit of parts for wiring and ducting the grill outdoors is also available from Jenn-Air.

When the grill is not in use, snug-fitting caps plug the exhaust ports in both the wall and

FOR PERMANENT installation, the grill can also be placed right in your kitchen countertop.

SEE ALSO

**Barbecues . . . Bars . . . Cookout bars . . .
Family rooms . . . Hutch tables . . .
Kitchen accessories . . . Serving carts**

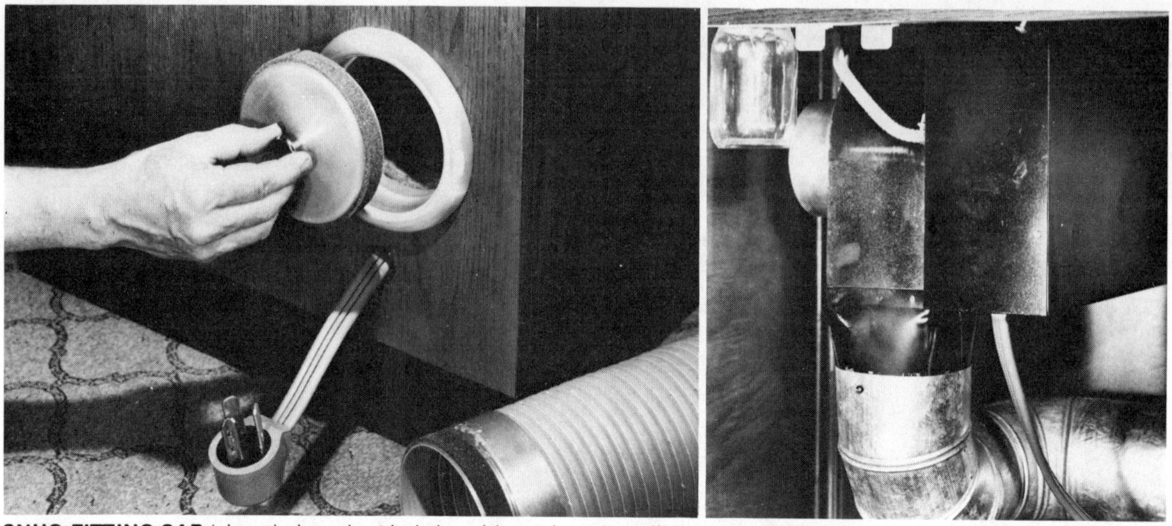

SNUG-FITTING CAP (above) plugs duct hole in cabinet when the grill is not used. Interior view (right) shows how the grill blower is piped outside with two 5-in.-dia. galvanized furnace pipe elbows fastened together.

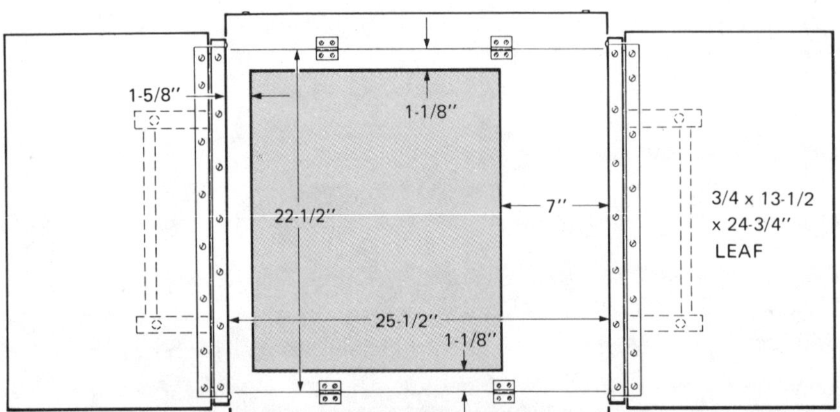

TOP VIEW
(OPEN)

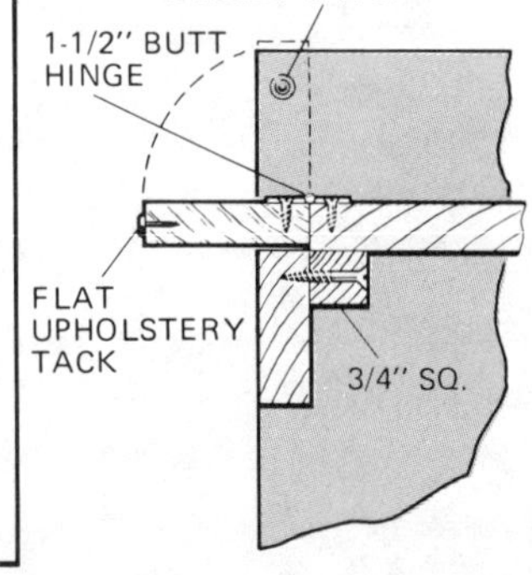

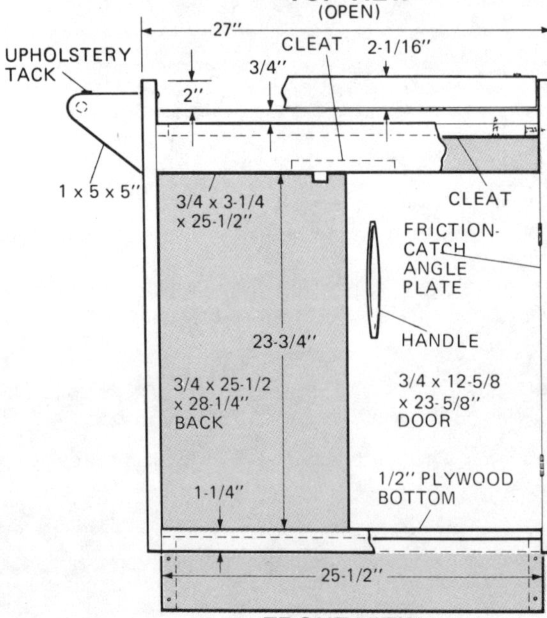

FRONT VIEW

PIANO HINGE

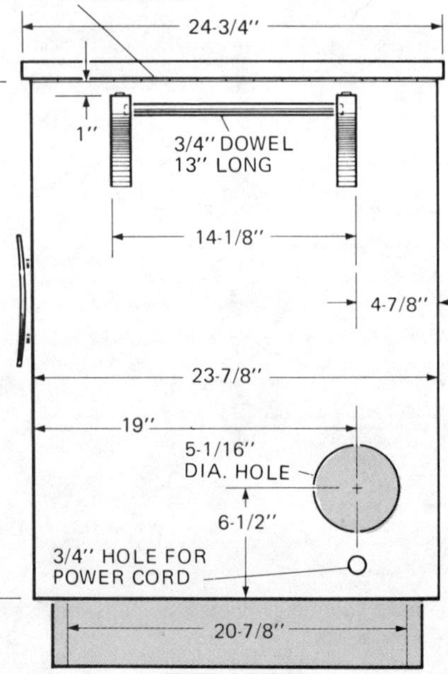

END VIEW
(RIGHT HAND)

cabinet. The duct and cable store inside and the cabinet top folds shut to hide the grill.

The boxlike design of the handsome Danish-modern cabinet helps simplify construction. It's made entirely of oak-veneer plywood, (stained dark brown) except for the black-painted base and the bottom shelf. Butt joints are used for the most part and reinforced on the inside with square blocks glued in the corners. Both ends are the same size, but right and left-hand, with a 5-in.-dia. hole being cut in the right-hand one. Both are blind-grooved on the inside at the front for the bottom crossrail. The back butts between the ends, as do the grill cutout, the 3⅜-in. crossrail and the bottom. The storage section of the cabinet is fitted with twin doors and equipped with suitable pulls and magnetic catches. There's a lot of storage room here for all of your cooking and party needs.

The two-piece top is joined with piano hinges and supported when open by handles on the ends of the cabinet. Flip-down aprons hinged to the grill cutout, front and back, support the top when closed; spring-loaded friction catches placed at the ends of the aprons hold them in an upright position.

The electric grill sits in the hole provided and is secured in place with locking screws. Two standard 5-in. elbows and a straight section of galvanized smoke pipe are needed to duct the

continued

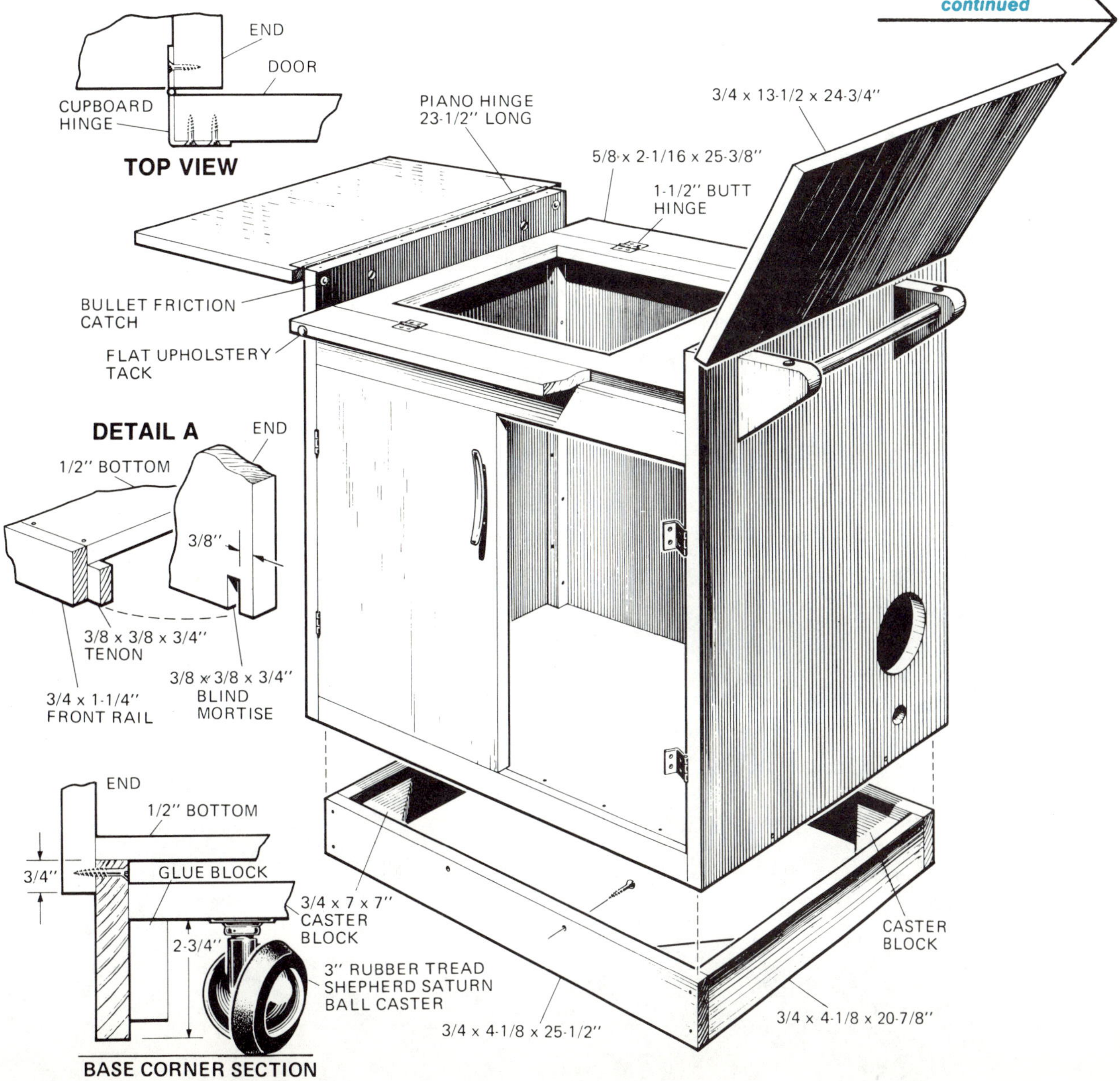

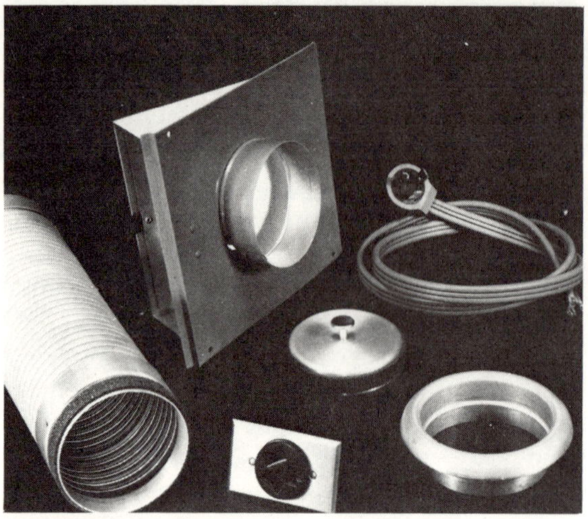

KIT OF PARTS includes two rings, two caps, flexible duct, damper, power cord and a 240-v. receptacle.

DUCT THROUGH house wall (above, left) is capped outside with butterfly damper attached with screws.

ventilating fan through the hole in the side of the cabinet. An aluminum ring that comes with the kit fits the hole on the outside. The outdoor exhaust port is installed by cutting a 5-in. hole through the wall and inserting a 5-in. section of 5-in. galvanized pipe. The pipe is then fitted with a ring on the inside and a damper on the outside. Since the unit is on ball casters it can be rolled from room to room, and additional outdoor exhaust ports can be placed in the kitchen or wherever you want to cook.

EXHAUST PORT in outside wall is located 12 in. from floor. The 240-v. receptacle is shown adjacent.

HANDY CONDIMENT rack is attached to left-hand door. Details (below) show how the rack is assembled.

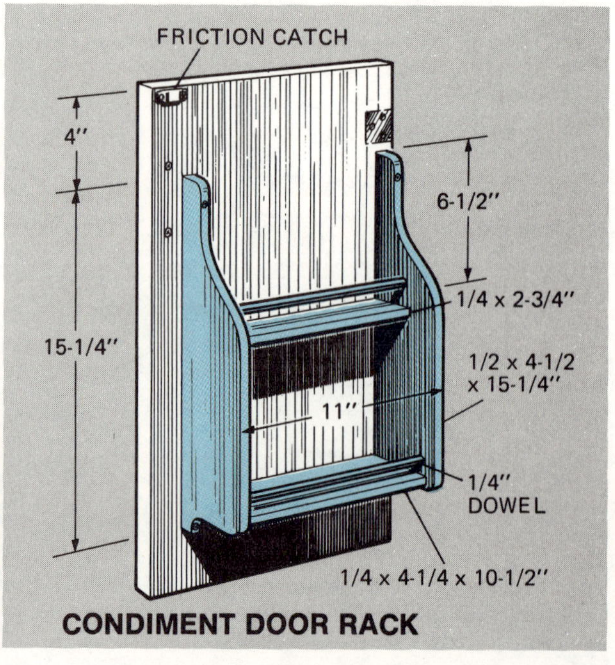

A weatherproof house for your grill

Nothing rusts faster than a portable grill and cooking utensils that are left exposed to the weather. This good-looking shelter provides protection and a handy work surface

■ OUTDOOR COOKING can be more work than pleasure if it means you have to round up the necessary gear each time—from the kitchen and a cluttered garage or basement.

With a weatherproof shelter for your grill, supplies and utensils, cookouts will be a lot less trouble. This shelter, designed by architect George Whittier, A.I.A., for Western Wood Products Assn., has a slide-out workshelf and room enough to keep everything handy. Materials should cost less than $200.

Before building, choose the unit's location carefully, making sure drainage is good. Since the

THE SHELTER keeps cooking equipment and supplies together. Shelf provides a work surface.

SEE ALSO

**Barbecues . . . Cabanas . . . Cookout bars . . .
Garden shelters . . . Gazebos . . .
Kitchens, outdoor . . . Patios . . . Summer houses**

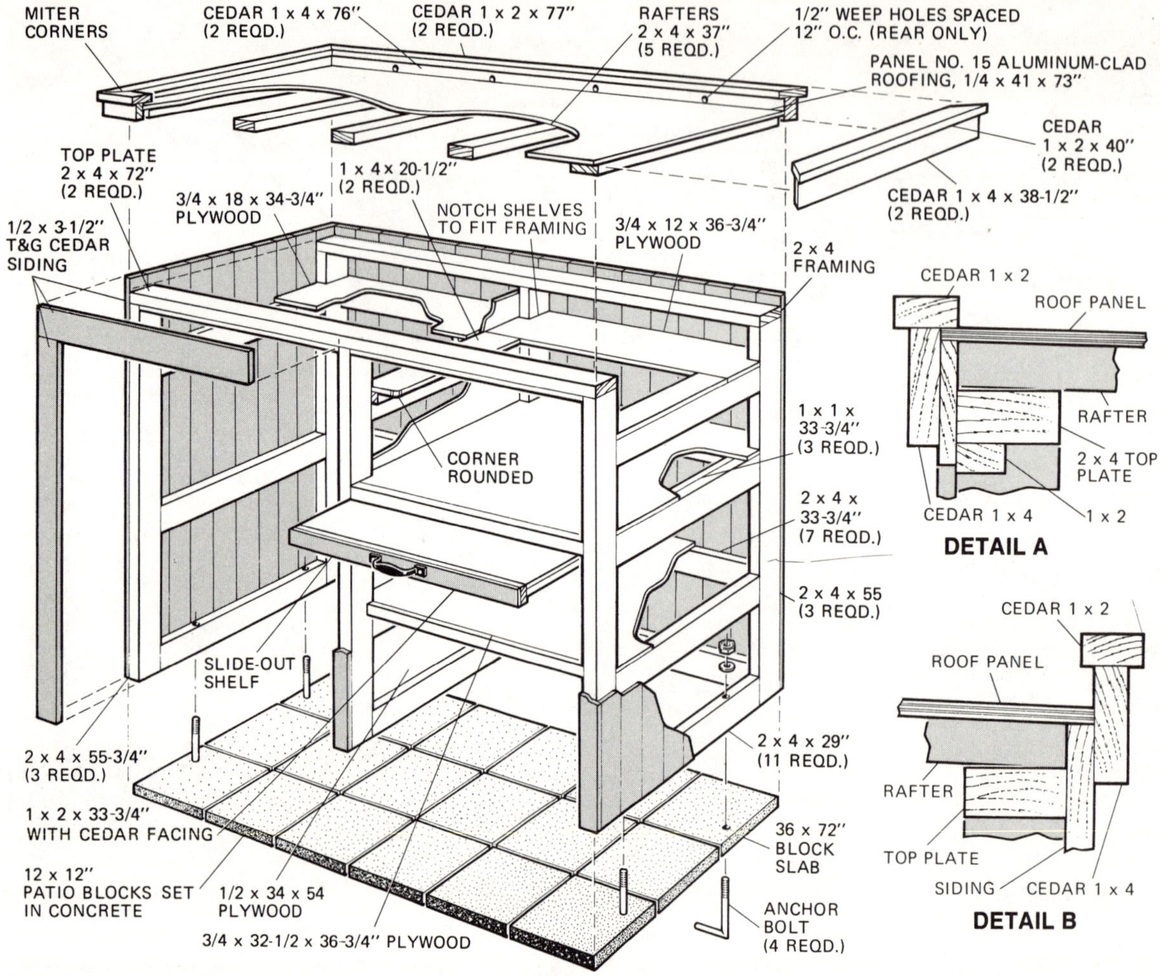

portable grill shelter, continued

structure may be considered a permanent addition to your property, check local codes to determine whether a building permit will be required. You may wish to attach the unit to your house or to a fence or privacy screen. If so, change the dimensions to suit; if it will butt against the house, it must be properly flashed to prevent leaks.

Begin construction by setting a floor of patio blocks in concrete, with anchor bolts protruding through holes drilled in four of the blocks. (This slab should rest on footings.) Framing is with 2x4s. Start the framing with one middle section and two end sections. Since the middle and one end are identical, one frame can serve as a pattern for the other. Horizontal members tie the sections together into a boxlike frame.

Both roof and slide-out shelf are made from Weyerhaeuser Co.'s Panel No. 15, a ¼-in. aluminum-clad plywood product available at lumberyards. Above the slide-out shelf is a wider storage shelf, which may be easier to install if sawed in half and rejoined in place. Fixed shelves are notched to fit framing. When shelves have been installed, the roof can be added and trimmed with 1x3s. Then ½ x 3½-in. tongue-and-groove western cedar siding is applied vertically and blind-nailed to the 2x4 cross members for a weathertight wall. Doors are made of the same siding, blind-nailed to 1x4 diagonal bracing using a jig of cleats nailed to your workbench or a sheet of plywood.

Use 10d common nails to spike the 2x4s together and 8d common nails to toenail them. Sid-

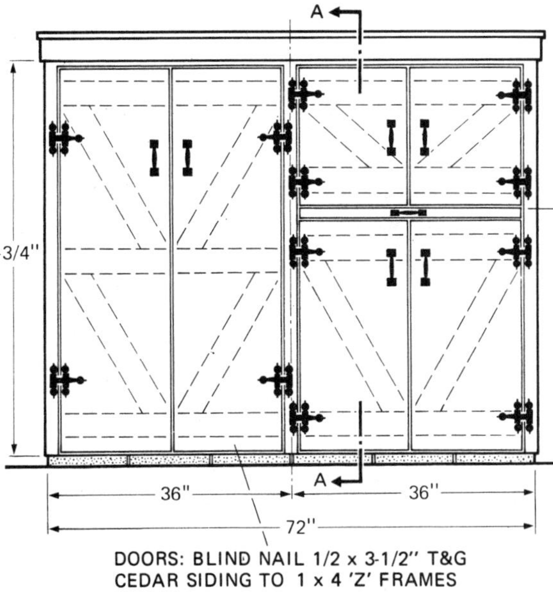

The closed shelter gives weathertight protection of its contents. The roof slopes 3/4 in. to the back and drains through weep holes in the rear fascia

ing and ¾-in. lumber require 6d finishing nails. The roof is attached to the rafters with neoprene washer roofing nails 12 in. apart, then caulked. Friction catches hold the doors closed.

The structure can be stained or painted after doors are hung; use saw-textured siding with stain. Wood siding other than cedar may be used, and other styles of siding are also possible. For best appearance, use the same material for both walls and fascia. Since the unit shown butts against house siding, its corner pieces were notched to fit.

The shelter is designed so that it can be readily adapted to other uses, such as for storage of garden tools or outdoor sports equipment. Poolside use is another possibility. The unit could also include a weatherproof electrical outlet, allowing temporary installation of a portable refrigerator in the lower cabinet for entertaining.

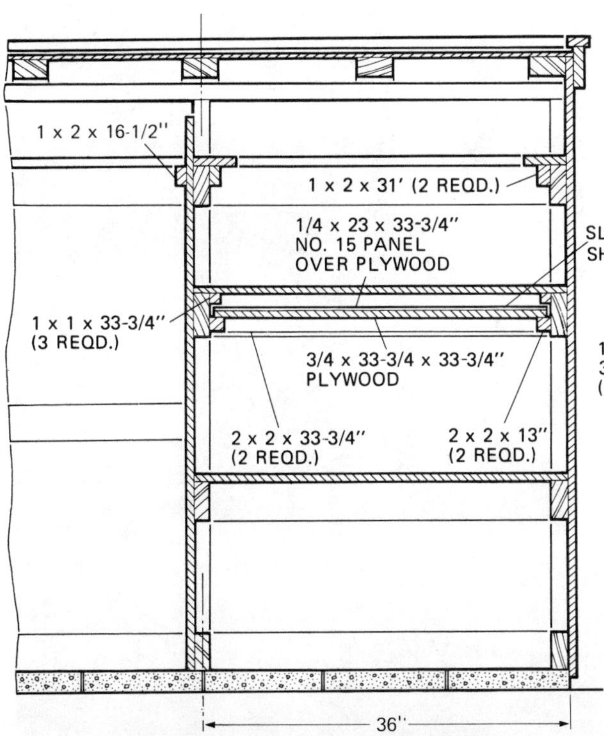

FRONT VIEW, SECTION B-B

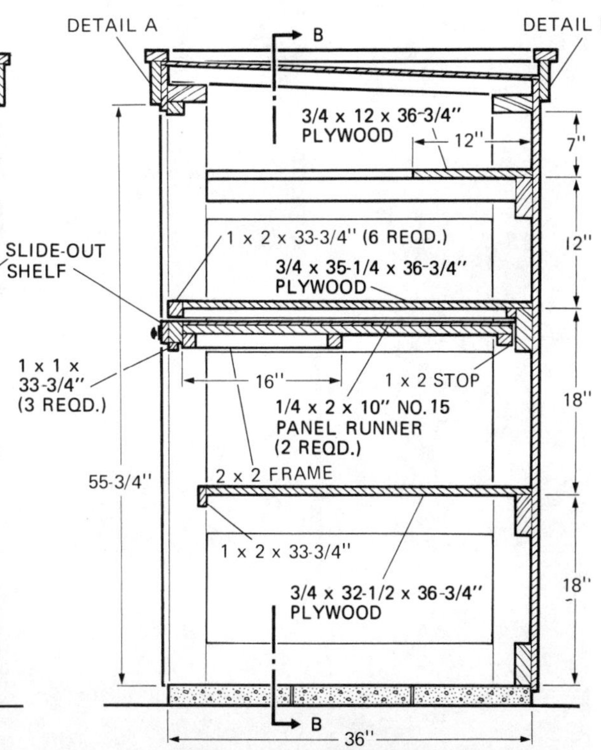

SIDE VIEW, SECTION A-A

A cabinet for your guns

To the buff, guns are handsome themselves. They'll look even better in this classic cabinet that you can build from the plans presented here. And, best of all, if you don't care for guns, you can use the cabinet for trophies, china or books

IF YOU TAKE PRIDE in showing off the guns you own, wait until you see them displayed in this beautiful solid-oak cabinet. It's truly a fine piece of furniture in Mediterranean design. And you can rest assured that the design will go with any furniture you have in your home—from traditional to the very latest modern. The cabinet is a project for the advanced craftsman with the proper kind of equipment at hand. It demands the best workmanship in both woodworking and finishing skills to make it the standout it is.

made for shelves, too

The cabinet will hold up to six guns and has storage for ammunition, scopes and cleaning gear. Doors lock to keep ammunition and guns out of reach, and sliding doors of polished glass keep them dust-free.

If you couldn't care less about guns, you'll find the cabinet equally useful when fitted with shelves and used as a trophy cabinet, a place for your wife to keep her best china and table linens, or a case for your fine bound books.

The cabinet consists of two separate assemblies, a top and a bottom. We used solid stock throughout in building the one you see on the opposite page although hardwood-faced plywood would be adequate for the side panels of each assembly.

Start the top assembly first by cutting the sides to size and rabbeting the top and back edges. The top board is cut ¼ in. narrower than the side members to accommodate the ¼-in. plywood back, and the back member is cut ¾ in. longer than the sides so it can be fastened to the bottom assembly.

Glue and nail the parts together and then face the front edges with a three-piece frame. This is made the same width as the assembled unit (31½ in.) but is cut ¾ in. shorter. It's doweled at the corners, then glued and clamped to the unit. You can use a few nails across the top in pre-drilled holes since they will be hidden. The top is finished with a molding that's mitered at the corners, glued and brought flush with the top board. So much for the upper assembly.

The bottom assembly is built similarly in that the top and rear edges of the sides are rabbeted as before. In addition, a ⅛ x ¾-in. dado is made in each side member for a bottom shelf. The latter is notched at the front corners so it will project ¾ in. across the front. Facing rows of ¼-in. blind holes (fitted with shelf brackets) hold the adjustable center shelf.

After the parts are glued and nailed together, a ¾ x 3¼-in. base molding is mitered and glued around the bottom. Finally, the three pieces which make up the top sill (E), are mitered and doweled, then shaped with a router along the outer edge. The sill is attached to the base with glue and screws, the latter being driven through pieces A and D from the underside.

use nails and screws

The top assembly is attached to the bottom with four screws driven through the side members from the inside. Nails can be used to fasten the plywood across the back.

Part A-A slips in place behind part E. While in each case it's rabbeted across the front for a plastic door slide, you can forget about cutting the gunstock pits in it if you plan to use the cabinet as a bookcase or china cabinet.

The stock pits are cut completely through the board, then backed up on the bottom. The neatest way to cut the pits is to bore holes at each end of the cutout and then saw out the waste. If you have a router, you can do the job quickly with a jig you make to guide the machine. Pieces of felt are later cut and glued to line the bottom

SEE ALSO
Bookcases . . . Chests . . . Cupboards, china . . . Glass cutting . . . Gun racks . . . Hunting

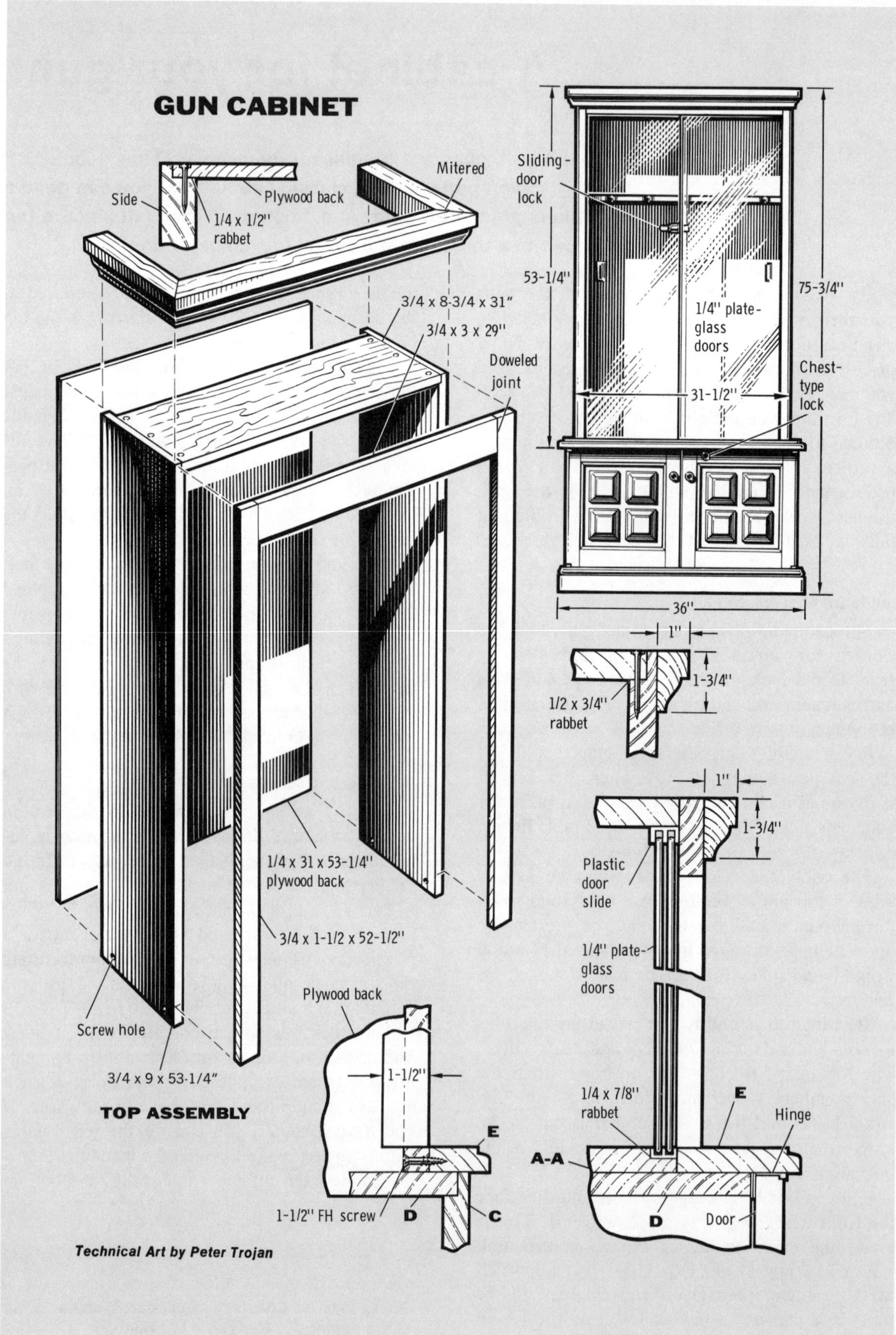

Technical Art by Peter Trojan

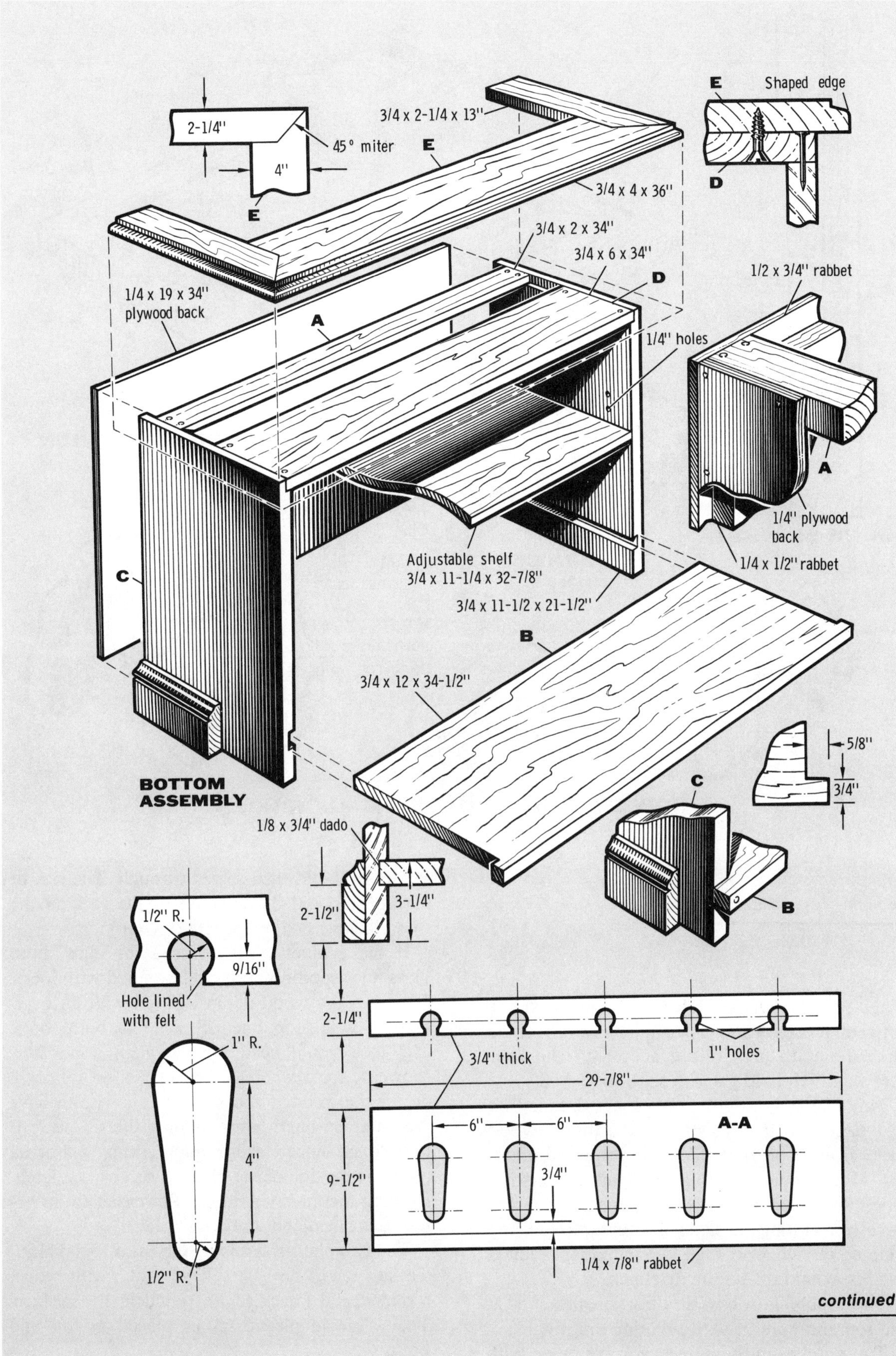

2-1/4"
45° miter
4"
E
3/4 x 2-1/4 x 13"
E
3/4 x 4 x 36"
Shaped edge
E
D
3/4 x 2 x 34"
3/4 x 6 x 34"
D
1/2 x 3/4" rabbet
1/4 x 19 x 34"
plywood back
A
1/4" holes
A
1/4" plywood
back
1/4 x 1/2" rabbet
Adjustable shelf
3/4 x 11-1/4 x 32-7/8"
3/4 x 11-1/2 x 21-1/2"
C
B
3/4 x 12 x 34-1/2"
5/8"
3/4"
C
BOTTOM
ASSEMBLY
1/8 x 3/4" dado
3-1/4"
2-1/2"
B
1/2" R.
9/16"
Hole lined
with felt
2-1/4"
3/4" thick
1" holes
1" R.
29-7/8"
6"
6"
A-A
4"
9-1/2"
3/4"
1/4 x 7/8" rabbet
1/2" R.

continued

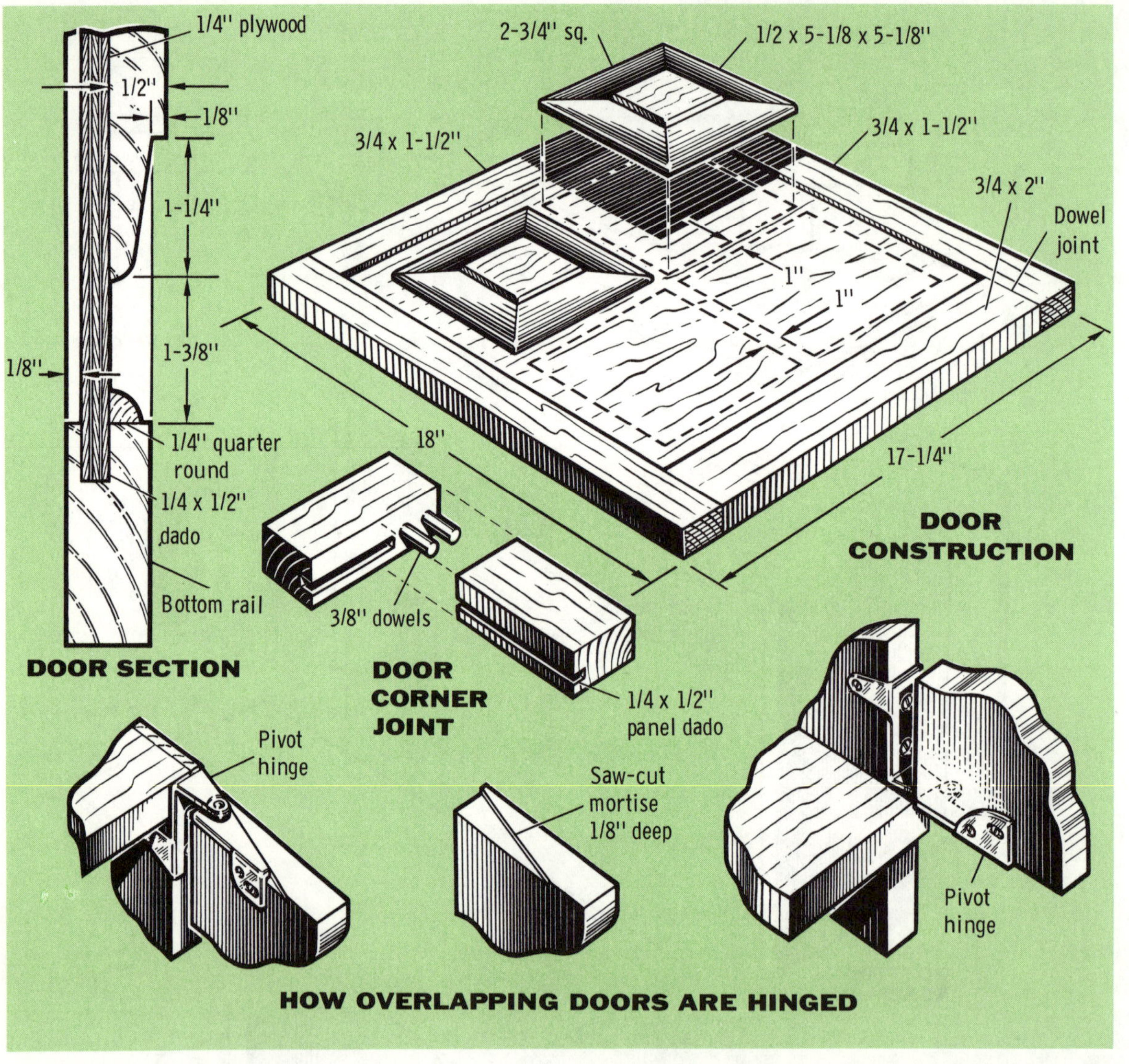

multi-purpose cabinet, continued

of the pits. Part A-A is left loose, and the space between pieces A and D permits piece A-A to be pushed out to give future access to the four screws which hold the top section.

This leaves the doors, which are detailed on this page. Each consists of a ¼-in. plywood panel framed on four sides with grooved members. Four square overlays cut from ½-in. solid stock are glued to the center panel. These are beveled by tilting the blade on your table saw and running the work on edge. A sandpaper block is used to round off the outer edges.

The details show how the doors are attached at the top and bottom with pivoting pin hinges.

The notches in the barrel rack are made with a 1-in. drill and then sawed through. The size of the notches and the location of the rack in the case are governed by the size of your guns.

If the cabinet is to be used for guns, both glass and wood doors should be fitted with locks. If one of the wood doors is fitted with an overlapping metal stop, one lock will lock both doors. The lock you'll need for the glass doors is a showcase lock, whereas a regular chest lock will do for the wooden doors. Here it is wise to have the latter on hand before adding the sill piece E to the base since it will require cutting a mortise on the underside of the piece to receive the latch. Routing the mortise will be a lot easier to do before E is glued and screwed in place.

The two plate-glass doors measure 15 x 51½". These you'll have to have cut, with edges rounded and finger grips ground in the surface. They slide in plastic tracks placed at top and bottom.

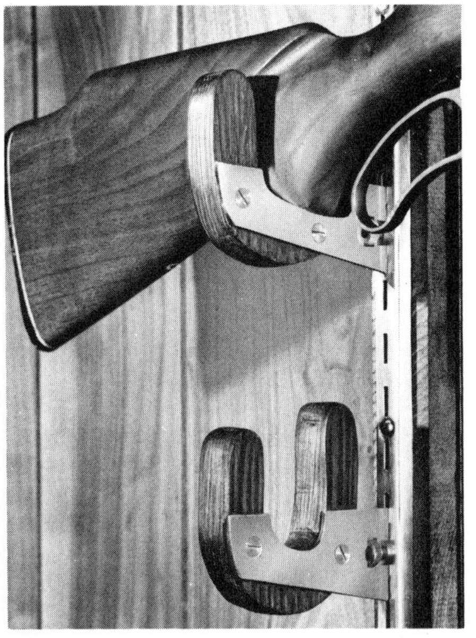

BASED ON standard shelf hardware system, this rack puts your present gun collection on display, with flexibility and room for future acquisitions. Guns are supported at both ends by blocks that are fastened to the cut-down shelf brackets.

Custom-fit gun rack

Using ordinary shelf hardware, a custom gun rack can be made for your collection of inoperatives. It grows by adding brackets as you acquire more for your display

PUTTING INOPERATIVE GUNS on display is quick work with a rack that makes use of shelf hardware for fast construction and flexibility. Each gun is fitted to its own brackets, assuring solid support and level display for best appearance. Guns can be repositioned and respaced easily and standards can also support a shelf, as shown above, for accessories.

The shelf system used here has satin-finish brass brackets, custom cut with a hacksaw blade. Support blocks were cut from ¾-in. pine and stained walnut. Scraps of an attractive hardwood such as walnut or birch could also be used. Blocks, used as templates for laying out cuts to be made on brackets, are shaped first to fit guns on a cut-and-try basis or, better, cut to cardboard templates fitted to gun contours. Rear (stock) supports are made first; then each gun is held in position and heights and depths of front (barrel) supports are figured so guns will be level.

BRASS SHELF brackets are surprisingly easy to cut with hacksaw blade in sabre saw. Wood block is first cut to fit gun, then temporarily attached to bracket as template for marking cuts. Final assembly is with ¾-in. No. 8 flathead brass woodscrews. Use a countersink made for metal on the brackets. Note: a locking cabinet and trigger locks should be used for display of operable weapons.

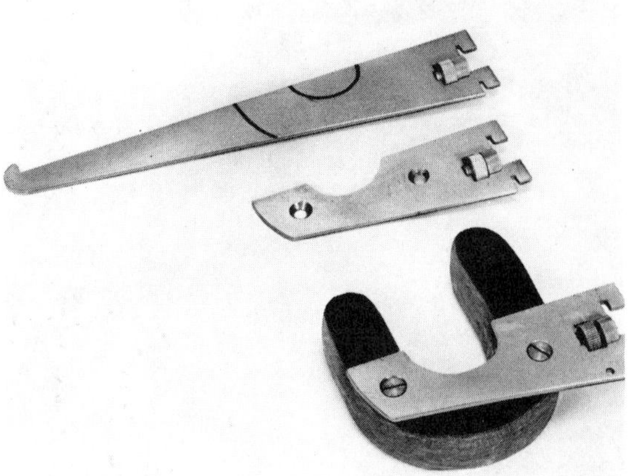

SEE ALSO
Gun cabinets . . . Muzzleloading . . . Shelves . . . Shooting . . . Shotguns

With a few basic tools and a little basic information you can easily install your own gutters and downspouts

By RICHARD DAY

How to install gutters and downspouts

GUTTER SEALANT, a nonhardening butyl rubber, is used on all joints to prevent leaks.

SEE ALSO

Basement waterproofing . . . Drainage, downspout . . . Fasteners . . . Home improvement . . . House additions . . . Roofs

■ INSTALLING GUTTERS and leaders is actually an easy job. That's a strong statement, but the fact is that the worst part of the job for most do-it-yourselfers is the height. If height bothers you and you have a tall house, your best bet is to call in a pro to do the job. But whether you decide to tackle the improvement yourself or not, the facts on these pages will let you know what a good gutter and leader system is all about.

Stated in simplest terms, a good roof-drainage system is designed to carry water away from the house quickly. To do it, gutters gather runoff water from the roof and move it to drop outlets. From here, leaders conduct the water into vertical downspouts (which should discharge directly into storm drainpipes or be extended away from the house to prevent foundation seepage).

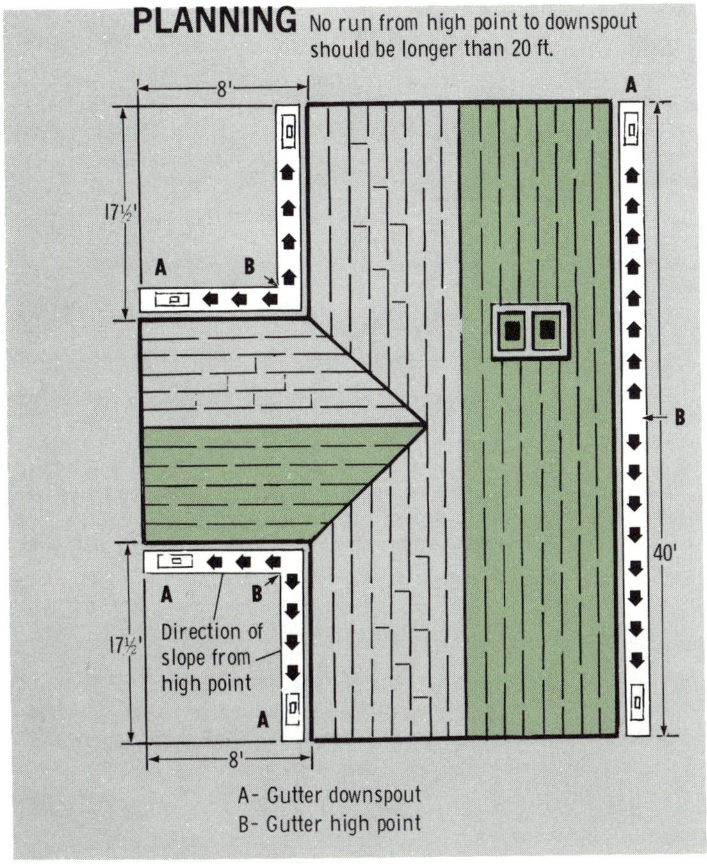

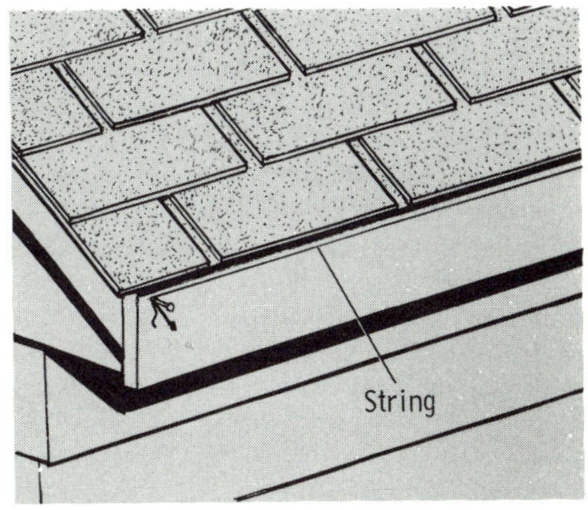

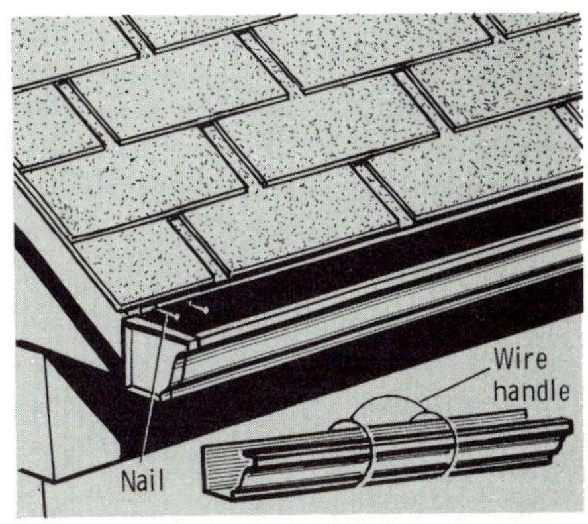

Tools needed for gutter installation include a hammer, screwdriver, pliers, tin snips, hacksaw, ruler, level, chalkline, caulking gun, drill and, if the gutter material requires it, a Pop RiveTool. (Aluminum gutter, for example, calls for riveted connections.)

Gutter materials are available in many sizes and shapes, including half-round as well as style *K* or ogee box-gutter cross section. Gutter lengths are usually 10 ft.; but in some materials, 16, 20 and even 30-ft. sections are offered.

Downspouts come round, rectangular or square in corrugated or plain styles. The corrugated type is better in freezing climates because it expands with the freezing water. Elbows come in bends of 30, 45, 60, 75 and 90°. You can choose from among many types of gutter hangers. End caps are made to seal the ends of gutter sections (both right and left). Miters, or corners, can be bought for both inside and outside turns. Slip-joints or expansion joints are available to connect gutter lengths. All necessary hardware, including screws, rivets and nails, can be purchased for compatibility with any system.

Gutter systems are available in galvanized steel, aluminum, copper, zinc, lead, vinyl and wood. Cost for a typical one-story ranch home ranges from about $85 for steel up to approximately $140 for aluminum.

Galvanized-steel gutters are generally the lowest in cost. They're now available with baked-on acrylic coatings that do away with the problem of painting raw galvanized surfaces. You simply add the finish coat of your choice after they're installed. Gutters come in varying gauges—the higher the number, the thinner the material. The most commonly used is 28 ga. but for extra strength use 26 ga. For economy, use 29 ga. Unlike steel, aluminum gutter material thickness is spelled out in inches (.027 and .032 in. are popular).

Never mix your metals, even small parts like screws. Electrolytic (galvanic) action between dissimilar metals will corrode them quickly. Choose one material and stick with it.

The problem is not so much in determining the size of the gutter, but in finding the size and number of downspouts to carry water away from the gutter. A general rule is to use one outlet for each 600 sq. ft. of roof area. A gutter run of more than 20 ft. needs a downspout at each end. If shorter, put a downspout at one end.

Determine the actual roof area to be served,

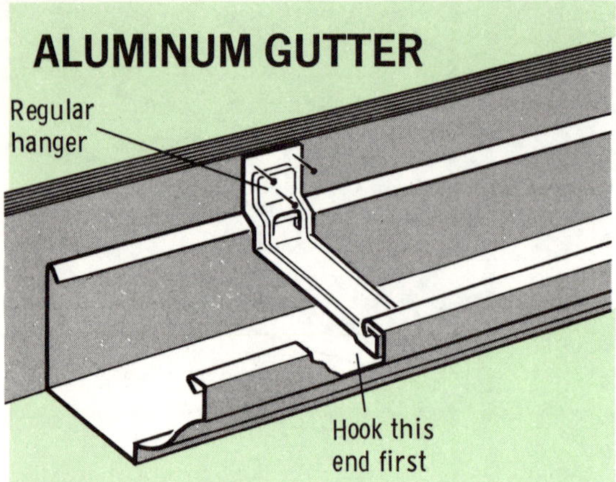

HANGERS ARE SPACED a minimum of 30 in. on center, preferably at the rafters. A hanger strap is hooked to the front and rear lips of the gutter prior to nailing. Then the back of the hanger is nailed to the fascia at the rafter points or directly to the rafter where fascia boards are not installed. Use 1½-in. nails.

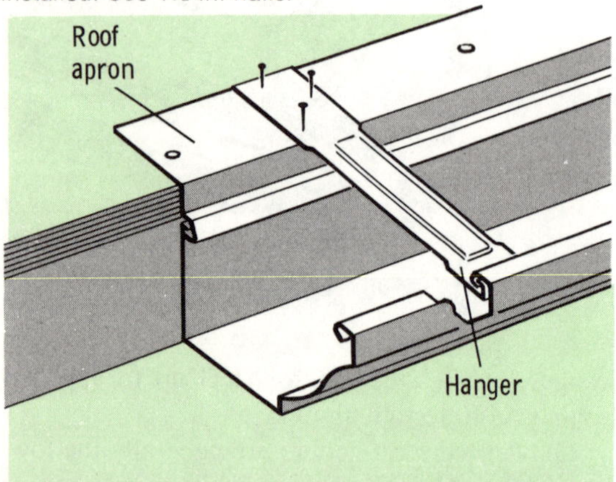

A ROOF APRON and hangers can be used on new work to provide additional flashing. The apron is engaged to the gutter along the back and then nailed to the roof sheathing at 12-in. intervals. The hanger straps are hooked into the gutter's front lip and nailed over the rafters every 30-in. Use 1½-in. aluminum nails.

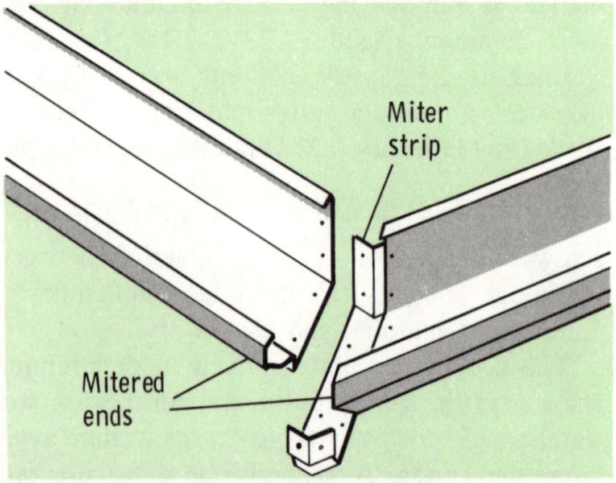

IN THE FIELD ASSEMBLY of a miter strip, cut both left and right-hand gutter sections at a 45° angle for both inside and outside miter strips. Apply sealer to the strip and rivet to the butted ends of the gutter sections. Joint sealer should be applied to all the rivet heads to prevent drip-producing holes.

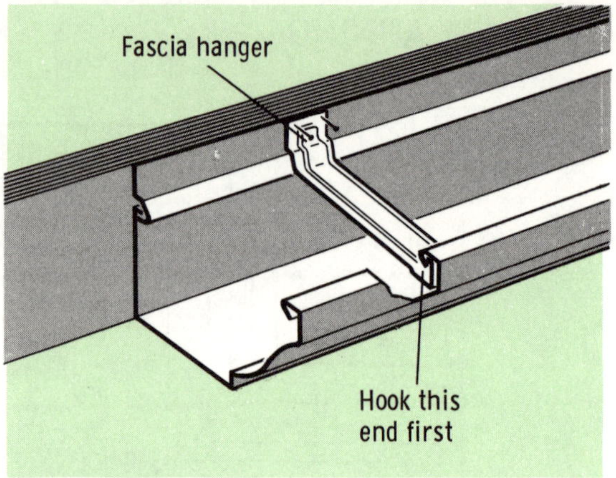

A FASCIA HANGER and apron are used on jobs where the roofing material is already in. To install, the hook of the fascia apron is engaged along the back of the gutter and secured to the fascia at 12-in. intervals. The fascia hangers are spaced 30 in. apart and hooked into the front lip of the gutter.

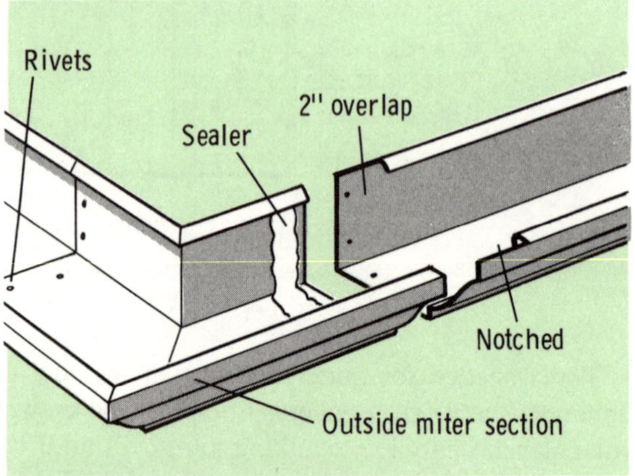

TO JOIN GUTTER AND MITER sections joint sealer is applied around one surface of the entire joint. After notching the front bead and the rear of the gutter as shown, lap the sections 2 in. Drill rivet holes and insert two rivets in each of the three sides. Apply a bead of sealer along inside edges.

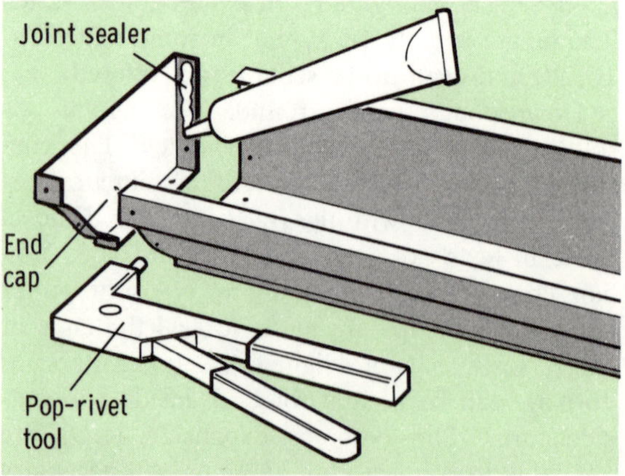

RIVET-TYPE CAP INSTALLATION is easy to do and gives a neat-looking job. After applying joint sealer to the end cap, it is slipped onto the gutter section. Drill rivet holes and insert the rivets. Use an adequate number of rivets since the joints must bear the weight of snow and ice in the winter months.

including all gables and roof surfaces. Don't use the horizontal length times width of your roof. Since rain seldom falls in a true vertical, all surface planes gather water during a storm. When the roof slope is increased, the roofline is raised accordingly and more surface is created to catch additional rainfall.

Downspouts should be placed near the corners of the house so that gutter water will not have to flow beyond the sharp turn. Of course, appearance plays a part in locating such outlets. If possible, keep them away from doorways and place downspouts flush against the front of the building when viewed from the street. If they protrude out to one side, downspouts can be an eyesore.

the correct size gutter

Size of gutter depends upon: (1) the number, size and spacing of outlets; (2) slope of the roof (a steep roof carries water to the gutter faster than a flat roof); (3) style of gutter used, and (4) the gutter's slope. Avoid a gutter less than 4 in. wide. And never use one that is smaller than the leader. If leaders are spaced 20 ft. or less, use a gutter the same size as the leader. But if they are more than 20 ft. apart, add 1 in. to the gutter width for every 30 ft. of additional spacing on peaked roofs. Add 1 in. for every additional 40 ft. of gutter length for flat roofs.

Gutter slope is a problem. It looks bad on the house, yet it is needed. The minimum slope from high point to downspout should be ½ in. in a 20-ft. run. A better slope is 1 in 20. Though a gutter can be set dead level, it requires using larger gutters and downspouts to drain off the water. With no slope, water pockets are a possibility. They encourage corrosion.

When installing a new gutter system, it's a good idea to first clean and paint the fascia boards. Next, stretch a chalkline along one fascia board to locate the top of the gutter. Allowing for slope to the downspout, run the line out to the other end of the fascia, then snap it.

Start gutter assembly at an end opposite the leader. Select the proper end cap, fill its grooves with gutter sealant and attach it to the gutter. A gutter should extend ½ in. beyond the rake edge of the roof.

Complete assembly of a manageable section of gutter, then lift it into place. Working alone, rest one end of the assembly on a 10-ft. stepladder. Or, you can fashion wire loops (as shown) around the gutter and hook them over nails tacked to the fascia or the roof.

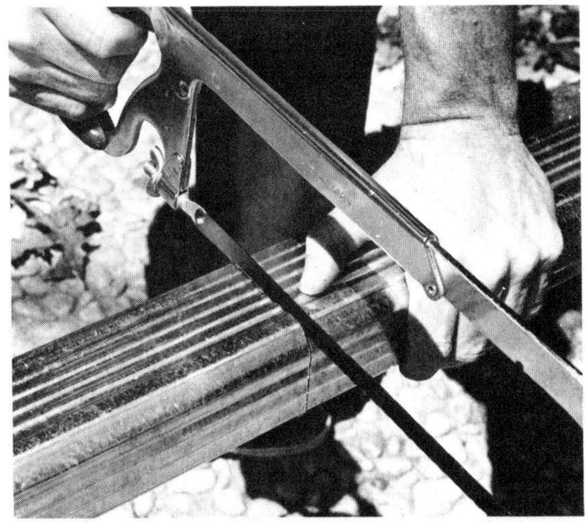

DOWNSPOUTS AND GUTTER SECTIONS are cut with a 32-point hacksaw. Support the section solidly and keep the blade as flat as possible.

FASTEN THE DOWNSPOUT to the wall with a strap and nails. Straps differ for masonry and wood walls. In masonry the studs are driven into mortar.

ELBOWS are used to bring the leader back from the roof overhang to a downspout on the house wall. After positioning, holes are drilled for the rivets.

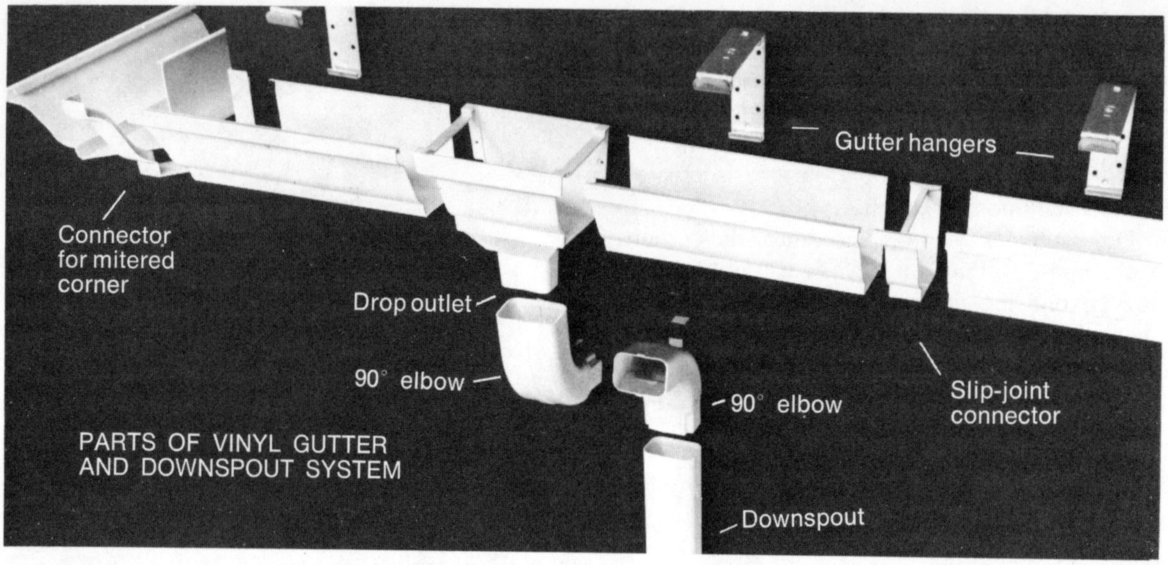

PARTS OF VINYL GUTTER AND DOWNSPOUT SYSTEM

continued from previous page

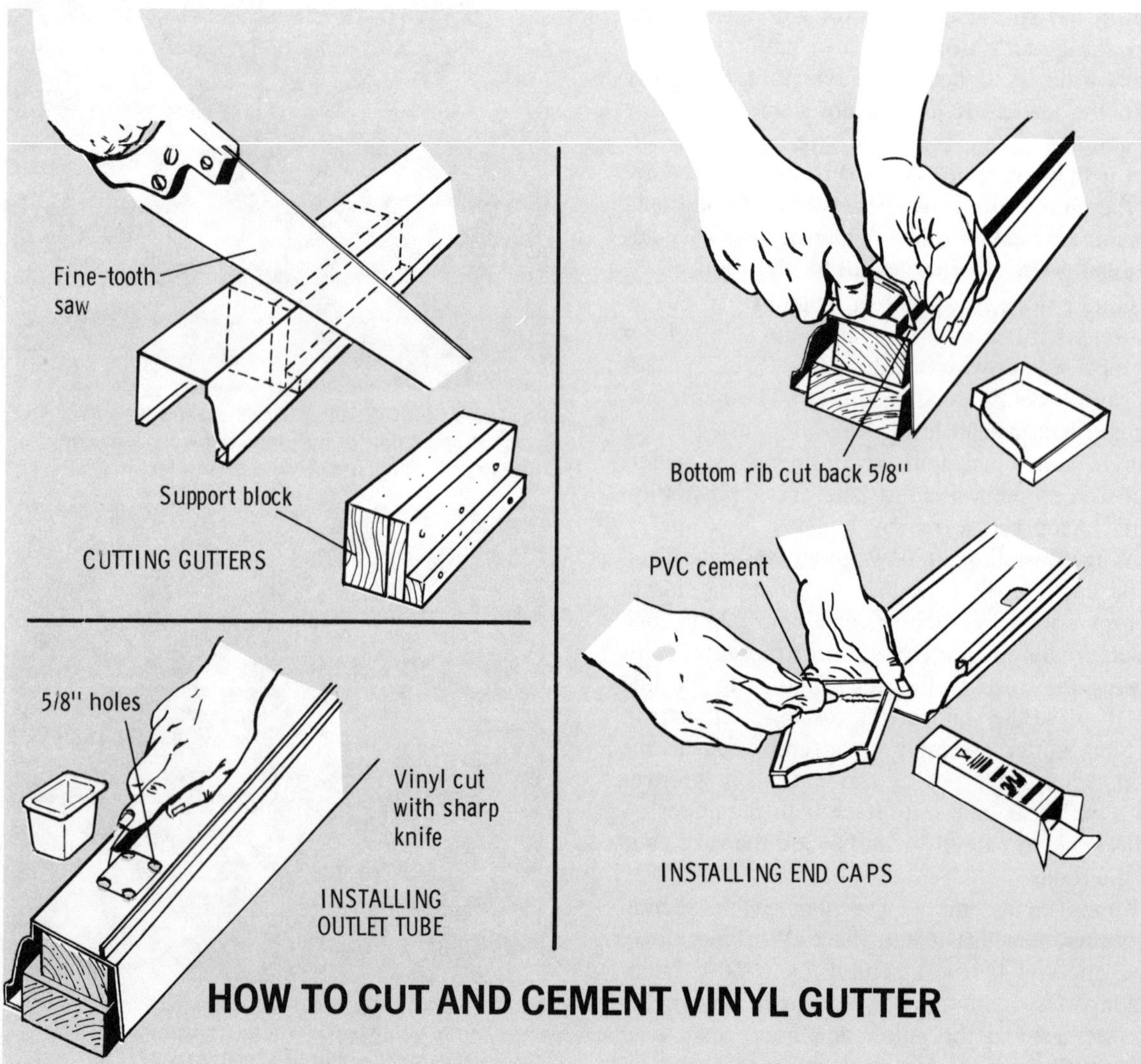

HOW TO CUT AND CEMENT VINYL GUTTER

When you reach a corner, attach either another end cap or an inside or outside miter. If the corner calls for a leader, use the special gutter section with a leader fabricated into it. The end cap or corner is then attached to this section.

making joints

Joints between lengths of gutter and fittings can be made by overlapping, or with slip-joint connectors. For a waterproof joint, treat slip joints the same as end caps, filling their grooves with gutter sealant and sliding the gutters into them from each side.

Lap joints are my personal choice. To make them, cut the top flange of the bead back at an angle (see drawings). Spread two ¼-in. rows of gutter sealant spaced about an inch apart on the uncut gutter. The beads should extend without gaps over the entire inside circumference of the gutter. Insert the cut length into the uncut one about 2 in., drill and rivet. The rivets and sealant provide a lasting, watertight bond.

With the assembled gutter tacked in place, attach the gutter hangers. Of two basic types, brackets fasten to the fascia and straps attach to the roof. Line up the top edges of the hangers with the chalkline. Slip the gutter into each hanger, making sure the back edge of the gutter is under the top lip of the hanger and the rear bottom edge of the gutter rests on the bottom of the hanger. Depress the top hanger flange with a screwdriver and hammer it down. Then insert a hanger strap under the front lip of the gutter and place the strap's slot into the hanger's hook with a twist. Punch down the hook with a screwdriver and hammer it down to hold the strap securely.

The procedure for fastening strap hangers (which go under the roofing) is similar, but it means lifting shingles and sticking them down again with mastic. To use strap hangers, position the gutter section so that its top edge is flush with the guideline. Nail the gutter to the fascia board with one 6d nail every 32 in. Hook the hangers into the underside of the front bead of the gutter and nail them to the roof underneath the shingles.

The wraparound hanger works like a strap hanger, except that it locks around the gutter.

Another method of attaching gutters is the spike-and-ferrule system. Position the gutter, then temporarily nail it to the fascia with 6d common nails at several places. Place the ferrule inside the gutter at bead height, lined up with the end of a rafter. Drive the spike through the gutter bead, ferrule and fascia board into the rafter. Locate the spikes at the first rafter and at every second rafter.

LEAF GUARDS in strip form fit between shingles and gutter bead and keep the gutter free of debris.

If the gable end of the roof has an overhang, you'll have to add a 45° elbow, a short, straight piece and another 45° elbow from the outlet opening to carry the downspout system back toward the wall of the house.

Expansion joints should be used on all hip-roof installations, on straight runs of 40 ft. or more and in any other spots where normal expansion and contraction is restricted. The expansion joints devised by one manufacturer of aluminum are made of neoprene and aluminum to provide the needed flexibility. The neoprene section is in the center of two aluminum end pieces. When joining gutter sections with an expansion joint, follow the method used with regular slip joints. The neoprene section will be hidden by the overlapping ends of the gutter sections.

Note that each section of downspout pipe and elbow has one end slightly smaller than the other. The parts are joined by fitting the larger end over the smaller and forcing them together. The sections are then anchored with sheet-metal screws. The smaller end must be on top so that flowing water is always running into the larger end of the pipe section. After snugging the downspout section against the wall, use two straps for each 10-ft. section of pipe.

The bottom of the downspout is completed with an elbow (or shoe) and a 4-ft. extension or splash block to direct water away from the foundation.

How to keep your gutters and downspouts functioning

By inspecting and maintaining your gutters and downspouts you can add 10 years to their life

A THOROUGH ANNUAL GUTTER and downspout inspection and maintenance program can add from 5 to 10 years of service to the gutters on your home. That's the kind of do-it-yourself work that keeps cash in your pocket.

Basically, gutter upkeep can be broken down into three categories: 1) cleaning, 2) repairing damaged and leaky areas and 3) preventive maintenance.

Because clogged drains prevent proper water runoff, water can back up under roof shingles or cause a damp or wet basement and unsightly stains on the house siding. You should also know whether your house is adequately guttered. For an average rainfall, a gutter will perform well with approximately 1 sq. ft. of surface for each 150 sq. ft. of roof to be drained.

Typical gutter and downspout component parts are shown below. These are available in both metal and plastic types.

Gutter sections come in 8, 10 and 12-ft. lengths—the 10-footers are perhaps the most popular length and are easy to handle. The various fittings, connectors and the like must be ordered separately: make certain that you include enough hangers to do the job. Assemble sections on the ground; then, with help, hoist and fasten them in position.

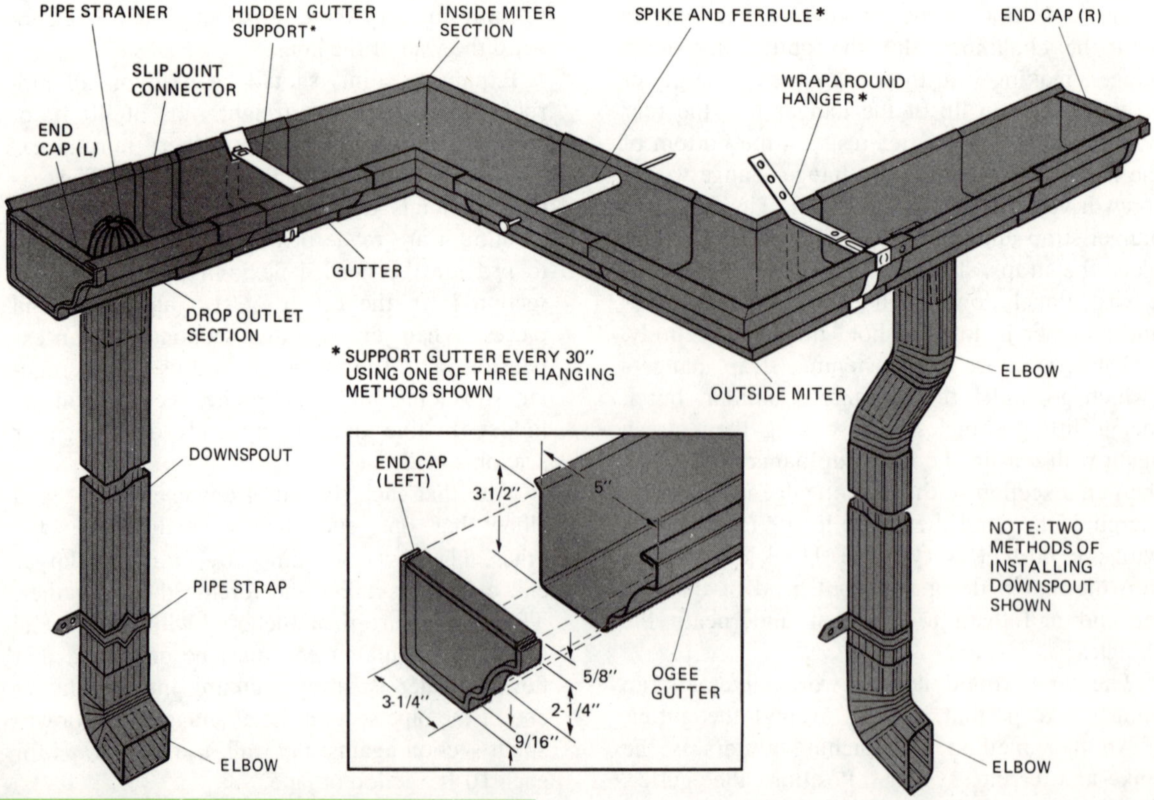

SEE ALSO

Basement waterproofing . . . Drainage, downspout . . . Home improvement . . . House additions . . . Roofs

WHEN TO CLEAN THE GUTTERS

The logical time to give your gutters an annual cleaning is in autumn, after all leaves have fallen. You'll find minerals and grit from your shingles in gutters as well. A whisk broom (1) is a perfect "tool" for this chore. After all leaves and debris have been scooped out (2), flush out the gutter using a garden hose. During this cleaning stage you can check for leaks and drainage pitch and make necessary corrections (see next two pages). Keeping gutters clean is extremely important; rotting leaves combined with soot and the like will form an acid that hastens rusting and corrosion.

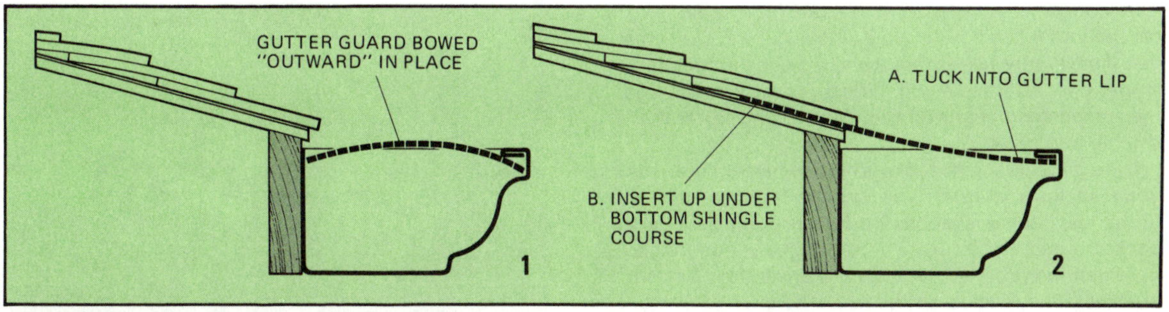

CONSIDER INSTALLING GUTTER GUARD

Installation of plastic gutter guard takes a lot of the work out of keeping gutters clean. Using the screen doesn't completely eliminate the leaf-cleaning task, but it does minimize it. Most types of gutter screening come in rolls 6 in. wide by 25 ft. long. The guard can be installed using either method shown above: By tucking one edge up under the bottom course of shingles with the other edge in the gutter lip, or by bending both edges into the gutter to create a pressure fit. Overlap end joints by at least 4 in. The only tool you'll need for this job is a pair of scissors for cutting the guard. In any event, the guard does not eliminate annual hosing down of gutters.

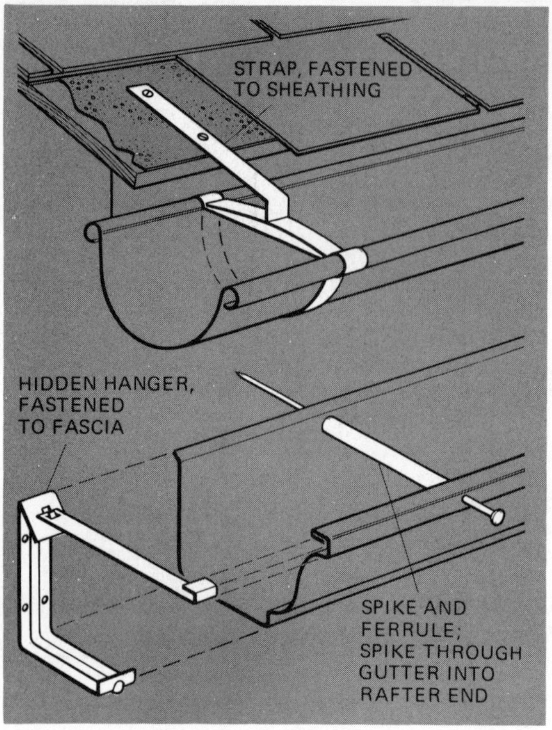

TYPICAL GUTTER HANGERS

Your yearly inspection should also include checking for sagging gutters (where water will collect instead of run off). Sags will inevitably cause water to spill over the gutter during heavy rains. If you have water spills during a cloudburst, and your cleaning assured that there were no clogs, you can assume that the gutter is sagging because of a hanger problem.

A sag can be caused by a loosened hanger—usually created by excessive weight of ice formed in an improperly pitched gutter. There are other reasons for sag, too—a ladder placed improperly against the gutter, a stray basketball or a fallen tree limb, for example.

If your gutter is fastened with straps (top sketch), carefully lift the shingle to avoid cracking it and check the nail. If necessary, take up slack and replace the nail with a longer one. After replacing the nail, cover its head and the surrounding area with roof cement and lower the shingle into place.

If the gutter is supported by a hidden-type hanger, the gutter section may have to be removed for inspection. If the hanger is loose, chances are that either the nails have backed out or too few were used originally. Add longer nails and make certain *all* nails are driven home so the bracket is fully seated on the fascia board.

The third type of hanger is the spike and ferrule. Carefully remove the old spike. After determining that the fascia is sound, carefully drill a hole in the gutter at least 2 in. away from the spot where the old spike was. Insert the spacer (ferrule) and drive home the spike. Patch both sides of gutter where it was pierced by the original spike.

REPAIRING HOLES IN WOOD GUTTERS

Wood-gutter repairs are similar to metal-gutter repairs except that a careful check should be made to assure that there are no soft spots under the surface of seemingly sound areas. Soft spots should be gouged out with a wood chisel and patched with a quality wood filler intended for outdoor use. When filler has hardened, proceed with the patching operation as described above for metal gutters.

PATCHING SMALL HOLES AND BREAKS

Small holes in the metal can be closed using a fabric patch and roofing compound. First clean the area and go over it with a wire brush. After dusting, apply roof mastic (1). Then press in a patch of either fiberglass, canvas or burlap. Use a wood "spatula" to smooth out all wrinkles (2) and apply a top coat of the roof mastic compound (3). Do not build up the area too high or you may restrict the flow of water. These patches can add years of service life to a gutter.

If corrosive damage is extensive, an external patch may also be required. Your best bet is to use one of the fiberglass repair kits that are available at auto supply stores. Read the manufacturer's instructions before applying. However, before tackling a patch job of considerable size, give thought to replacing the damaged section of gutter entirely. In the final analysis, replacing the section may be cheaper, and accomplished with less time and effort.

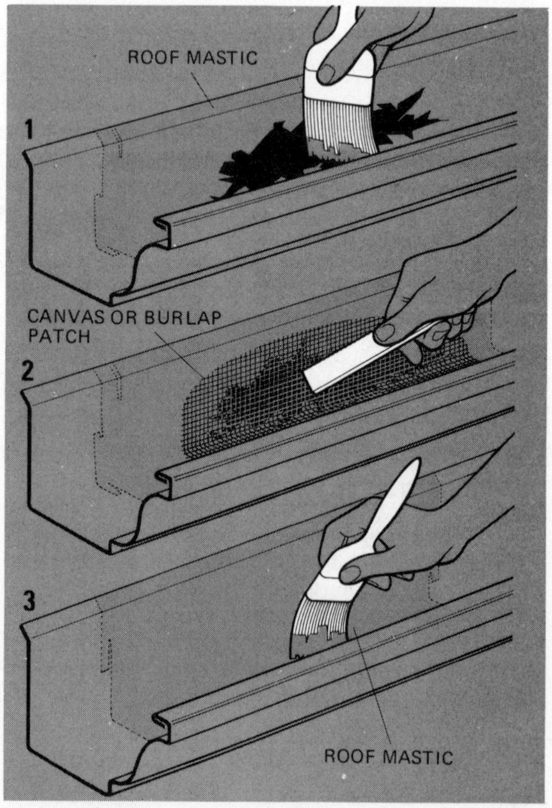

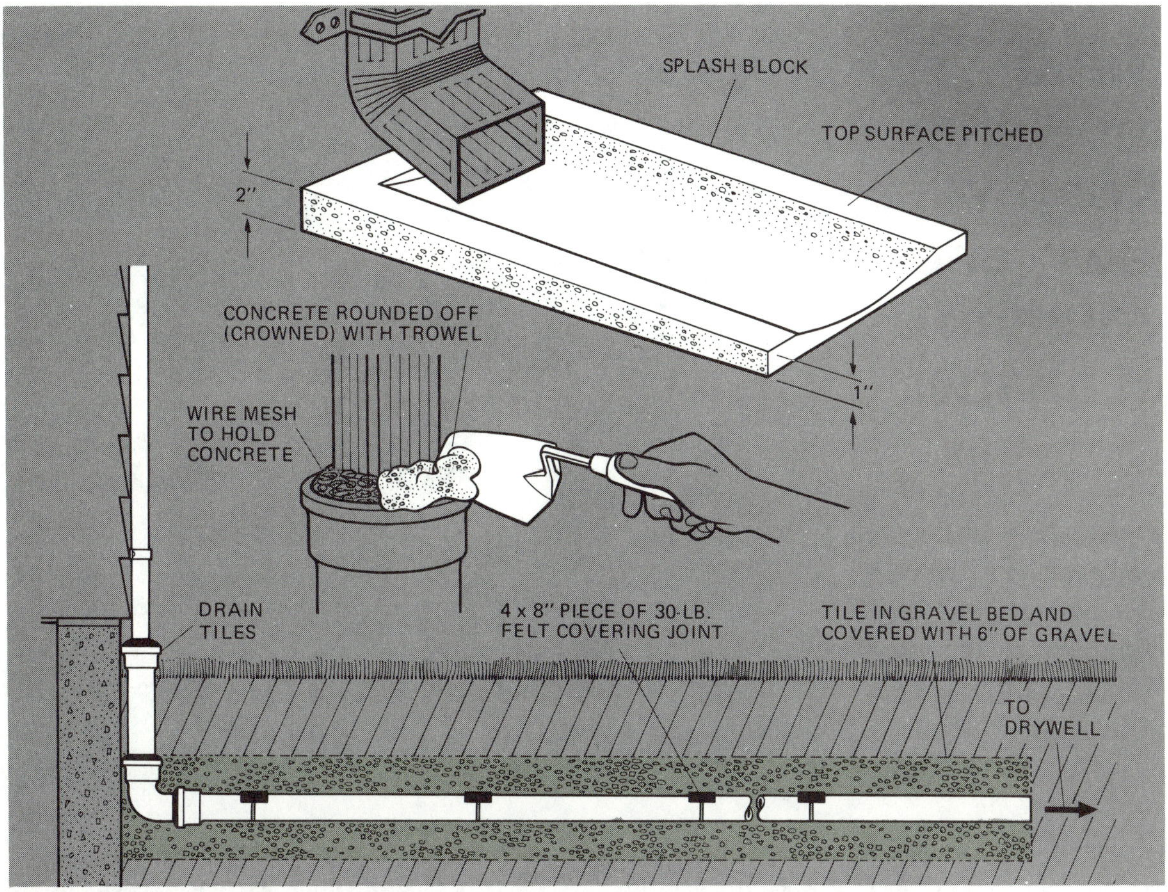

INSTALLING SPLASH BLOCKS AND DRAIN TILES

Unless you provide for water discharge at ground level, soil will be washed away. And if drainage away from the foundation wall is poor, water may seep into the basement.

If there is good drainage away from your foundation, a flat stone placed beneath each downspout will do an adequate job of dispersing water. It is better, however, to install concrete or plastic splash blocks; you'll have a more permanent job.

☐ In some soils, a run of open-end drain tiles installed below grade as shown above will serve as an effective dispersal unit. If desired, drain tiles can be connected to a dry well filled with gravel and capped with concrete. On long runs, wells are usually not needed; water is adequately dispersed at joints along the length of the tiles.

ANNUAL PREVENTIVE MAINTENANCE

After gutters have been thoroughly cleaned and any necessary spot-patches completed, they should be given the appropriate annual maintenance. Follow these steps:

☐ *Wood gutters.* Keep inside surfaces thoroughly coated with brush-on asphaltic cement.

☐ *Metal gutters.* If of galvanized iron, they may show rust spots. After wire brushing and dusting off, apply a quality rust-preventing prime coat of paint. Consider painting the entire gutter lining, but make certain the surfaces are clean or the primer will peel off.

☐ *Aluminum gutters.* Require minimal maintenance because they will not rust. Aluminum gutters provide their own oxidation which helps the paint to adhere. They are not as strong as steel however, and are more prone to damage from ladders, tree limbs and the like.

☐ *Polyvinyl chloride (PVC) plastic gutters.* This type requires practically no upkeep (other than annual cleaning). It is not as strong as metal when used as a ladder support and has the disadvantage of great expansion and contraction in heat and cold. Thus, when you are installing PVC gutters be sure to use the prescribed connectors that allow for expansion at the joints.

Hand mowers: Keep your lawn and yourself in shape

Save energy and tone up your muscles by pushing a reel-type lawnmower. Here's how to revivify that old 'monster'

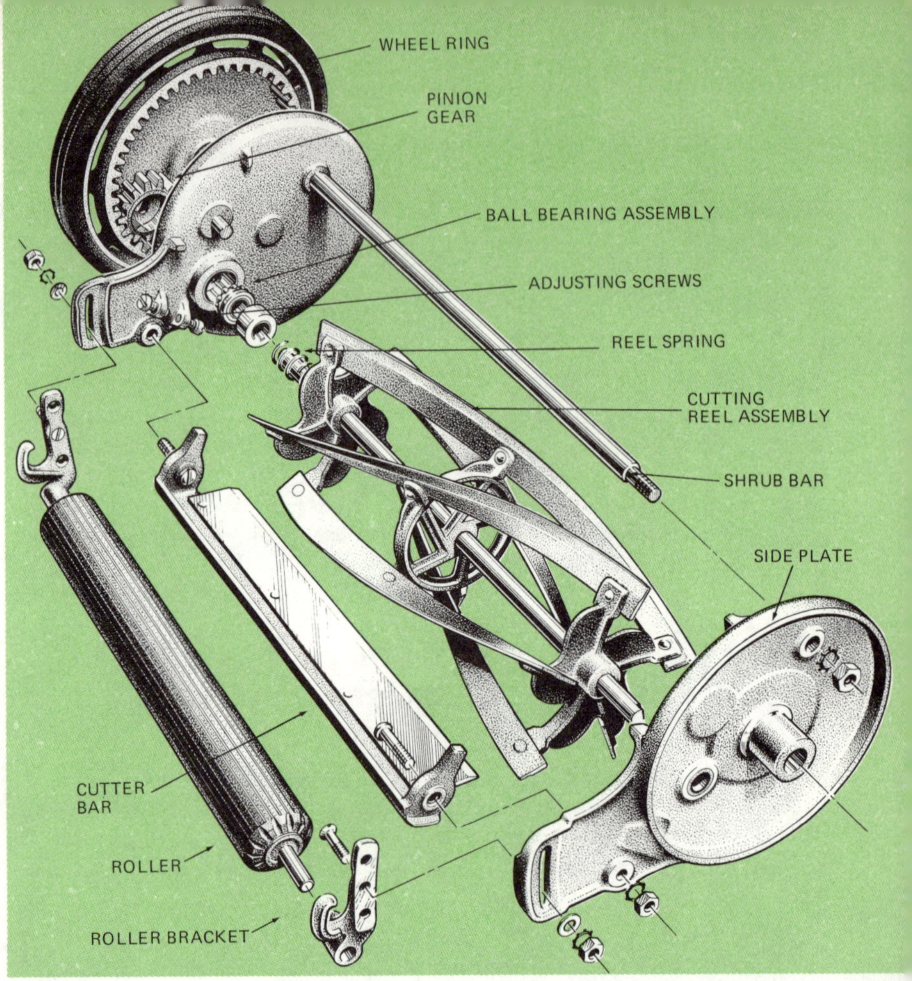

PUSHING a hand mower hasn't quite achieved the status of jogging when it comes to exercise. But you *can* work up a nice, warm glow behind a mower and at the same time keep up with your neighbors in exhibiting a neat, trim lawn.

If you have an old manual mower out in the garage or if you run across one at a tag sale, you can get it in working shape fairly easily and at very little expense.

Manual mowers need minimal maintenance. Spend a small amount of your time keeping them in shape, and they'll cut grass every time you want them to go to work.

You can make even a long-neglected reel mower work again by performing the simple maintenance procedures shown here. Basically, you'll need to disassemble it and clean its parts, replace worn or damaged parts, apply lubricant, then prime and paint it. After you've sharpened the blades, your mower will be ready for use.

Pay special attention as you disassemble the mower, so that you can replace the parts in their original positions. If not replaced properly, some parts, such as the right and left pinion gears, will cause problems when you try to put your lawnmower to use.

cleaning mower parts

To get parts thoroughly clean, you may have to apply a rust remover. Wear rubber gloves as you brush the solution onto the rusty surfaces. Then let it soak. Finally, wire-brush parts, rinse with water.

SEE ALSO
Grass . . . Landscaping . . . Lawns . . . Mowers . . . Paths, garden . . . Retaining walls . . . Stepping stones . . . Transplanting . . . Trees

1 Strip down the mower completely. If necessary, use oil to loosen parts frozen by rust.

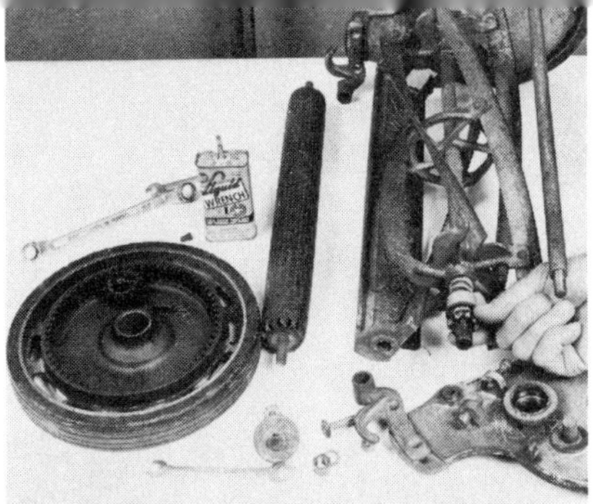

2 Pay particular attention to the reel-shaft bearings. Replace damaged balls or install an entire new bearing if necessary.

3 If rust is severe, clean parts with solvent to remove grease and oil. Apply a rust remover such as Naval Jelly. Wear rubber gloves when using remover.

4 Apply masking tape to parts that won't be painted, including shaft ends, tires, hubs and treads. Peel off excess after carefully cutting with a razor.

5 Apply oil to the cutting edges of the reel and cutter bar; then spray on red oxide or other primer. Oiled areas won't retain oxide. Wipe them later.

6 Spray several light coats of quality paint that can be used on metal. We used Plasti-Kote Aluminum on reel and cutter, Swift Red on other parts.

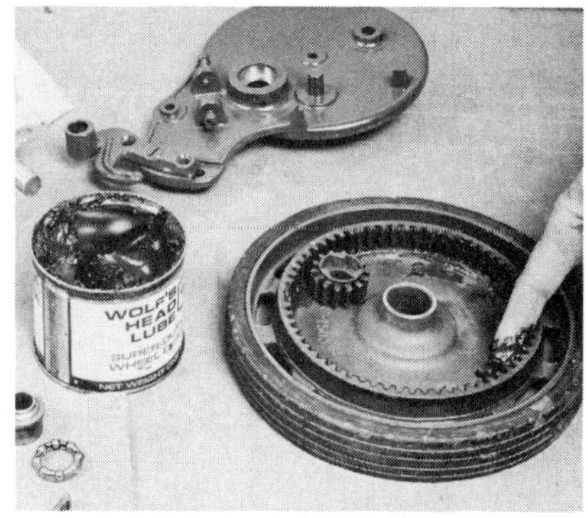

7 Grease gears, bearings and hubs. Carefully replace wheel rings and pinion gears in their proper places or reel will turn in reverse direction.

8 Stand the mower on end to facilitate replacing the wheels. Jiggle the wheel after it meets the hub to ensure that the gears mesh properly.

9 Sharpen the cutter bar while it is clamped in a vise. Make flat passes with a smooth, single-cut file on top edge *only*. Stroke with whetstone.

10 To sharpen reel blades, turn mower upside down, if needed, to adjust cutter bar at ends so it lightly contacts reel blades. Perform steps 11 and 12.

11 Apply fine-grit grinding compound. This is available at auto-supply stores. This should be applied directly to the inside edge of the cutter bar.

12 Then rotate the reel *backward* by hand so blades make contact with the bar about a dozen times, lapping up the abrasive along the leading edge.

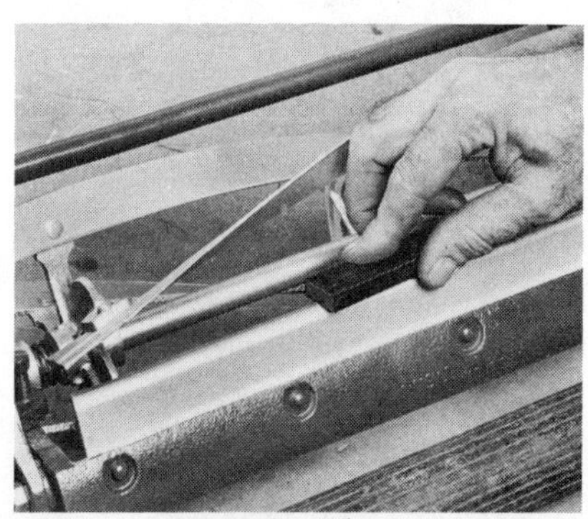

13 You can give the cutter bar a touch-up sharpening without removing it. Turn the mower over and firmly slide a whetstone across bar's top edge.

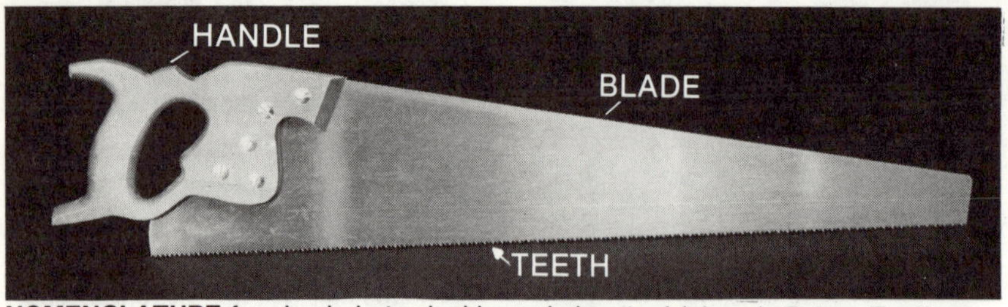

NOMENCLATURE for simple but valuable workshop tool (above). Below: Teeth of cross-cut saw, set alternately to both sides of blade plane, cut like two rows of knife points. Ripsaw blade has teeth that resemble chisels lined up in a row.

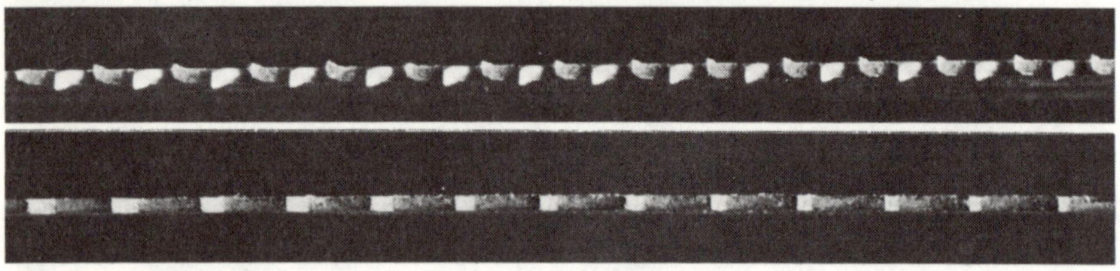

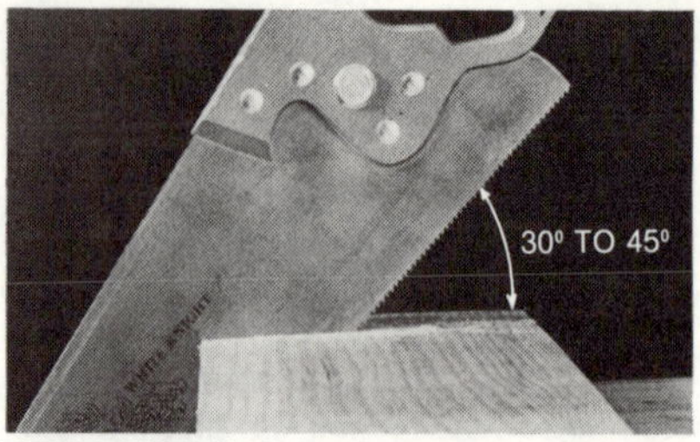

BEST CUTTING angle is when saw is held so teeth are within above degree range.

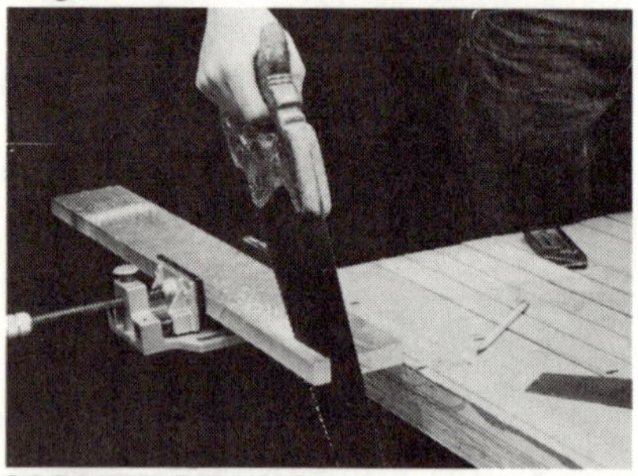

GREATER RIPPING accuracy is assured if you clamp work in vise when possible.

Handsaw basics

■ THERE IS A LOT MORE to the handsaw than most beginning woodworkers suspect. Did you know, for example, that a saw's blade is slightly thicker along the edge with the teeth than the rest of the blade? That's the way high-quality saws are made in order to give firmness to the cutting edge. You should know that there are two types of general carpentry saws—the crosscut saw for cutting across the grain and the rip saw for with-the-grain cuts. You should have at least one of each in your toolbox.

■ Pick a tool with a quality handle, one that feels comfortable and is securely fastened to saw blade.

■ A crosscut saw has teeth much like small knives set far enough apart to keep the saw from binding. The crosscut does about 80 percent of its cutting on the downstroke and cleans the kerf on its upstroke. For a first crosscut saw, pick one about 26 in. long with 7 or 8 points.

■ Rip saw. Since there is less resistance when cutting with the grain, a rip saw requires fewer teeth. Here, pick a 5½ or 6-pointer.

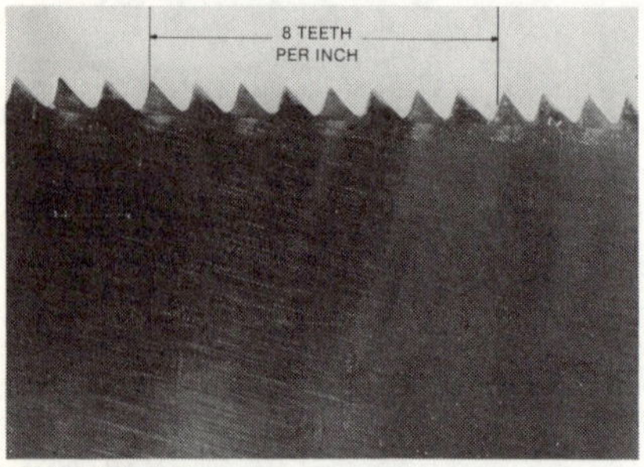

MEASURE IN teeth or points per inch. There will be one more point than teeth.

BASIC CARPENTRY RULE: Always position saw to cut on waste side of line.

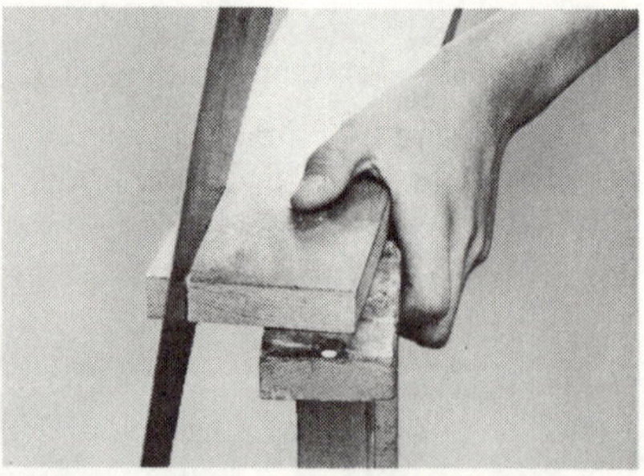

TO RIP board on a sawhorse, hold work securely, using other hand like vise.

WHEN STARTING cut, guide blade with thumb, form kerf by several upstrokes.

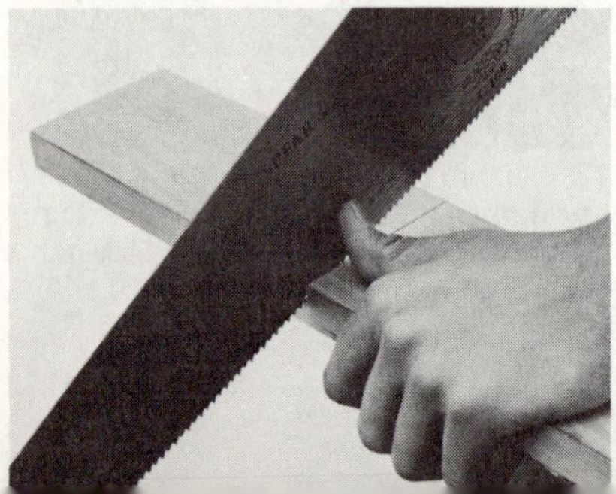

SAW MUST be held at 90° to the board face or you will create a bevel cut.

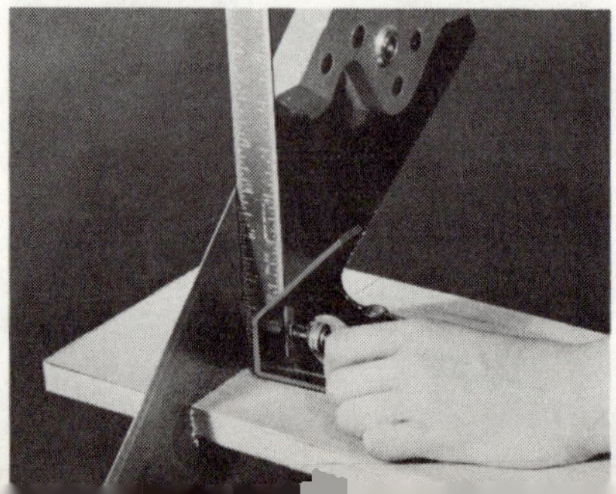

IF POSSIBLE, clamp workpiece in the vise when making cross cuts as well.

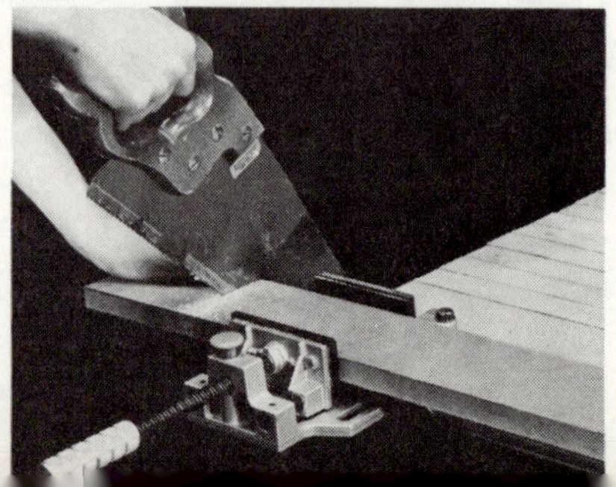

EXTRA BLADES for a sabre saw are stuffed in a user's pocket so they'll be often handy. A better way to keep them together is to "string" them on a shower curtain hook. A typical hook will hold more than enough blades for a heavy work session, and holes in pockets will be eliminated.—*Andrew Vena, Philadelphia.*

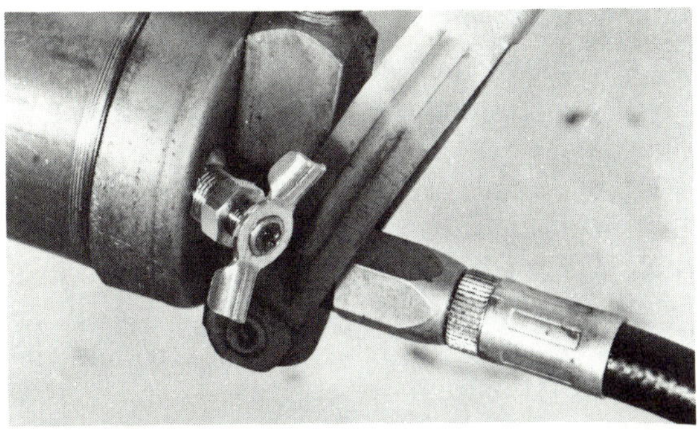

AIR LOCKS in a hand-operated grease gun inevitably cause loss of pumping action. Such locks can be immediately relieved if you replace the gun's filler plug with a radiator drain cock. A standard cock with an ⅛-in. pipe thread will fit most guns. When the gun fails to pump, just let air escape through the drain cock.—*Edward E. Smith, Jackson, MI.*

SHOE POLISH is an excellent wood-finishing material. By simply rubbing in the polish with 00 steel wool and buffing with a cloth, a very fine patina can be achieved. For exotic effects, try intermixing polishes such as oxblood and blue. On softwoods, apply thinned shellac before polishing.—*Albert J. Zulkowitz, Woodmere, NY.*

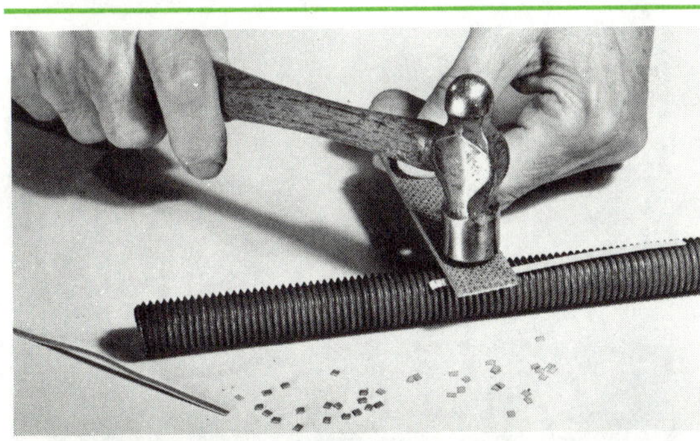

YOU CAN CUT uniform confetti-size rectangles of paper and sheet for craft projects with a ¾-in. threaded steel rod. Position a strip of the material at a slight diagonal to the rod so that thread-edges are at a right angle to strip edges. Then, lay cardboard over the strip and tap with a hammer; thread edges will do the cutting.—*Walter E. Burton, Akron, OH.*

MOST PEOPLE have a small metal box at home for safeguarding jewelry, insurance policies, birth certificates and other valuable papers. Next time you leave home for a vacation or trip, put this box in the refrigerator. In case of fire, the refrigerator is generally the one household article that is not totally destroyed.—*William Swallow, Brooklyn, NY.*

All about hardboard

Hardboard, manmade from materials which once were wasted, is now a standard item in the home, in the shop and for construction. You should know the types available and the tricks of working with it.

By LEN HILTS

IN 1924, WILLIAM MASON invented hardboard while seeking a use for the wood chips left as waste behind the nation's sawmills. Experimentally, he reduced the chips to their component fibers in a roaring blast of steam which removed impurities and left each wood fiber encased in lignin, the natural bonding agent of wood.

He made mats of the damp wood fibers, felting them with their own coating of lignin. Then he applied heat and pressure, expecting to produce a soft insulating material. To his surprise, he made a smooth, tough, grainless panel—the world's first hardboard.

SEE ALSO

Basement remodeling . . . Fasteners . . . Fences . . . Floors . . . Home improvement . . . Paneling, hardboard . . . Plasterboard . . . Remodeling

ELEGANT PECKY CYPRESS decorative hardboard panels help to give this small living room a spacious feeling.

THE DECORATIVE HARDBOARD PANELING here is deeply embossed and provides a French Provincial look.

Since that time, hardboard has become a standard material for home construction, remodeling, repair and furniture making. Its use increases each year because, while it has most of the characteristics of wood, it has some advantages.

The surface of hardboard is dense and smooth, ready for finishing. There is no grain, so there is less tendency for the finish to check. The panels are equally strong in all directions, and there are no knots or other imperfections. Hardboard won't splinter, resists cracking, can be curved, and worked with ordinary tools.

Standard hardboard, the basic material, is light brown, with a fairly hard, smooth surface on one side and a rough screen impression on the other. It is recommended for most interior uses, such as partitions, ceilings and cabinets. It should not be used where there is excessive moisture or where subjected to considerable abrasion.

Tempered hardboard is impregnated with a special compound which produces a much harder wearing surface, increases the strength, and reduces moisture absorption. It is a deeper brown color and suitable for both interior and exterior use. It can be used in basements and bathrooms, where the moisture is high. If you doubt which kind to order, go for the tempered. It costs a little more, but will wear much better.

Black hardboard is tempered hardboard treated with a black dye. Use it only where a flat black effect is desired—blackboards, for example.

Panel hardboard, used for walls, ceilings and soffits, is somewhat denser than standard hardboard, but not as dense as tempered. It is usually finished smooth on one side.

Underlayment is made specifically for use over wood floors and subfloors to provide an extremely smooth, flat surface on which to lay linoleum, tile or carpeting. The standard size is 4 x 4 ft.

Hardboard smooth on both sides is available in both standard and tempered, for applications where both sides may be seen. Common thicknesses are ⅛ in. and ¼ in.

Hardboard tile panels are exceptionally hard, with a very low water-absorption rate. Only ⅛ in. thick, they are scored to give the appearance of 4 in. wall tiles. Used primarily in bathrooms, kitchens and laundry areas.

TYPES AND SIZES OF HARDBOARD

Sizes and thicknesses shown are those generally available at lumber and building materials dealers, or which can be ordered through dealers. Some special sizes may not be listed. If you need a size not listed, check with your dealer.

Nominal Thickness (inches)	Sizes
Standard hardboard	
1/8	4 x 4, 4 x 7, 4 x 8, 4 x 9, 4 x 10, 4 x 12, 4 x 16
3/16	4 x 4, 4 x 7, 4 x 8, 4 x 9, 4 x 10, 4 x 12, 4 x 16
1/4	4 x 4, 4 x 7, 4 x 8, 4 x 10, 4 x 12, 4 x 16
5/16	4 x 4, 4 x 8, 4 x 9, 4 x 10, 4 x 12
Panel hardboard	
3/16	4 x 8, 4 x 10, 4 x 12, 4 x 16
1/4	4 x 8, 4 x 10, 4 x 12, 4 x 16
Underlayment	
1/4	4 x 3, 4 x 4
Standard, both faces smooth	
1/8	5 x 8, 5 x 16, 4 x 8, 4 x 16
3/16	5 x 8, 5 x 16, 4 x 7, 4 x 8, 4 x 16
Perforated hardboard (standard and tempered)	
1/8	4 x 4, 4 x 8
1/4	4 x 8
Tempered hardboard	
1/8	4 x 4, 4 x 7, 4 x 8, 4 x 9, 4 x 10, 4 x 12, 4 x 16
3/16	4 x 4, 4 x 7, 4 x 8, 4 x 9, 4 x 10, 4 x 12, 4 x 16
1/4	4 x 4, 4 x 8, 4 x 10, 4 x 12, 4 x 16
5/16	4 x 8, 4 x 9, 4 x 10, 4 x 12
Black tempered hardboard	
1/8	4 x 4, 4 x 8, 4 x 10, 4 x 12
1/4	4 x 4, 4 x 8, 4 x 10, 4 x 12
Tempered, both faces smooth	
1/8	4 x 4, 4 x 8, 4 x 10, 4 x 12
3/16	4 x 4, 4 x 8, 4 x 10, 4 x 12
1/4	4 x 4, 4 x 8, 4 x 10, 4 x 12
5/16	4 x 8, 4 x 10, 4 x 12
Die-cut filigree hardboard	
1/8	16″ x 6, 2 x 4, 2 x 6, 4 x 8
Hardboard tile panels	
1/8	4 x 4, 4 x 8, 4 x 10, 4 x 12, 4 x 16
Embossed Hardboard	
1/8	4 x 4, 4 x 6, 4 x 8, 4 x 12, 4 x 16
1/4	4/7, 4/8, 4/10
Concrete form hardboard	
3/16	4/8, 4 x 12
1/4	4/8, 4 x 12
Siding (in panels) (Thickness and lengths available vary with design and with manufacturer)	
7/16	4 x 6, 4 x 7, 4 x 8, 4 x 9, 4 x 10, 4 x 12, 4 x 16
Siding (lap) (Thickness and lengths and widths vary with design and manufacturer)	
1/4, 5/16, 7/16	9″, 12″, 16″, 24″ widths; 8, 12, 16-ft. lengths

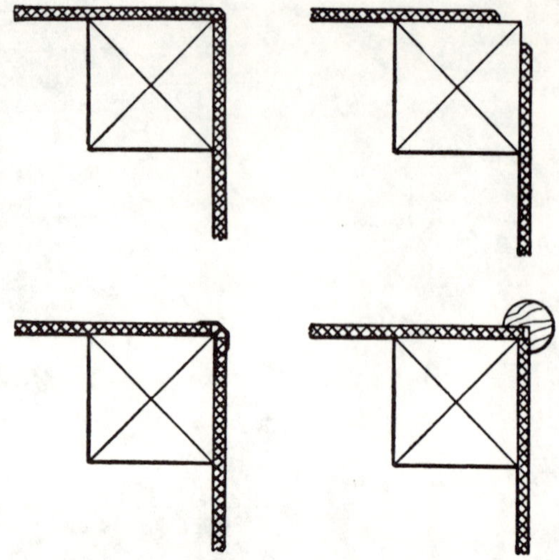

CORNER TREATMENTS

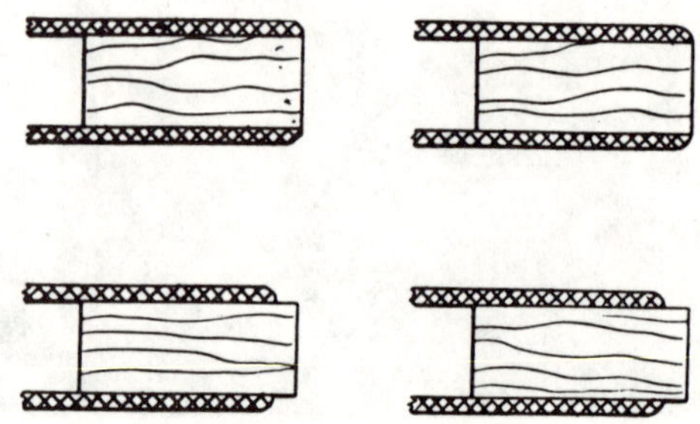

FOR SHELVES

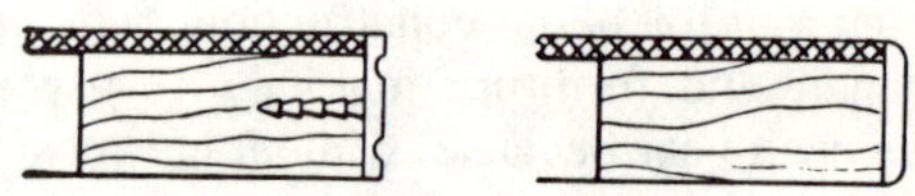

FOR COUNTERS

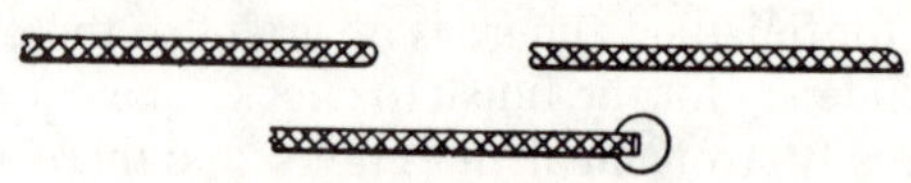

FOR UNSUPPORTED PANELS

EDGE TREATMENTS

Embossed hardboard is tempered with a patterned surface embossed into one side. One very popular finish looks like fine-grain leather. Many patterns are available and new ones are constantly being introduced for decorative wall paneling.

Filigree hardboard is a die-cut panel for interior use, available in several patterns and in standard widths of 16, 24 and 48 in. It is widely used in room screens and dividers, ceiling installa-

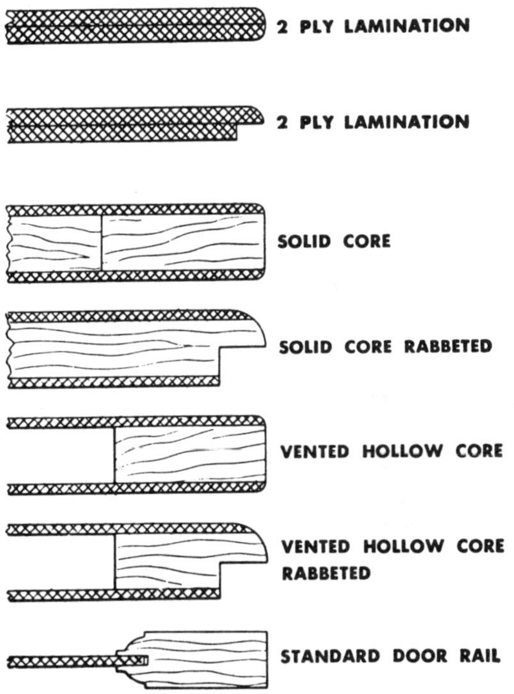

DOOR CONSTRUCTION

EXPOSED JOINTS

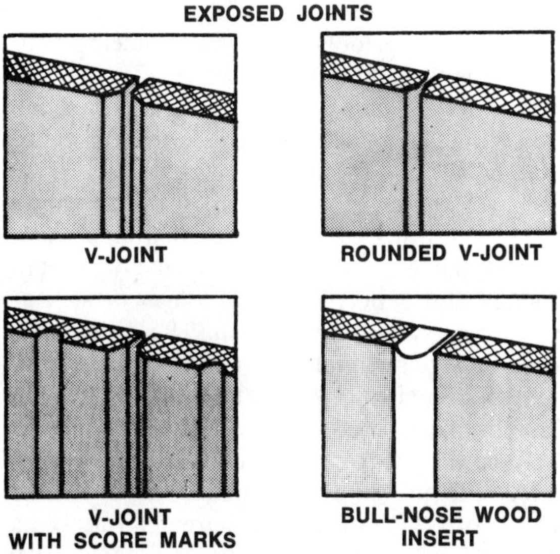

COVERED JOINTS

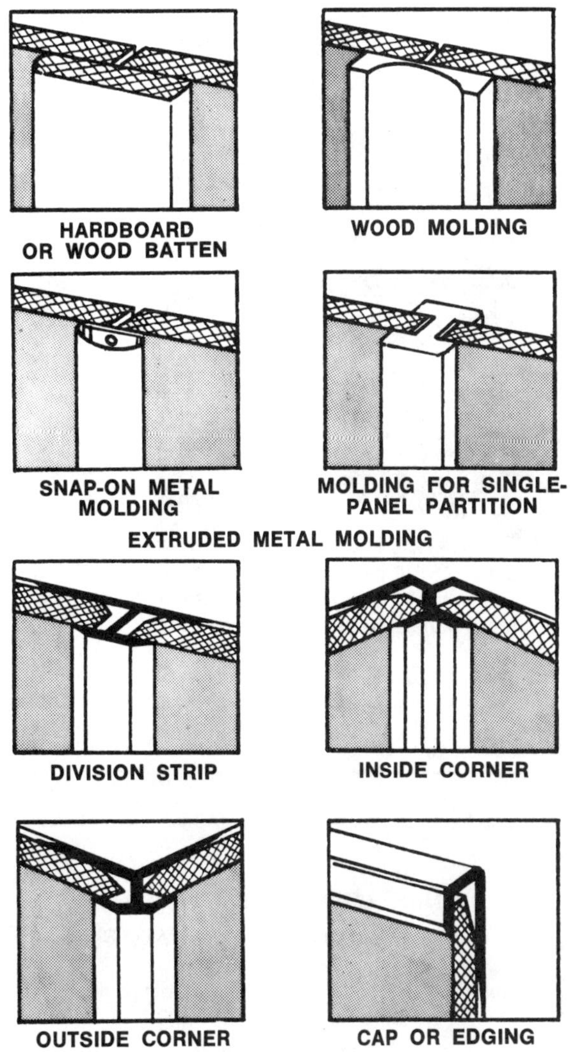

tions, and other places where an unusual design effect is desired.

Concrete-form hardboard is specially tempered for use in building forms for pouring concrete. Because it can be bent to smooth curves, it is useful in making unusual, irregular, or freeform shapes. It imparts a smooth finish to the concrete.

Hardboard siding has gained wide usage and comes in a number of designs and types. You can buy it unfinished, prime-coated, or precoated in a wide variety of colors. It comes both in large panels and in lap siding, with sizes and thicknesses varying from one brand to another. You don't waste much in using this material and you get a surface completely free of knots and checks. House paint applied to it doesn't suffer from bleed-through of knots as sometimes happens with poor-grade wood siding.

Perforated hardboard is one of the most popular hardboard products. It is a wall panel with holes $^3/_{16}$ in. in diameter drilled in it on ½ and 1 in. centers. Mounted on spacers on a wall, the perforated hardboard provides excellent hanging and storage space. Various wire hangers are available to be pushed into the holes, to hold

VINYL ADHESIVE packed for use in standard caulking guns is now the easy and preferred method of mounting hardboard panels. No nailing is necessary.

FOR BELOW-GRADE INSTALLATIONS, such as basement walls, a plastic vapor barrier should be put in place between the concrete wall and the hardboard.

all about hardboard, continued

MINIMUM BENDING RADII (in inches)

Thickness Of Stock	Cold Dry Bends		Cold Moist Bends	
	Smooth Side Out	Smooth Side In	Smooth Side Out	Smooth Side In
Standard Hardboard				
⅛	12	10	7	5
3/16	18	16	10	8
¼	27	24	15	12
5/16	35	30	22	18
Panel Hardboard				
3/16	20	18	12	10
¼	30	27	18	15
Both Faces Smooth				
⅛	10		7	
3/16	16		12	
Tempered Hardboard				
⅛	9	7	6	4
3/16	16	14	9	6
¼	25	22	14	10
5/16	35	30	20	16
Tempered, Both Faces Smooth				
⅛	10		7	
3/16	16		12	
Embossed Finishes				
⅛	10		7	

everything from tools and kitchen implements to small shelves and magazines.

You'll find some prefinished hardboard available, though most of this goes to the makers of wall panels and furniture.

Check the chart on page 1400, which shows the standard sizes of each type of hardboard that are available. Note especially that there are "long" and "short" panels—longer or shorter than the standard 8-ft. length. These often are easier to use and more economical when finishing rooms with 7, 9 or 10-ft. ceilings. These lengths may not be stocked by all dealers, so you may have to make a special order.

All lumber yards and home centers carry hardboard, but some have a greater variety on hand. Many will cut a panel to size for a small cutting fee. They also may charge you on the basis of the next 24-in. multiple, regardless of where the cut is made in the board.

If you're looking for an odd-sized piece, smaller than the standard, check the cutting department. Most yards have a rack where they put remnants at special prices.

Ordinary woodworking tools can be used on all hardboards. The material cuts easily with a fine-toothed saw. When sawing hardboard, always work with the smooth surface up. This

HARDBOARD UNDERLAYMENT is specially prepared for use over wood floors and subfloors to provide a smooth surface for vinyl tile, linoleum or carpeting.

produces a clean sharp edge. When making long cuts, always support both pieces. If one side is left unsupported, it may tear away as you near the end of the cut.

For cutting with power saws, a cross-cut or combination semi-high-speed or high-speed steel blade is best. Because of its density, hardboard will dull saw blades quickly, so if you intend to do considerable cutting of the material, use a carbide-tipped blade.

Use any of the standard woodworking glues or adhesives on hardboard, but for good adhesion on the smooth surface, you should roughen the surface a little with sandpaper. The rough side of the board provides tooth for the adhesive without further preparation.

Use high-speed twist drills rather than auger bits when drilling hardboard. Drilling should be done from the smooth side, not the rough or screened side, to make a clean hole.

Hardboard panels can be bent to simple, one-directional curves if the radius is not too small. To make a bend, first fasten one side, then bend the board and fasten the other side.

For sharper bends, the hardboard panels should be soaked in cold water for a minimum of 40 minutes, or scrubbed with water on the screened side and stacked for a day or more to permit the moisture to be absorbed. If you plan to bend only one panel, lay wet rags or newspapers on the screened side for the same period.

Almost any type of nail, wood screw, bolt, staple or rivet can be used to fasten hardboard. Always nail at right angles to the panel. Don't try to toenail hardboard and don't drive nails too close to the edge of the panel. Allow a minimum of ⅜ in. from the edge. When attaching large panels, always nail in the center first, and work your way toward the edges.

Every hardboard joint must have solid support behind it. Don't use the hardboard itself as a nailing base. Nails won't hold satisfactorily in it. When fastening hardboard with screws, predrill the screwholes, using a bit which drills a countersink for the screwhead.

Most hardboard paneling today is installed with a vinyl adhesive rather than nails. Normally, a ¼ in. bead of the adhesive is applied to framing members or furring strips. The adhesive comes in tubes which fit the standard caulking gun, and one tube is sufficient to mount three 4 x 8-ft. panels. Follow the directions on the tube for drying time. The adhesive is also used to put up the furring strips on cement or masonry walls.

One-eighth-inch hardboard is often used to provide a new surface for cracked plaster walls. The hardboard can be nailed through the old plaster to the studs. Adhesive can be used to mount the hardboard if the plaster is sound enough to hold it. For a completely smooth final wall, make sure the hardboard panels butt over wall studs, and nail the edges of the board to the studs with finishing nails driven flush.

The ⅛-in. hardboard is too thin to use unsupported and should always be attached to a solid surface. Other thicknesses may be fastened to furring strips, joists, studs or other framing members not more than 16 in. on centers.

When paneling large areas, scrub the screened side of the panels with water and stack them for a few days. This causes a slight swelling in the hardboard and prevents trouble at the seams later. Never butt two panels of hardboard tightly against each other. If the panels absorb moisture and swell, they may buckle at the joint. Allow a slight space at the joint to avoid this problem.

When painting or enameling hardboard, use a 3-coat application. Begin with a primer, follow this with an undercoat, and then the final coat. If you are finishing a hardboard siding, read the directions supplied with the material. Some sidings are too smooth and hard to provide a tooth for certain alkyd exterior paints.

How a heat pump works

By ALAN R. TRELLIS

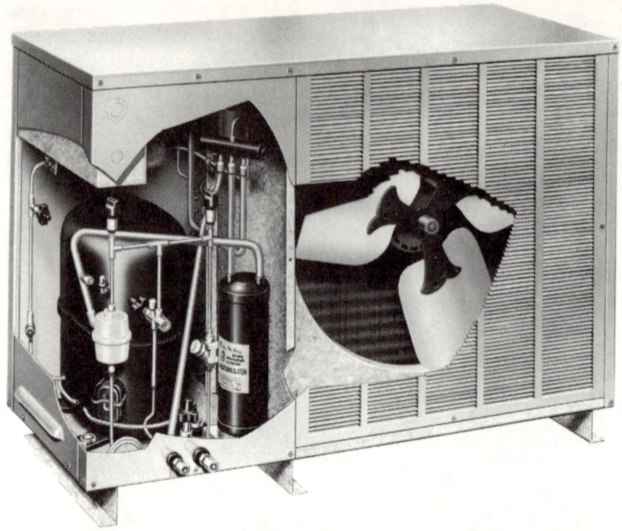

OUTDOOR SECTION of typical split-system heat pump contains compressor, coil, reversing valve and controls.

IT LOOKS LIKE a something-for-nothing appliance. In a way, it's a solar device. It's an airconditioner that works backward and forward. It's a heat pump—the old idea for home heating and cooling that's been getting lots of new attention.

It doesn't really give you something for nothing, but it does operate at more than 100-percent efficiency. It does use solar energy, although indirectly.

The heat pump is a refrigeration machine, like an airconditioner, refrigerator or freezer. It absorbs heat from one environment and transfers it to another. When this process is used to take heat from within a building and put it outdoors, we call it airconditioning. To supply heat *to* a building, the heat pump reverses the flow, absorbs heat from outdoors and feeds it to the building interior.

At the most basic level, a heat pump is a solar device, because the environmental heat it picks up outdoors is the result of solar radiation. That's where the efficiency of more than 100 percent comes from—the energy absorbed and moved is greater than the energy the unit requires to operate.

Virtually all residential heat pumps sold today are the air-to-air type. That is, they remove heat from air and transfer it to air. The drawing on page 1405 shows typical operating cycles of such a unit in both heating and cooling modes.

Although outdoor temperatures of 20° F. or 30° F. are quite cold compared to our body temperatures, they are warm compared to the extremely cold refrigerant used in the heat pump. Since heat will always flow from warm surfaces or objects to colder ones, the cold refrigerant moving through the outdoor coil absorbs heat from the outdoor air. This temperature difference between air and refrigerant is a key factor in heat-pump performance. The amount of heat the equipment can remove from outdoor air is roughly proportional to this difference and thus to outdoor temperature—the warmer the air, the more heat is available.

Unfortunately, this situation is contrary to the demands placed on the heating equipment. As outdoor temperatures drop, the need for heat inside the building increases while the heat available from the outdoor air decreases. The point at which the heating capacity of the heat pump just equals the heat requirement of the building is known as the balance point. Below this point, usually around 35° F., the heat-pump output must be supplemented with heat from another source. This extra heat is most often provided by electric resistance elements—but may be from a gas or oil furnace.

Heat pumps give maximum performance in areas with mild climates. In regions where temperatures are below the balance point a lot of the time, heat-pump efficiency is reduced and supplemental heat is needed more often. The map on page 1406 is based on recorded weather data and shows heat-pump seasonal performance factors (SPFs) throughout the 48 contiguous states. An SPF of 1 is equal to a seasonal efficiency of 100 percent; 1.5 means 150 percent, and so forth.

In colder climates, during cold, humid weather, frost can form on a heat pump's outdoor

SEE ALSO
**Boilers . . . Energy, saving . . . Furnaces . . .
Heaters, solar . . . Heating systems, home . . .
Heating systems, solar . . . Humidifiers . . .
Solar energy . . . Stoves, wood-burning . . .
Winterizing, homes**

coil just as it forms in your refrigerator. So the heat pump periodically defrosts itself by temporarily operating on the cooling cycle, forcing hot refrigerant through the outdoor coil. During the defrost cycle, the supplemental heat source is used to maintain the indoor temperature.

pros and cons

Behind all the ballyhoo, several strong advantages of heat pumps can be seen:

■ *Heat pumps save energy and money.* Their over-100-percent efficiency translates into substantial dollar savings when compared to electric resistance forced-air heating. Energy savings of 25 to 50 percent can easily mean hundreds of dollars per year.

■ *Heat pumps are electric systems.* With restrictions on new natural-gas connections in many parts of the country, more and more totally electric homes are being built. Heat pumps offer a useful alternative to oil heat for those who cannot obtain natural gas. Additionally, in the long run, heat pumps can help improve the mix of our natural energy consumption. A heat pump, unlike a gas or oil furnace, can operate on electric energy created from coal or nuclear fission.

■ *Heat pumps are central forced-air systems.* As such, they're compatible with humidifiers and electronic air purifiers. Heating systems without ducts require separate installation of ductwork for those functions, or for central airconditioning.

Critics of heat pumps have also been vocal, most often raising the following objections:

■ *Heat pumps are inefficient as airconditioners.* To provide reliable, low-cost heat pumps, some manufacturers have sold products whose efficiency in the cooling mode is lower than that of other central airconditioning equipment. Many heat pumps, however, have excellent energy efficiency ratios (EERs). The potential buyer should carefully evaluate EERs, for both heating and cooling. (EER ratings are certified by the Air-conditioning and Refrigeration Institute and are published in product literature or are available on request from the manufacturer.)

■ *Heat pumps cost more than other systems.* The initial cost of a heat pump in a new home will normally be \$300 to \$600 more than the cost of an electric-resistance, gas or oil forced-air system plus central airconditioning. A comparison of total cost for the life of the equipment is virtually impossible to calculate, however, because of uncertain fuel prices. In my opinion, though, electricity should prove to be one of the more price-stable energy sources, and the economic advantages of heat pumps should be excellent in the years ahead.

■ *Heat pumps force the purchase of central airconditioning.* Since heat pumps operate as both heating and airconditioning systems, their total energy consumption on an annual basis may be greater than that of a less efficient heating system without airconditioning. But, in general, the cost of a heat pump compared to the cost of other heating without central airconditioning will be sufficiently high to dissuade those who had not

IN WINTER OPERATION, cold liquid refrigerant is pumped to the outdoor coil where it evaporates, absorbing heat. This heat is then given up at the house by the refrigerant at the indoor coil.

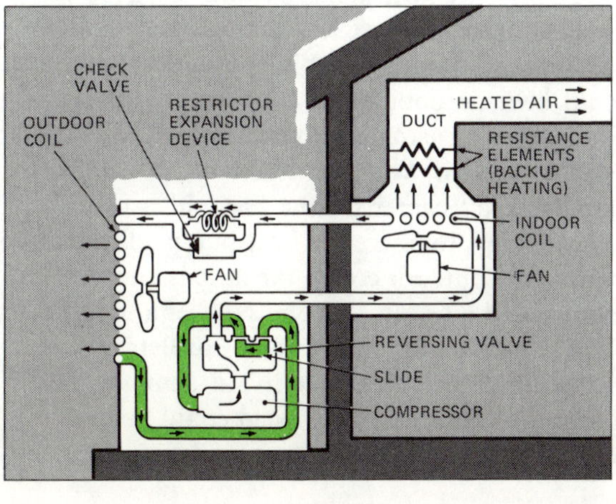

IN SUMMER, the direction of heat movement is reversed. Cold refrigerant absorbs heat from the house interior, then gives it up to outdoor air at the outdoor coil—just as in an airconditioner.

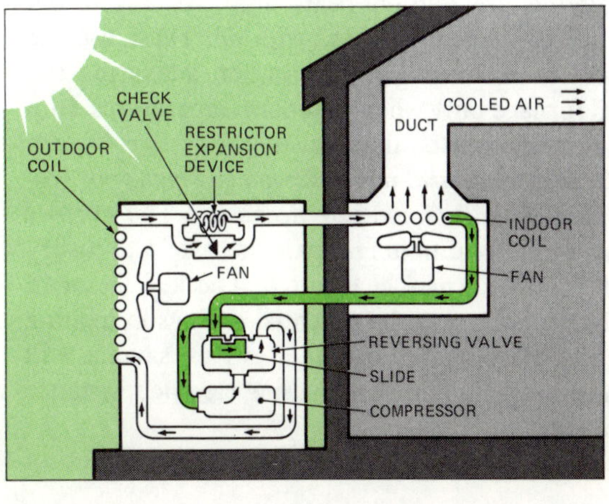

SEASONAL PERFORMANCE FACTORS

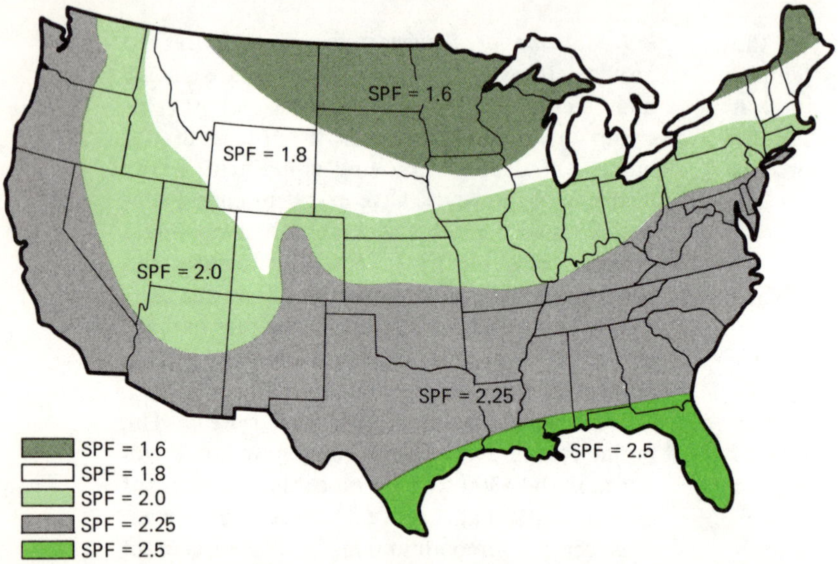

THE SEASONAL performance factor (SPF), which takes climate into account, is the realistic measure of heat-pump efficiency. The number is the ratio of energy put out by the system (as heat) to energy put in, over the course of heating season.

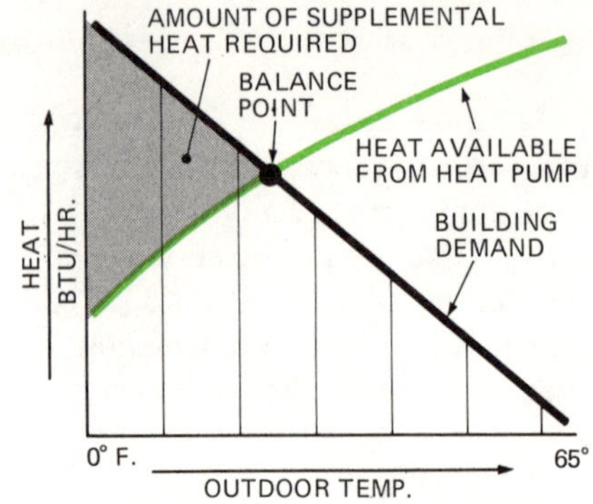

AS OUTDOOR temperature rises, heat-pump output (colored line) increases, while building's heat requirement (black line) decreases. Below the balance-point temperature, the heat-pump cannot meet the building's heat demand, and a source of supplemental heat must be turned on in the building.

planned on central airconditioning from buying a heat pump. For those who do buy heat pumps for their heating efficiency, self-control is the only way to minimize airconditioning use.

existing houses

Startling utility bills have made many homeowners consider installing heat pumps in their present homes. While each case must be considered individually, the cases below are those in which conversion to heat pumps is most likely to be cost-effective:

■ *Adding central airconditioning to previously unairconditioned homes.* Heat pumps are particularly attractive for houses currently using forced-air, electric-resistance heating. Also worth considering are add-on heat-pump systems if the house is currently heated with oil. These use the heat pump during mild weather, activating the oil furnace only when outdoor temperatures drop below a predetermined level.

■ *Major central-airconditioning repairs or replacement of compressor necessary.* The cost of major airconditioning repairs may help to justify the cost of a new heat pump. The key factor in the decision must be potential savings in heating costs. Here again, at today's prices, savings will be greatest in homes now using electric resistance heating.

Heat pumps are relatively costly pieces of equipment which offer substantial operating efficiencies. Unfortunately, they use electricity, which *in many areas* is much more expensive than other forms of energy such as natural gas.

on the horizon

Heat pumps have come a long way, but the potential for still better efficiency and performance is staggering. Research now underway could radically change the entire heating and cooling picture. Noteworthy projects include:

Variable-capacity heat pump: With a compressor that can change its effective size, a unit sized correctly for cooling could grow to supply heat in winter with little or no supplementary heat. The increase in SPF would be large.

Heating-only heat pump: A unit designed just for heating could cost less than current models with airconditioning capability. Such heat pumps could become popular in areas where airconditioning is not customarily needed.

Solar-assisted heat pump: Many possibilities exist here; all center on the basic idea of using solar energy to increase heat-pump efficiency. Putting the outdoor coil in the attic is one way to do this, and a test in Lincoln, NB , of a modified Carrier heat pump has yielded excellent results.

Hot water with heat pumps: In summer, heat that would otherwise be wasted could be used to produce domestic hot water.

How to repair portable room heaters

By MORT SCHULTZ

■ ON FROSTY MORNINGS or whenever you want some quick heat in a small area, a portable room heater can provide it. And, happily, the units are simple mechanisms that you can fix yourself.

There are basically three types of portable heaters: *bowl-type heater,* in which the heating element is composed of nichrome wire coiled around a ceramic core; *rod-type heater,* with one or more heating elements consisting of nichrome wire wrapped around a porcelain insulator in rod-fashion; and the *ribbon-type heater,* in which the heating element is a ribbon of nichrome wire that is strung between insulators on each side of the reflector pan. Once you've determined what ails your heater (the troubleshooting chart will guide you), strip it down for repair work as outlined.

Before proceeding to repair your heater, there are several variations in heaters that you should know:

TROUBLESHOOTING GUIDE

No heat

1. Tighten loose connections or replace broken wire.
2. Replace defective power cord.
3. Replace defective temperature control, tip-over switch assembly.
4. Replace open heating element.

Heater heats, but there's no fan action

1. Replace broken wire.
2. Replace wave washer if motor works, but blade doesn't turn.
3. Replace blade if hub is worn.
4. Service or replace defective motor.

Temperature control out of calibration (Too much or not enough heat for setting)

1. Replace the temperature control and tip-over switch assembly.

Heater is noisy when operating

1. Foreign object is hitting fan.
2. Fan binds or sticks against case.

Intermittent operation

1. Tighten loose connections.
2. Replace faulty temperature control.

Unit won't shut off if tipped over

1. Replace faulty temperature control and tip-over switch assembly.

■ Most heaters possess a reflecting panel and motor-fan assembly which produce both radiant and forced air heating. However, some heaters have no motor-fan assembly and provide only radiant heat.

■ Some heaters have a cooling feature. When set for cooling, the fan alone operates. The heating element is shut off.

■ Most heaters have an adjustable thermostat or temperature control. You can set the temperature control knob at one of a variety of settings to provide more or less heat.

When you turn the heater on, contact points close, energizing the unit. The heater provides heat until the temperature increases sufficiently to cause the bimetal thermostat contact points to bend apart. When contacts break, electricity ceases to flow.

Manipulation of the temperature control knob allows greater or lesser tension on contacts. Thus, it takes more or less heat to cause contact points to break.

The terms "thermostat" and "temperature control" are interchangeable.

■ Practically all room heaters manufactured in recent years are equipped with a safety tip-over switch, normally combined with the thermostat in a single assembly. This switch takes the form of a weighted arm that swings on a pivot. When the heater tips over, the weighted arm swings and causes contacts to break, shutting off the heater.

■ Most room heaters operate on 110-volt 50-cycle a.c. or 120-volt 60-cycle a.c. Some possess one heating element that is usually rated at 1000, 1320 or 1620 watts. You select the desired heat range by setting a low-high heat switch.

Important: Never try to repair breaks in heating wire by twisting ends together. Replace the element. Replacement parts are available from dealers or the manufacturer.

SEE ALSO

Energy, saving . . . Heaters, solar . . . Heaters, space . . . Solar energy . . . Stoves, wood-burning

bowl-type heater disassembly

Caution: disconnect heater during the entire operation.

In bowl-type heaters, where the heating element is nichrome wire coiled around a ceramic core, the bowl acts as a reflector. A line cord attaches to the core and when plugged into an electric outlet, allows the coil to glow. Heat is radiated from the polished bowl.

This is the simplest room heater. Failure occurs if the line cord or heating coil malfunctions. To make repairs, remove the screw holding the line cord and heating element housing to the back of the bowl. Disconnect the line cord from the screw terminals in the base of the heating element. Replacement heating elements are available.

rod-type heater

Caution: This heater must be disconnected during the operation.

1. Remove screws **(1)** holding the guard; also clamps if your heater has them. Take off the guard **(2)**.

2. Remove the power-cord strain relief **(3)** which is around the power cord where it enters the unit. A special tool called Heyco pliers permits you to remove this part without breaking it. Ask an appliance or hardware dealer to order one for you. If you break the strain relief, get a replacement or wrap the power cord heavily with electrician's tape.

3. Remove fasteners, if any, and carefully slide the complete heating element and reflecting assembly **(4)** from the case **(5)** so you can reach leads to disconnect them.

4. Disconnect the power cord **(6)** by detaching it from the thermostat and tip-over switch assembly **(11)** and the motor lead connector **(8)**. Consult the wiring diagram.

5. Disconnect the heating element lead **(9)** that goes from the heating element lead assembly terminal **(7)** to the thermostat and tip-over switch assembly **(11)**.

6. The thermostat and tip-over switch assembly can now be removed by pulling off the control knob **(12)** and removing the thermostat hex retaining nut **(13)**.

7. The heating element **(10)** can be removed by pulling off the heating element cap **(14)** and detaching the motor-to-heating element lead **(15)** at the element.

8. Two screw assemblies normally hold the motor **(16)** in place. Unscrew them to remove the motor.

9. The fan assembly is positioned on the rotor shaft of the motor. Disassemble it by removing the snap ring in groove at the tip of the rotor shaft. Working toward the motor, remove the washer, blade **(17)**, wave washer, washer and clip, which is flush with the motor.

10. Reassembling this heater is done in reverse of disassembly. Before putting things back together again, spread a light coat of SAE 30 motor oil on the motor's rotor shaft. This reduces wear on the fan and motor assembly. Make sure all terminal connections are re-engaged tightly.

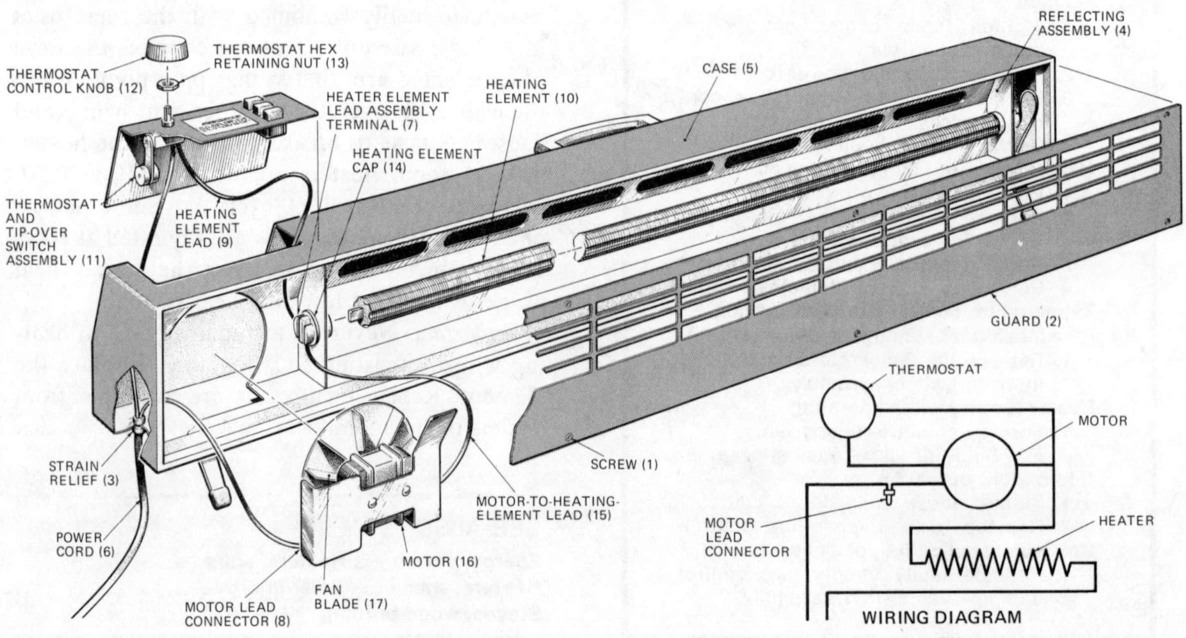

RIBBON-TYPE HEATER

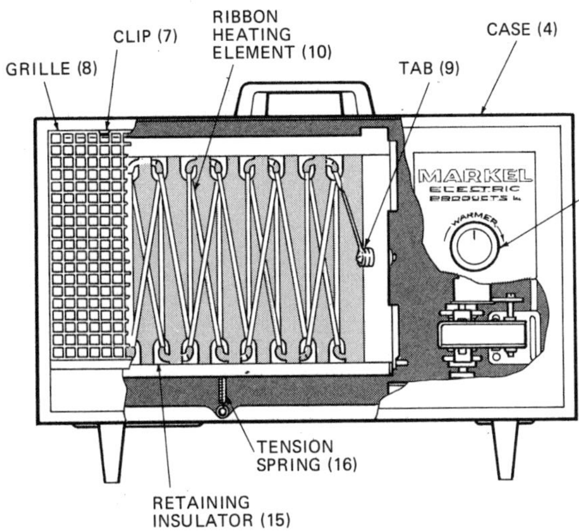

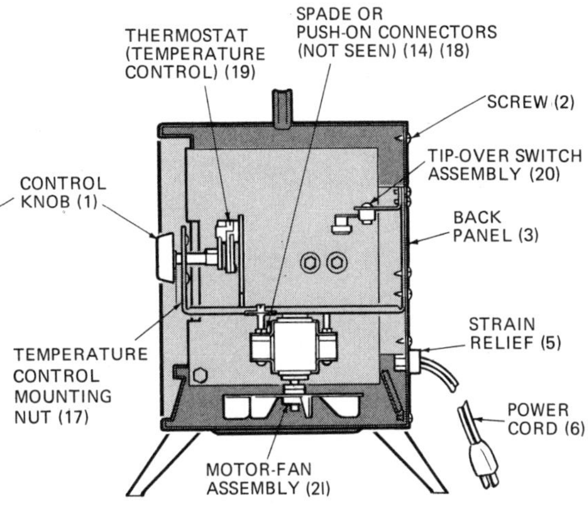

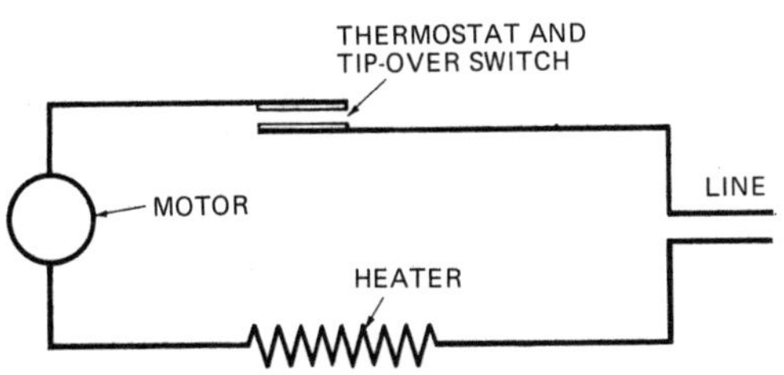

WIRING DIAGRAM

RIBBON-WIRE ELEMENT

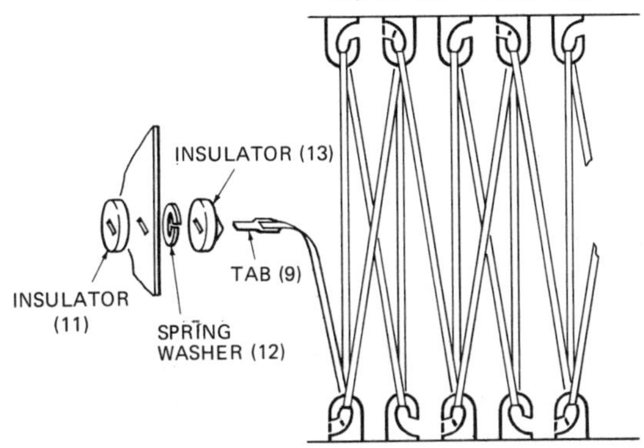

ribbon-wire type heater

Caution: This heater must be disconnected during this entire procedure.

1. Remove the control knob **(1)**. The knob may be held by a setscrew, so look for one, or it may be pressed on. Knobs are often glued on the temperature control shaft. Heavy pressure may be needed to get one off.

2. Withdraw the screws **(2)** in the back panel **(3)**. The heating unit and back panel can now be removed from the case **(4)** as a unit.

3. Remove the power cord strain relief **(5)** and power cord **(6)** as described for rod-type heaters.

4. Pull the push-type clips **(7)** off the tip end of the grill **(8)** and remove the grill.

5. With pliers, twist the tabs **(9)** on the ends of the ribbon heating element **(10)** to a straight flat position. Remove the end insulator assemblies. These normally consist of an insulator **(11)**, spring washer **(12)** and another insulator **(13)**.

6. Unhook the spade connector **(14)** coming from the motor and remove the ribbon-wire heating element. **(10)**.

Note: Consult the wiring diagram.

7. You can now remove any retaining insulator **(15)** that is cracked or broken and has to be replaced. Insulators are generally held by tension springs **(16)**.

8. Remove the temperature control mounting not **(17)**. Pull the other spade connector coming from the motor **(18)**. Disconnect the temperature control thermostat **(19)** and tip-over switch assembly **(20)**.

Note: Check the wiring diagram.

9. Withdraw the fastener assembly holding the motor and fan assembly **(21)** and remove the motor-fan assembly.

10. *Reassembly.* The following procedure will help you replace the ribbon-wire heating element:

A. Wear rubber gloves to keep moisture on your hands from getting on the element.

B. Insert one tab of the ribbon-wire element through one end insulator. Twist the tab so the element is held in place at this end.

C. String the ribbon-wire element over the retaining insulators and insert the second tab through the other end insulator assembly. Twist the tab to lock element in place.

Caution: After assembly, no part of the ribbon-wire element should sag. If the element touches the case it presents a shock hazard.

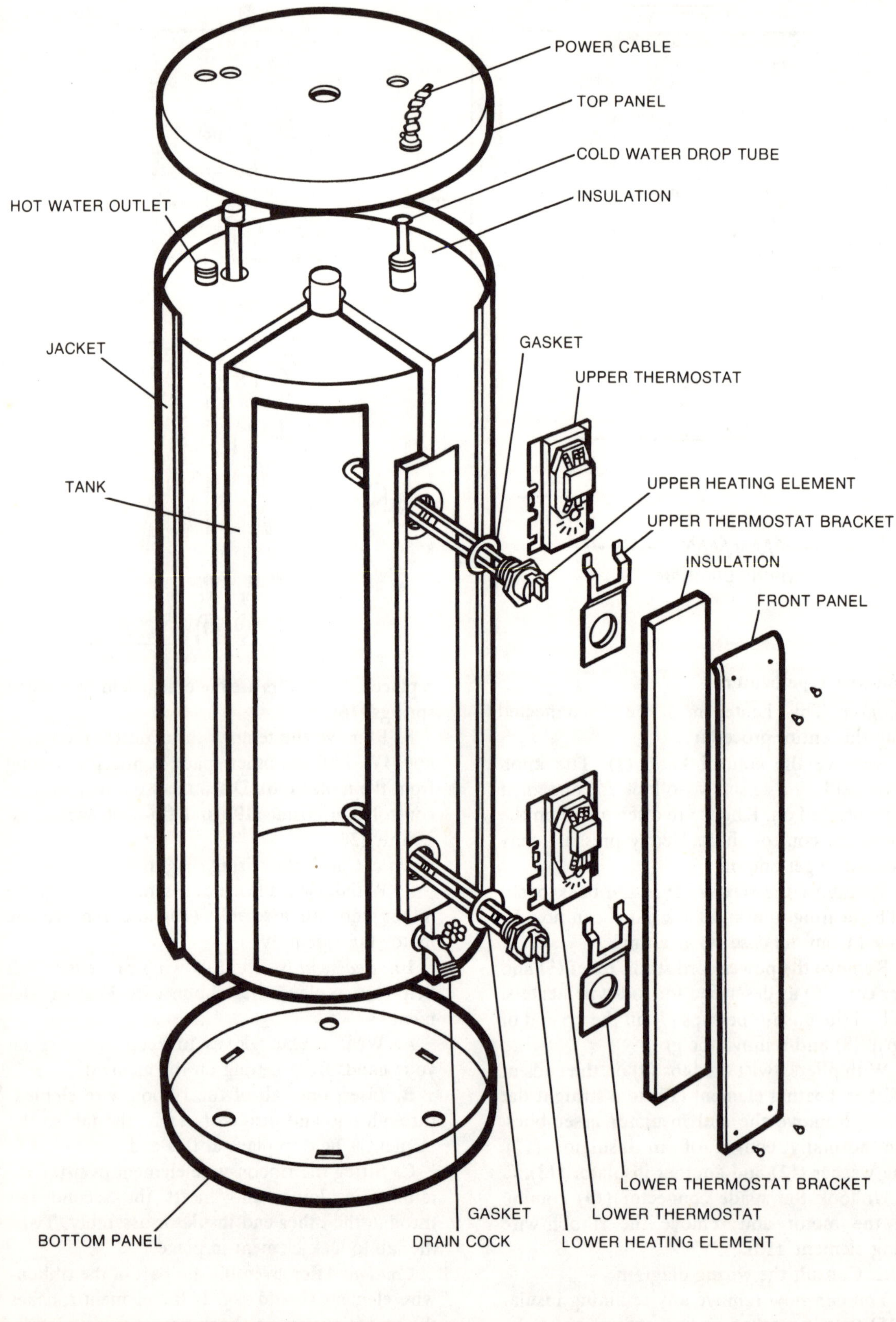
POWER CABLE
TOP PANEL
COLD WATER DROP TUBE
INSULATION
HOT WATER OUTLET
JACKET
GASKET
UPPER THERMOSTAT
TANK
UPPER HEATING ELEMENT
UPPER THERMOSTAT BRACKET
INSULATION
FRONT PANEL
LOWER THERMOSTAT BRACKET
GASKET
LOWER THERMOSTAT
BOTTOM PANEL
DRAIN COCK
LOWER HEATING ELEMENT

How to troubleshoot a water heater

■ IF YOUR WATER HEATER fails to perform satisfactorily, the fault may not lie within the heater at all. Leaking faucets or hot-water demands in excess of heater capacity may be the problem, or impure water may have damaged the heater and thus caused the trouble. The charts on the following pages will help you pinpoint and correct most common hot-water problems. The illustration at the left shows the major parts of a typical electric water heater and their locations. Other illustrations show components made by different manufacturers, and gas-heater details.

Average monthly hot water requirements

FAMILY SIZE	CONSUMES PER MONTH
2	700 gallons
3	950 gallons
4	1200 gallons
5	1450 gallons
6	1700 gallons
7	1950 gallons

A water heater is basically a storage tank. Cold water enters through the top and goes to the bottom through a pipe called a drop or dip tube. The water is heated by either electric elements or a gas (or oil-fired) burner rises to the top of the tank, and is discharged through the outlet pipe there. Thermostats are used to regulate the heat source in order to maintain a constant water temperature within the tank.

Hot-water requirements vary with different family sizes, locations, washing methods and number of water-using appliances in the home. A tub bath generally requires 7 or 8 gal. of hot water, a quick shower 2 to 3 gal. A dishwasher will use 9 gal. for each load; washing dishes by hand will use from 2 to 7 gals. Figures in the chart are average. When replacing a faulty heater, estimate the tank size you need by dividing the number of gallons shown for the number of

SEE ALSO
Dishwashers . . . Plumbing . . . Washing machines

Methods of heating water electrically

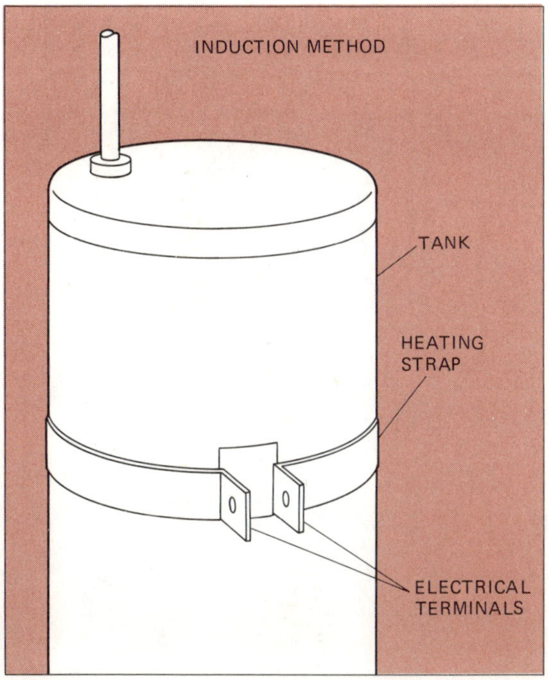

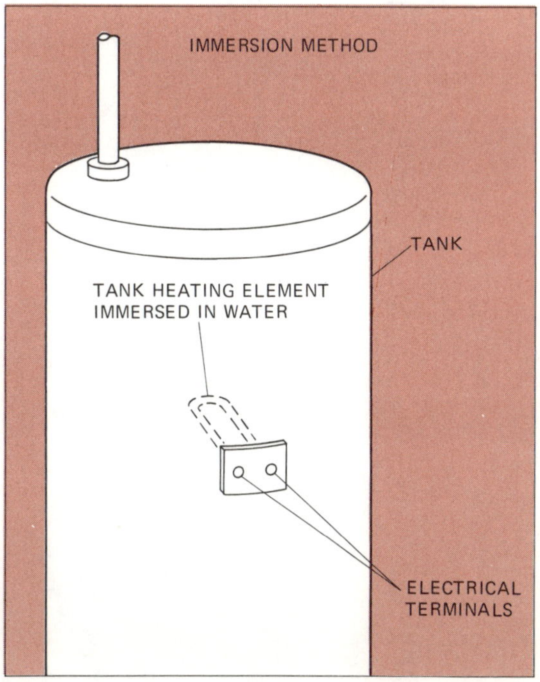

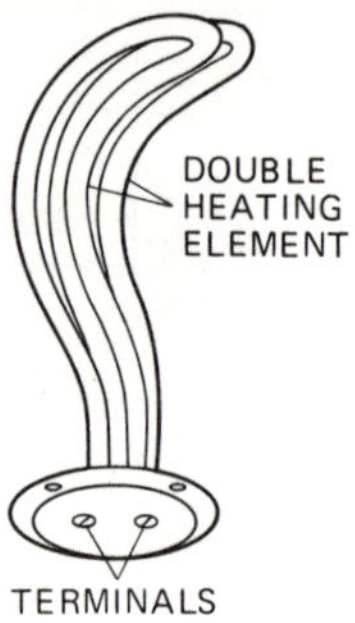

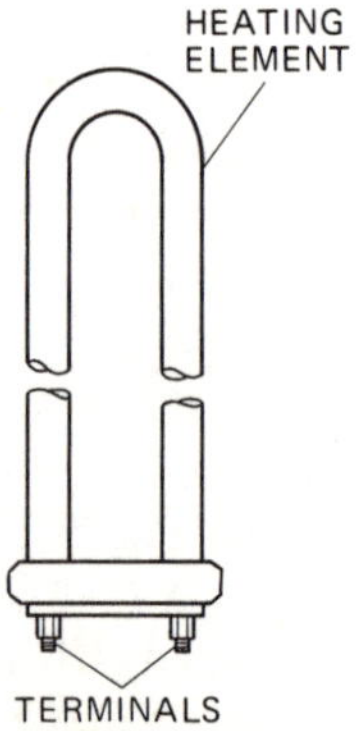

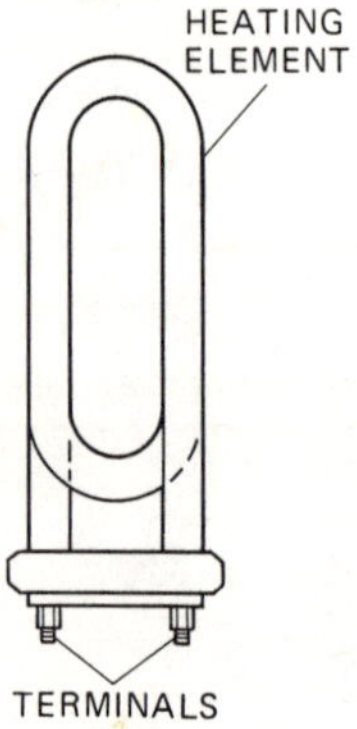

No hot water

POSSIBLE CAUSES	WHAT TO TRY
1. Blown fuse.	Replace fuse. If new fuse blows, a short circuit exists in water heater. Disconnect power. Remove panel and make visual inspection of wiring. If wiring is good, call serviceman.
2. Heating element burned out.	Disconnect power. Place continuity tester across heating-element terminals. No reading indicates an open coil in element. Before replacing immersion-type element, close cold-water inlet valve and drain tank past element. Install new element. Refill tank, check for leaks and turn on power. On band heaters, loosen snap or bolt, slip band off tank and replace with new one. Retighten fasteners, replace insulation, turn on power.
3. Calcium buildup on heating element (immersion type).	Remove element. Use a vinegar-and-water solution to clean off all calcium deposits; then reinstall element.
4. Thermocouple defective (gas).	Clean pilot orifice. Turn thermostat valve to Pilot. Depress pilot button and light pilot. Hold button in for 30 to 40 seconds. If pilot fails to stay lit, replace thermocouple.
5. Thermostat defective (gas).	Turn thermostat valve to On position and temperature control to Hot position. Run hot water. If burner fails to light after two or three minutes, replace thermostat.

Typical gas water-heater controls

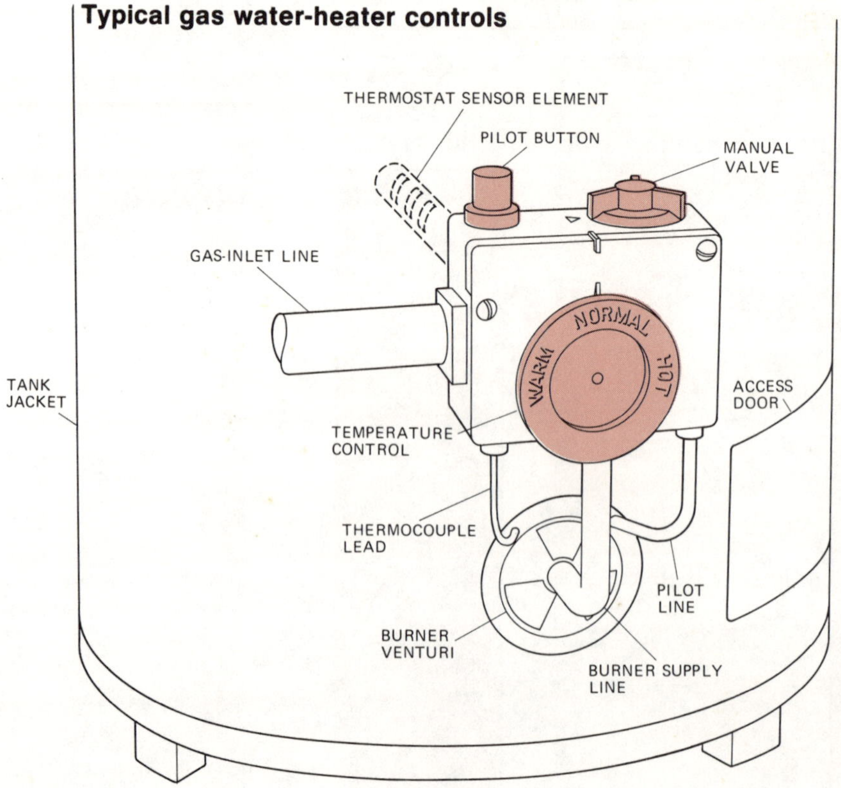

Not enough hot water

POSSIBLE CAUSES	WHAT TO TRY
1. Thermostat setting too low.	Turn setting to Normal (140°-150° F.)
2. Lower heating element burned out (immersion type).	Turn off power. Check element with continuity tester. No reading indicates an open coil. Replace.
3. Undersized tank.	Check quantity of water used by family and appliances. See hot water requirements chart.

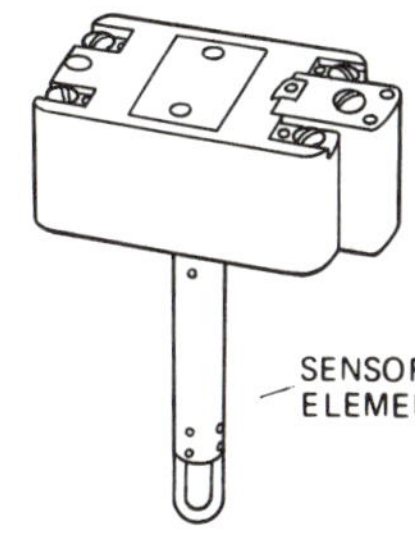

Slow recovery between demands

POSSIBLE CAUSE	WHAT TO TRY
1. Top heating element burned out.	Turn off power. Check top heating element for continuity across terminals. If there is no reading, replace element.

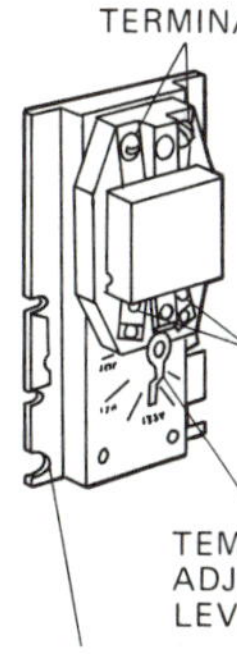

Steam in hot water

POSSIBLE CAUSES	WHAT TO TRY
1. Thermostat contacts burned (electric).	Look for shorted or burned terminals. Replace thermostat.
2. Thermostat set too high.	Lower setting to Normal (140°-150° F.).
3. Thermostat runaway (gas).	Check whether thermostat is cutting off main burner. If burner fails to go out when temperature control is turned to Low, replace thermostat.

people in your family by 30. This gives your average daily hot-water requirement, which is also the tank size needed. To be on the safe side, allow a little extra capacity. For example, a family of five consumes 1450 gal. of hot water per month; 1450 divided by 30 is about 48 gal. A 50-gal. heater is indicated.

Recovery time is the time a water heater takes to replace hot water. A minimum recovery rate would be eight hours to heat a tankful of 50° F. water to 150° F. This would allow the heater to recover overnight, so a family could start the day with a new tankful of hot water. For practical reasons, most water heaters sold today have a much quicker recovery rate than eight hours.

Any hot water that goes to waste will, of course, leave less hot water available to use. A leaking faucet is one of the most common forms of water waste. A slow drip—about one drop per second—wastes about 200 gal. of water a month, 5 tankfuls in the case of a 40-gal. heater. A more serious leak, such as a smooth stream that runs about 3 in. before breaking up into droplets, wastes about 1000 gal. a month. Other factors in hot-water waste are the amount of water standing in pipes and the number of running feet of pipe in the system; they should be taken into account when you plan any new water-heater installation.

There are two types of electric water heaters, induction and immersion. An induction heater has a heating element strapped around the outside of the tank and covered with insulation. Heat passes through the wall of the tank to the water. In an immersion heater, the heating elements (usually two) pass through the tank wall directly into the water, with flanges and gaskets to keep the tank watertight where the elements enter. Some common types of immersion elements are shown on page 1412. The wattage rating of the elements and the size of the tank will determine the time required for water to reach the desired temperature (recovery time). A large tank, holding more water than a small one, will also naturally require more electricity to heat a tankful of water.

High water-heating cost

POSSIBLE CAUSES	WHAT TO TRY
1. Leaking hot-water faucets.	Replace washers in all leaking faucets.
2. Thermostat setting too high.	Turn thermostat to Normal setting (140° to 150° F.).
3. Scale deposits appearing on heating elements.	Remove and clean elements. See "Not enough hot water"

Water under heater

POSSIBLE CAUSES	WHAT TO TRY
1. Thermostat leaking.	Check flange and gasket around thermostat. Replace gasket if leaking.
2. Plumbing connections.	Check all sweated (soldered) connections in and around tank. If leaks are found, make any necessary repairs.
3. Condensation.	Check for moisture buildup in insulation if basement is cold or damp. Moisture resulting from condensation will not drip steadily as it would from a leak.
4. Leak (hole) in tank.	Use boil plug for temporary repair if hole is accessible. Replace tank eventually.

Water black or discolored at faucets

POSSIBLE CAUSE	WHAT TO TRY
1. Magnesium in water.	Magnesium rod in tank is probably corroded. Shut off power and water supply. Remove metal band or screws from top panel of water heater. Remove insulation and then remove head of magnesium rod with socket wrench. Replace with a new rod, using sealer or Permatex on threads. Reassemble, turn on water and power. Allow about 24 hours for the lines to clear.

Gas-burner assembly

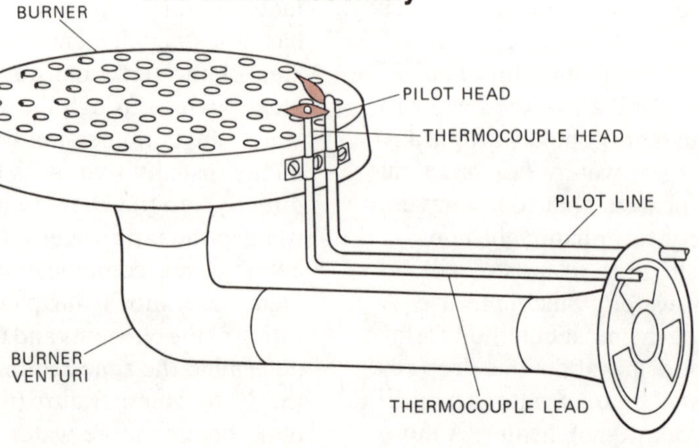

Location of pressure-relief valve

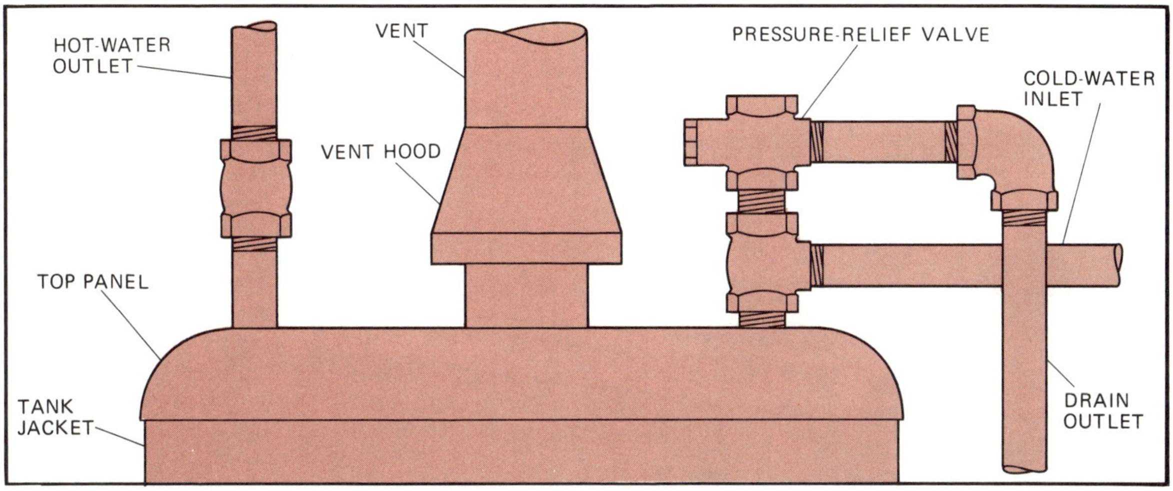

A typical two-element, electric water heater has a "load-limiting" circuit to keep both elements from drawing current at the same time. It operates as follows: With a tankful of cold water, the upper (secondary) heating element is turned on by the upper thermostat. About 25 percent of the total volume of water in the tank is heated by this element. The lower (primary) element is turned on only when the upper thermostat has sensed that the water at the top of the tank has reached the desired temperature and is ready for use. The lower element now heats the remainder of the water in the tank. If some of the hot water is used, cold water entering the tank through the drop tube is heated by the lower element. When all the water in the tank has been heated, the lower element is turned off by its thermostat. In the load-limiting circuit, wiring is usually color-coded with a blue lead to the upper element, a yellow lead to the upper thermostat and then to the upper element's other terminal, a red lead to the upper thermostat and then to the lower element and a black lead to the lower thermostat and then to the lower element's other terminal.

Gas water heaters have a single immersion thermostat, located near the bottom of the heater, a burner and a thermocouple-governed pilot light. Heater controls are a temperature dial, a pilot reset button and a manual valve with OFF, PILOT and ON positions. A thermocouple screwed into the base of the thermostat is attached to the burner and enveloped by the pilot flame. Gas from the main line enters the thermostat at one side.

The gas water heater is lit as follows: The pilot button is depressed, the pilot light is lit with a match or igniter, and the pilot button is held down for 30 to 45 seconds. The pilot flame striking the thermocouple head makes it generate a current that actuates a magnetic valve in the thermostat; this is a safety device that shuts off the supply of gas to the pilot light when it goes out. The pilot button is released and the manual valve is turned to the ON position. The burner is now lit by the pilot light.

If the burner does not light, turn the temperature dial to a higher setting, then return it to NORMAL. The thermostat maintains a constant water temperature by means of a bimetal or bellows regulating the supply of gas to the burner.

With both types of water heater, a pressure-relief valve is installed in the cold-water line just above the tank. This valve gives protection from pressure buildup in case of thermostat failure. Most of these valves are set 25 to 35 pounds per square inch above normal water pressure, to a maximum of 125 p.s.i. Valves may be spring-operated and resettable or replaceable lead plugs that melt at high temperature.

Normal hot-water temperature is 140-150° F. Most water heaters also have temperature settings for WARM, about 120° F., and HOT, about 160° F.

Because water often contains corrosive impurities, water-heater tanks usually are made of copper and are glass lined. In addition, some heaters have a magnesium-rod anode. Corrosive agents will attack the rod instead of the tank, but when the rod has become badly corroded, it will discolor hot water and must be replaced.

COLLECTOR MADE by Solarcell is a nontracking concentrating type that focuses sunlight onto ¾-in. copper tubing that has a heat-absorbing black coating.

MORE COMMON in hot-water systems are flat-plate collectors like these from Sunworks. Installation shows a relatively small collector area is needed for water heating, even in New England.

How to get hot water from the sun

Solar domestic hot-water systems are becoming cost-effective now in most parts of the country. You can retrofit it to your current hot water system and start saving

SEE ALSO
Energy, saving . . . Heat pumps . . . Heaters, water . . . Solar energy . . . Solar water heaters . . . Winterizing, homes

■ WHEN YOU'VE DONE all you can to cut energy use and waste in your home, the only way to trim those bills more is to *add* energy somehow. One way to do that—without spending your life's savings—is to install a solar domestic hot-water system.

Even though sunlight is free, the equipment needed to capture it isn't. Yet you can probably install a system that provides 50 percent of your hot water (60 sq. ft. of collectors, as a rule, for a family of four) for about $1200, or twice that if you opt for professional installation. These prices are far less than the $6000 to $12,000 you'd have to shell out to get solar space heating—which is usually too complicated for do-it-yourself installation, especially in existing homes.

Solar hot water is relatively easy to retrofit. A small collector array can go on the roof, against a wall, or on a separate support frame in the yard—while solar space heating requires a collector area equal to one-third to one-half the floor area to be heated. You need a large, strong, properly angled roof for such an array.

An Energy Research and Development study (done a number of years ago, when fuels were cheaper) has shown that solar water heating, at a total system cost of $20 per square foot of collector, is cost-effective in most parts of the country, beating electric resistance heat-

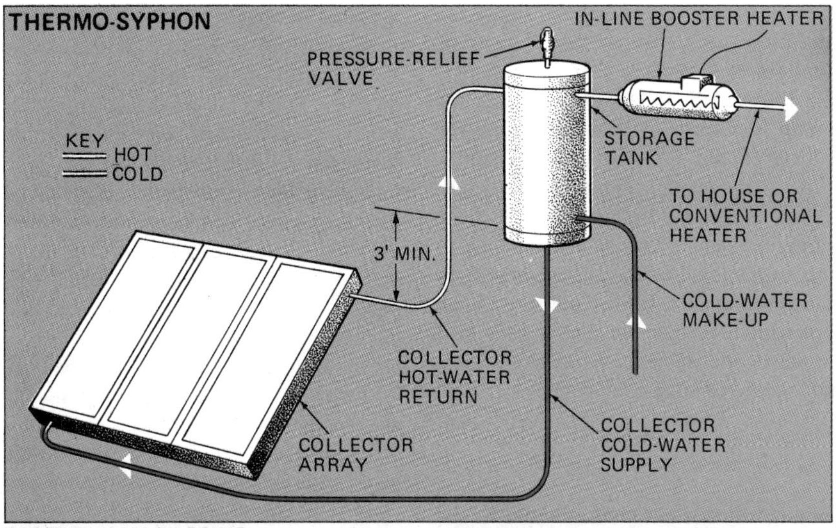

ESSENTIALLY PASSIVE system relies on gravity and convection to circulate water: Cold water flows from bottom of tank to bottom of collector, returns when warmed.

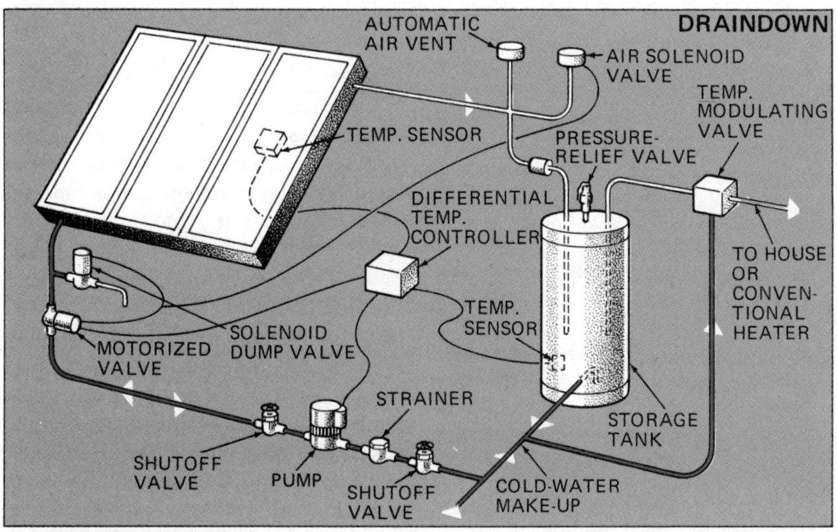

ELABORATE CONTROLS are needed to assure automatic drainage of collectors and pump cutoff when temperature falls to freezing or collectors can't warm water.

SIMPLER SYSTEM loses efficiency because water must be heated to keep it moving through collectors during periods of below-freezing temperatures.

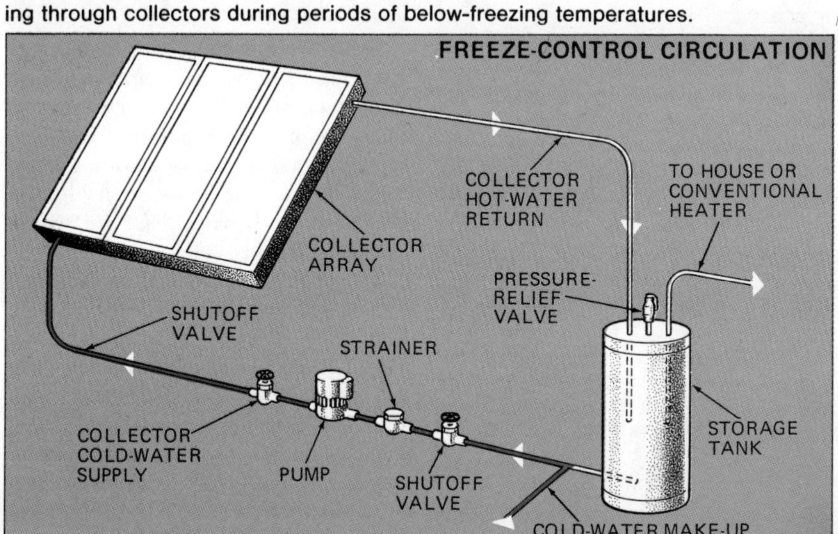

ing in all but one of the 13 cities considered. Payback time (system cost divided by annual savings) ranged from 9 to 13 years in the other 12. The payback period will keep getting shorter as conventional-energy prices go up.

ERDA also notes that if new technology and government incentives combine to reduce system costs, solar hot water and solar space heating will then be competitive with all conventional fuels.

system basics

The collector is the guts of any solar system. As commonly used for solar hot water, it has an absorber plate covered with a special selective surface or painted flat black to collect light and convert it to heat, plus tubing attached to the plate to carry the heat-transfer medium (water, water plus antifreeze, or air) that gathers the absorbed heat and takes it to the point of use. The absorber plate is enclosed in an insulated frame and covered with glass or transparent plastic.

Collectors should be pitched at an angle equal to local latitude, but a variation of 10° either way (to suit a roof's pitch, for example) can be accepted—and in some cases it can pay to tip them forward to pick up sunlight by reflection from a horizontal surface. This can be especially effective in areas of the country that have snow cover for most of the winter. Similarly, collectors are usually oriented to point due south, but variation of up to 20° either way is acceptable and may be necessary to make the installation practical. Other factors that need attention are shading of collectors by trees or parts of the house and snow accumulation on the array.

A solar hot-water system is really a preheater, using conventional heating to give the water a final boost to the desired temperature. It requires much less conventional energy than a normal system. Most solar systems use a separate storage tank that supplies the tank of a conventional heater—which also provides backup for night and for cloudy days.

five systems

With all the many kits and components coming onto the market, there are still just five basic types of solar hot-water systems in common use.

Simplest is the thermo-syphon setup, which depends on gravity and convection to circulate water through its collectors. It requires a water storage tank located near and slightly above the collector array. Such a system is fine where there's plenty of sunshine and the temperature rarely dips to 32° F., but in most parts of the country, water can freeze and wreck the whole works. Frequent manual draining—a nuisance—or a resistance booster heater can prevent freeze-ups, but flow rate and temperatures remain difficult to control in a thermo-syphon system.

The four other systems allow a more remote tank location. In the draindown type, a pump moves water through the collectors only when there's enough sunlight to prevent freezing and to produce useful heat. At other times, the pump is automatically shut off and the collectors are simultaneously drained.

A less common system uses what's called freeze-control circulation from storage. Warm water is kept moving in the collectors when the temperature drops to freezing. It's less efficient than a draindown system because it uses heat to warm the collectors, but it gives the advantage of simpler controls.

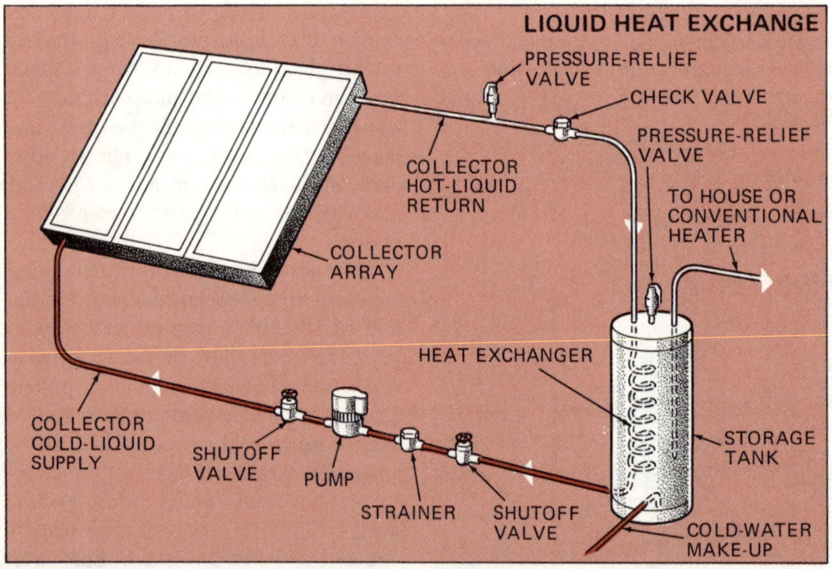

LIQUID MEDIUM in collectors won't freeze since it's an antifreeze solution—but there must be absolutely no mixing of antifreeze with domestic water supply.

USING AIR as a heat-exchange medium eliminates both the hazard of collector freeze-up and the danger of contamination of house water with antifreeze.

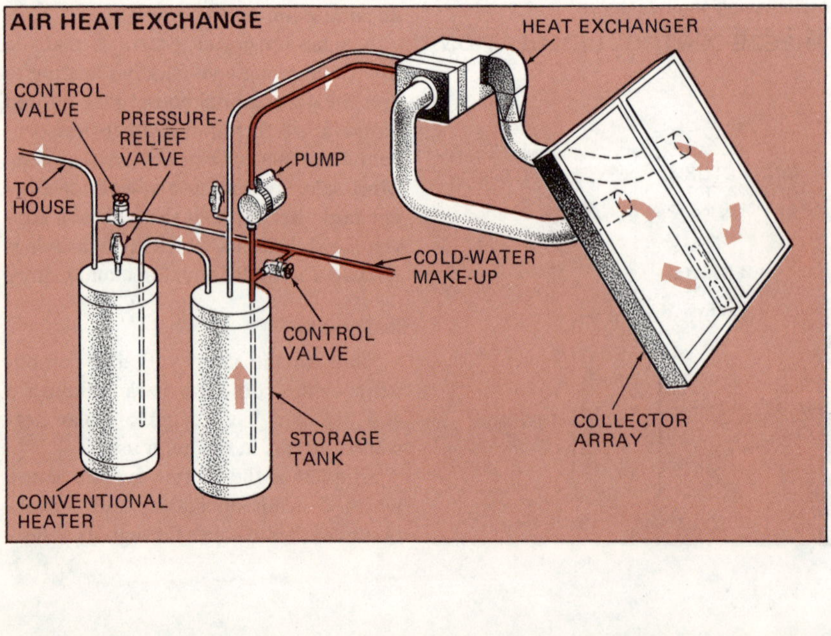

using antifreeze

An obvious way to keep collectors from freezing is not to run plain water through them. You can use an antifreeze solution instead and make this liquid surrender its gathered heat to the water through a heat exchanger, usually a coil of tubing inside or around the outside of the tank. But this requires care. Most antifreezes are poison, and some local codes require a double-wall heat exchanger to keep house water and collector medium separate. The antifreeze solution also must be replaced periodically as it tends to become corrosive.

The heat-exchanger idea can also be used with air as the medium. Water from the tank is pumped out to a motorized heat exchanger, then returns to the tank. Both liquid and air heat-exchange setups are less efficient than heating the water directly, but they do eliminate the freezing problem.

Cautions: Regardless of the system you're considering, be wary when shopping for solar equipment—some manufacturers make impossible claims. A good guide to self-protection is *Buying Solar,* about $1.85 from the Superintendent of Documents, U.S. Government Printing Office, Washington, DC. 20402 (ask for Stock No. 041-018-00120-4). Also ask anyone who wants to sell you solar equipment for names of other customers, and check with them. Get a guarantee, too. Systems can vary greatly in cost, yet work about equally well. How long they'll last is the question that's still hard to answer. Tests being performed now in many areas of the country may soon yield the answer.

manufacturers

Explosive growth of the solar-energy field makes it virtually impossible to keep track of all the firms active in it—there are new ones almost daily. The most comprehensive listing of manufacturers in the solar hot-water field is included in the booklet *Solar Hot Water and Your Home.*

To get this free booklet, as well as a list of solar-equipment distributors in your state, write to the National Solar Heating and Cooling Information Center, Dept. PM, Box 1607, Rockville, MD. 20850. It should be understood that inclusion in either list does not imply endorsement by *PM* or by the government of a company's products or business practices.

FREESTANDING FIREPLACE, though not as efficient as a stove, is cheery and easy to install. This El Fuego unit supplies heated air through vents.

How to choose the right space heater

By JOHN H. INGERSOLL

■ GEORGE WASHINGTON warmed his Virginia home with "zoned heat"—or, more simply, fireplaces. Since then, we've come a long way—at least until recently. Up to 1973, we basked in the luxury of controlled comfort from marvelously efficient, conveniently automatic, relatively economical central heating systems—the product of modern technology.

Then the crunch came.

Today, we're relearning some old truths. The "primitive" heaters of Washington's time no longer seem so crude—in fact, they make a lot of sense. What we're rediscovering now is that zoned heat can save energy and cut fuel bills by reducing the workload on the central system and supplying heat only when and where it is needed most—without costly and unnecessary waste.

What's more, zone heaters—or "space heaters," as they have been more popularly known in the past—make it possible to tailor the heat source to your individual tastes and requirements.

Wood and coal stoves give a cheery warmth and sense of good fellowship that are hard to get

PREFAB FIREPLACES MAKE INSTALLATION EASY

Self-contained prefab fireplaces circulate heated air through double-wall metal enclosure, are more efficient than open masonry type and come as complete, ready-to-install units. Zero-clearance Preway model (photo at right, drawing at lower right) can be built flush into a combustible wall without surrounding masonry. It draws in air for combustion from outside the house and has optional blowers to boost heat circulation. If space doesn't permit mounting in a wall, it can be installed in a corner of a room with simple stud framing around it. Heat-distributing fireplace (left, below) is one of newest types, works like a small warm-air furnace. Blower in plenum above firebox directs heated air to several rooms at once through system of furnace-like ducts. Arrangement shown here is for Octa-Therm fireplace sold by Martin Industries. Like Preway model, it also draws combustion air in from outside the house. This helps to prevent the loss of room heat that would normally be drawn up the chimney flue.

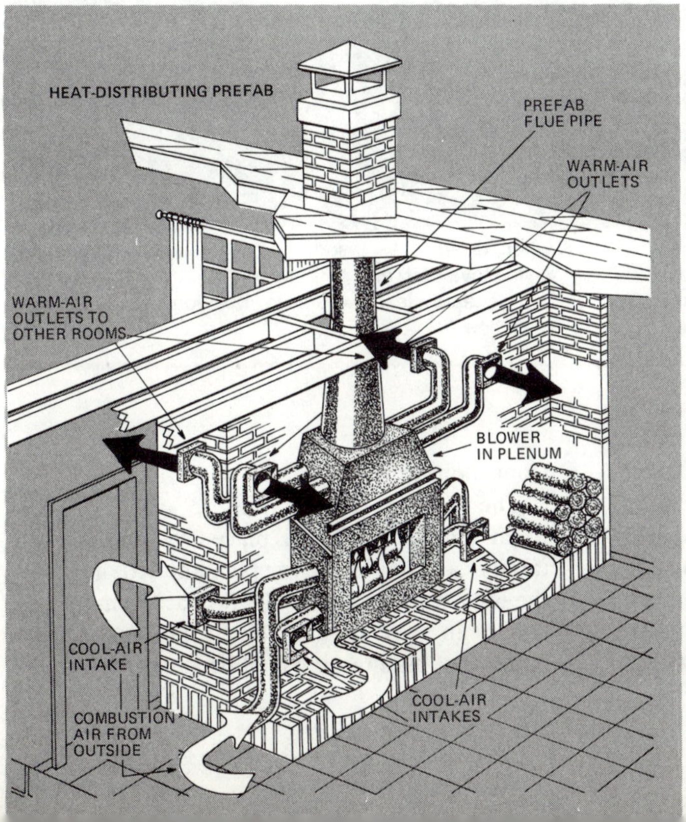

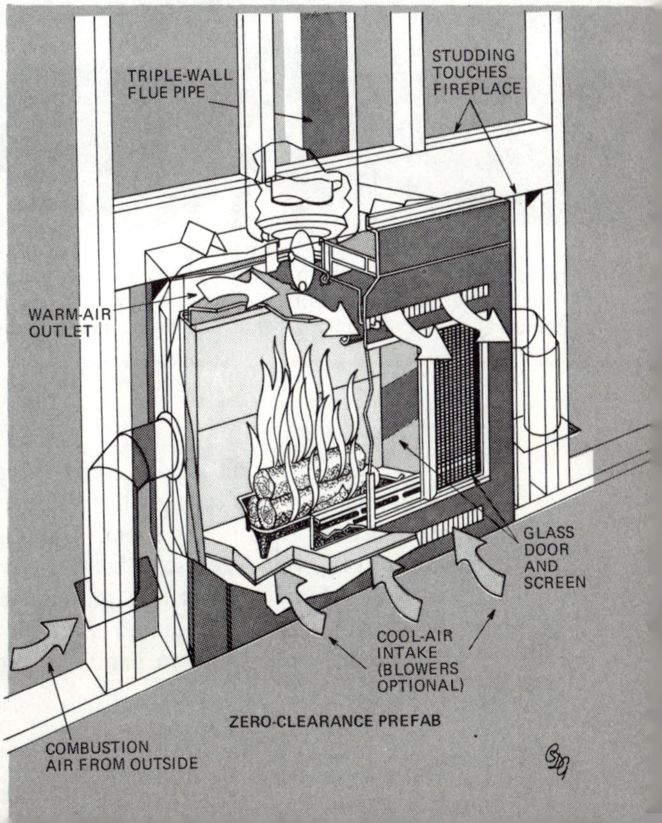

UPDATE A FIREPLACE WITH A SLIP-IN INSERT

Modern fireplace inserts fit into an existing fireplace to reduce waste heat and improve efficiency. Cool room air is drawn in at bottom, heated as it circulates around firebox in a double-wall enclosure, then flows back into room instead of up chimney. Inserts come in two types. Natural-flow heaters, such as this El Fuego model (photo above, drawing center), circulate air by convection. Forced-air heaters, like Bennett-Ireland (drawing, far right), have built-in blowers to aid circulation, are somewhat more expensive.

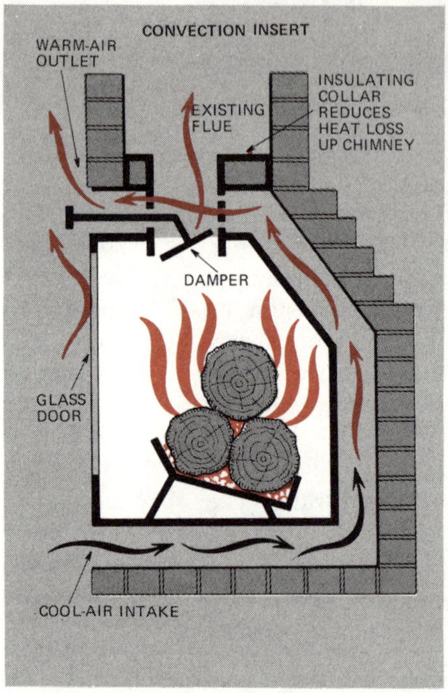

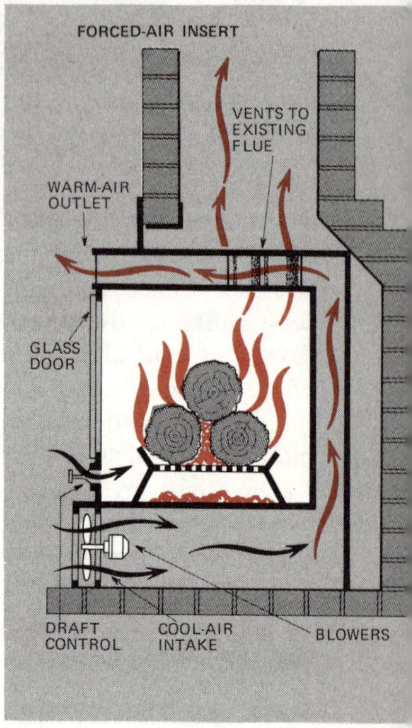

FOUR TYPES OF RADIANT WOOD STOVES

Airtight stoves like Jotul from Kristia Associates (far left) are rated tops in wood-burning efficiency, come in many styles. Crest model (far right), from Washington Stove Works, is a combination fireplace/stove that functions as an airtight when doors are closed. At center are traditional Franklin-style stove (left) and potbelly (right). These have rustic charm, are generally less expensive, but don't feature airtight construction.

from a furnace in the cellar. Prefab fireplaces make it relatively easy to enjoy the pleasures of a roaring fire in virtually any room. Trimly styled electric, gas, oil and kerosene heaters come on quickly and shut down instantly, putting out heat only for as long as it's required. Portable units can be used anywhere and are handy for carrying from room to room.

The concept of creating a special "warm room" in the house—a place where the whole family can congregate for pleasant activities over the long winter months—is fast becoming a new American way of life. The traditional British practice of maintaining cool bedchambers, where

HOW TO HAVE A FURNACE THAT BURNS ANYTHING

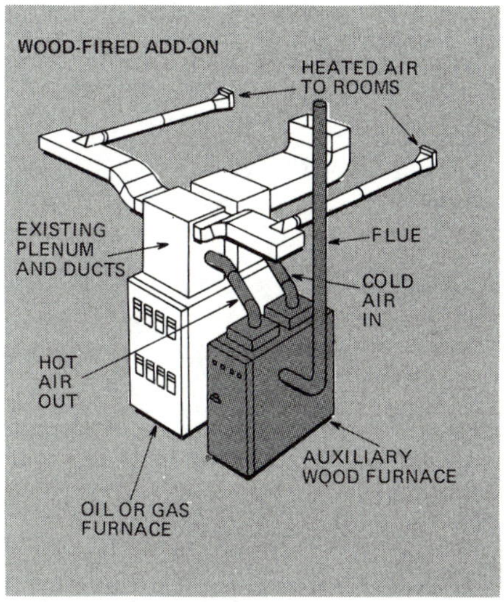

Wood-burning add-on furnace can be hooked into any central hot-air system to supply supplementary heat. Heated air is fed into plenum for distribution through existing ducts. Regular gas or oil burner provides automatic backup, coming on only if needed. This Ashley model can also be installed as central wood furnace by itself.

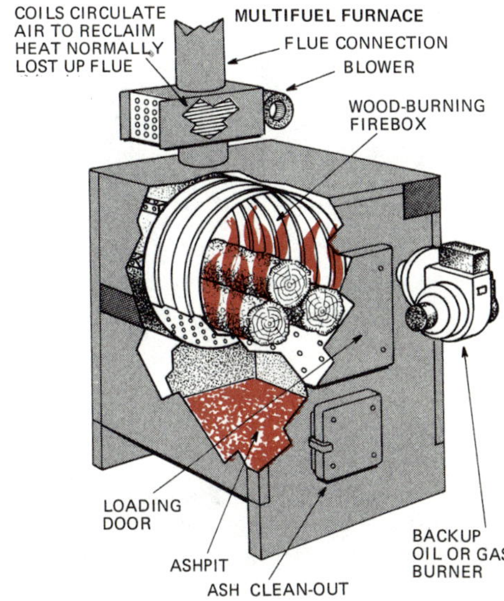

Central wood-burning furnace has backup gas or oil burner that comes on if fire burns low or you're away from home. This Longwood Dualfuel system can be connected to new or existing hot-air ducts. Coils help reclaim heat normally lost up flue.

little heat is needed for comfortable sleeping, is also catching on. Zone heaters lend themselves perfectly to these trends. Moreover, many are "blackout-proof," continuing to pump out welcome warmth even when winter storms down power lines.

Surprisingly, when you add up all the wood, coal, gas, oil, electric and kerosene heaters that exist, and all the varied forms they come in, you'll find at least 31 different kinds to choose from. To help you buy, we have compiled data on these in two charts—one for wood-burning stoves and fireplaces and another for electric, gas, oil and kerosene heaters. You'll also find information on multifuel furnaces and furnace add-ons that can conserve your regular fuel.

Which is best for you? This depends on what you want to use it for, where it will be located, how much heat it must produce, how often and for how long it will be operated, and how much you'll have to pay to fuel it in your area.

how efficiencies compare

While a heater's rated efficiency is important to know, buying on the basis of efficiency alone can be misleading—as we'll see. Also, don't confuse efficiency with output—they aren't the same thing. A high-efficiency heater may actually put out less room heat than one of lower efficiency but greater capacity. You need to consider both figures to shop wisely.

The efficiency ranges listed in the charts represent the percentage of usable heat extracted by a given type of heater from the available heat contained in a given type of fuel.

A pound of dry oak, for example, contains 8600 B.T.U. of *potential* heat. (B.T.U. stands for British Thermal Units, a standard measure of heat.) But when that pound of oak is burned in an open fireplace, at least 90 percent of its energy goes right up the flue. You derive no more than 10 percent—or 860 B.T.U.—in radiant heat. In some cases, you can even wind up with a *minus* percentage. Not possible? Oh, yes. The reason for this is that, under certain conditions, a fireplace can draw more heat *out* of a room than it delivers to it. It is actually *cooling* the room by pulling in cold air from outside the house!

You might be equally amazed to discover that the heating efficiencies for electric heaters all run to a neat 100 percent. How come? The answer here is that electric energy, when converted across a resistance element from watts to B.T.U., loses none of its potential (except for a small amount in visible light, its red glow). Nearly 100 percent is delivered to the room as heat—and there's no flue to let it escape.

PORTABLE HEATERS YOU CAN USE ANYWHERE

Portable electric and kerosene heaters put out 2000 to 17,000 B.T.U./hr., are handy for carrying to any room. Kingston (top) is typical of electric floor models. Kerosene heaters like this Aladdin model (center) come in many styles and sizes. Krups two-way electric (bottom) can mount on wall or floor stand, has timer control.

HOW ZONE HEATERS COMPARE

	Type of Heater	Rated B.T.U./Hr.*	Efficiency	Vented	Blower	Price Range**
Gas	Circulating floor model	15,000 to 70,000 (I)	80%	Yes	Yes	$175-$450
Gas	Gravity/radiant floor model	15,000 to 40,000 (I)	80%	No	No	$90-$200
Gas	Circulating/radiant floor model	35,000 to 70,000 (I)	80%	Yes	Yes	$250-$550
Gas	Circulating built-in wall model	15,000 to 70,000 (I)	80%	Yes	Yes	$250-$425
Gas	Counterflow vertical wall model	17,500 to 48,750 (O)	80%	Yes	Yes	$175-$550
Gas	Gas logs	40,000 to 50,000 (I)	10%	Through existing flue	No	$150-$550
Oil	Circulating floor model	38,000 to 65,000 (O)	70%	Yes	Yes	$195-$525
Oil	Convection floor model	38,000 to 50,000 (O)	70%	Yes	No	$125-$275
Oil	Circulating built-in wall model	60,000 to 70,000 (O)	70%	Yes	Yes	$650-$950
Electric	Baseboard convector	1280 to 8530 (O)	100%	No	No	$8-$16/ft.
Electric	Circulating wall model	2559 to 16,832 (O)	100%	No	Yes	$50-$190
Electric	Circulating ceiling model	4080 to 5120 (O)	100%	No	Yes	$45-$85
Electric	Radiant wall model	2559 to 10,240 (O)	100%	No	No	$30-$100
Electric	Radiant ceiling model	1706 to 3400 (O)	100%	No	No	$35-$75
Electric	Circulating kickspace model	1706 to 6826 (O)	100%	No	Yes	$75-$125
Electric	Electric fireplace	5120 to 10,290 (O)	100%	No	No	$125-$500
Electric	Portable baseboard convector	1700 to 5120 (O)	100%	No	No	$45-$75
Electric	Portable circulator	3413 to 17,060 (O)	100%	No	Yes	$30-$100
Electric	Portable radiant	3410 to 5120 (O)	100%	No	No	$25-$125
Kerosene	Portable radiant	7200 to 12,500 (O)	70%	No	No	$35-$250

*(I) indicates input rating; (O), output rating. Output is the more meaningful figure since it tells what a heater actually delivers. Some units are listed only by input. Output is roughly 70% input.
**Prices do not include installation cost in cases where installation is required.

WOOD-BURNING HEATERS

Wood-burning Appliance	Efficiency Range (%)*	Price Range**
Open masonry fireplace	−10 to 10	$1500-$3000
Masonry fireplace with glass screen	−10 to 5	Screen: $50 to $175
Prefabricated zero-clearance fireplace	−10 to 10	$350-$600
Prefabricated fireplace with natural or forced-air circulation and optional outside combustion air	10 to 30	$450-$1000
Freestanding fireplace	−10 to 20	$200-$700

Wood-burning Appliance	Efficiency Range (%)*	Price Range**
Franklin-style stove	20 to 40	$150-$600
Potbelly, box and other radiant stoves	30 to 45	$125-$200
Circulator stoves	40 to 55	$250-$475
Airtight stoves	50 to 70	$300-$1300
Fireplace inserts	Variable, see text	$450-$1000
Central wood furnaces	40 to 60	$1200-$2250

*See text for explanation of efficiency ratings.
**Prices do not include installation except for a traditionally constructed open masonry fireplace.

the case for wood

If you believed only your pocket calculator, all this might lead you to the conclusion that it's just as well to forget about wood as a fuel and use only electricity. Not so.

If you cut your own wood or have access to an inexpensive supply, a wood stove can be more economical than heaters of higher efficiency. If you live in an area where wood is scarce or costly, it will, of course, make less sense, but there are other factors to consider, too. The charm and romance of a wood fire are hard to put a value on—you're paying for something more than just another household appliance.

gas, oil and electricity

The problem with electricity is its cost. Despite its superb efficiency, full-time electric heating, at today's prices, would hit you with a yearly utility bill approaching the size of the national debt.

This is not to say there isn't a place for electric heaters—there is. Their clean heat, instant warm-up, compact size and ease of installation make them ideal for certain applications—if used for short periods and in relatively small spaces. They come in many styles—freestanding floor models, fixed and portable baseboard strips and wall and ceiling built-ins. Those with blowers for forced-air circulation generally have a higher B.T.U. output than radiant and convector types of comparable size, but are more expensive.

The same is true of gas and oil space heaters—they have their special uses, too. Like electrics, they churn out heat at impressively high efficiencies, but this isn't the only factor to consider. They won't cost you a penny less per B.T.U. than your present gas or oil furnace, but they won't be heating the whole house or running all the time. The fact that they heat only a specific area is what can make them practical, even though they burn the same fuel.

Like electrics, gas and oil heaters come in floor and built-in models, and in both natural convection and forced-air circulator types. If natural gas is not available in your area, there are gas models that burn propane in tanks.

All oil and most gas heaters require a flue or other form of venting to the outside. However, there are now some gas models on the market that do not call for venting. These are cheaper to buy and easier and less expensive to install.

While there is still some controversy over the venting question, the American Gas Assn. (AGA) has approved many unvented gas heaters for home use. According to an AGA spokesman,

TYPICAL AIRFLOW

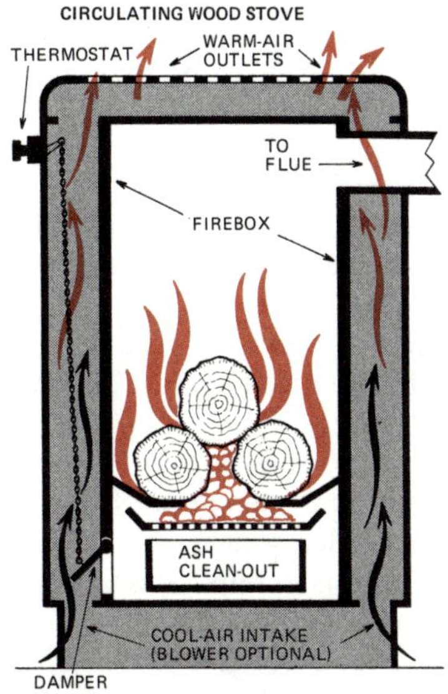

THIS DIAGRAM shows the airflow in a typical wood-burning stove. Cool air enters through vents at floor level and rises as it is heated to exit at the top. Combustion is controlled by a damper hooked to a thermostat.

"These heaters are perfectly safe for indoor use, provided they are used as directed."

Some units are not approved for heating mobile homes or similar tightly constructed living quarters, where there may be little fresh-air ventilation. Whether you choose a vented or unvented style, buy only makes that carry the AGA label.

Kerosene heaters do not need outside venting because kerosene burns more cleanly than other fossil fuels. Because of this, plus the fact that their fuel supply is self-contained, they are completely portable and are a good choice where no permanent installation is desired. Be sure, however, that you choose a model approved for *indoor use* by Underwriters Labs (UL).

how much heat do you need?

Most heaters are rated according to the maximum amount of heat energy they put out in B.T.U. per hour (B.T.U./hr.). Use this as a guide in determining the output you need to heat a given area. Outputs for electric, gas, oil and kerosene heaters are given in the chart, but these are general ranges. Look for the output on the particular model you buy.

Most wood stoves are also rated in B.T.U./hr., but you'll usually find three output figures for three different burning rates—low, medium and high—depending on how you fire the heater. A small stove may be listed as putting out 25,000, 35,000 or 45,000 B.T.U./hr. A bigger one might give 55,000, 65,000 and 75,000 B.T.U./hr. Large stoves can go all the way up to 90,000 B.T.U./hr.

Many heating experts now believe that one of the biggest mistakes some homeowners make is in buying a heater too big for their needs. This is especially true of wood stoves.

"People are buying units rated at 50,000 or 60,-000 B.T.U./hr. to warm up a family room," says Dr. Timothy Maxwell, co-director of the wood-burning appliance labs at Auburn University, Auburn, Ala. "Charged up, that big stove gets so hot no one can stay in the room. The normal response is to cut back the air supply to slow down the fire, but an air-starved log fire will deposit creosote in the flue, which can cause a chimney fire. The answer is to buy a stove sized correctly for your needs."

So how do you determine your needs? Here's a simple rule of thumb to follow: Multiply the size in square feet of the area you want to heat by 55. The result will roughly represent the B.T.U./hr. output required for that area.

If, for example, you want to warm a 16x20-ft. family room, multiply 16 by 20 by 55. This comes to 17,600 B.T.U./hr. Now buy a heater that delivers between 16,000 and 22,000 B.T.U./hr. This should give you enough capacity to heat the immediate area as well as provide some spillover into adjoining spaces.

should you buy an airtight?

Of all wood stoves, the most efficient is the airtight design, as you see from the chart (page 1422). There's a catch. The most efficient burn is not necessarily the safest or most desirable. Top efficiency comes from a slow-burning, air-starved fire, but this produces the largest amount of unconsumed creosote. You can crank up the fire to get a roaring-hot blaze (which will cut down the creosote), but this just consumes your wood faster and sends more heat up the flue.

Then why pay for an airtight stove? Because there's a burning rate for an airtight midway between roaring and air-starved that conserves wood and produces low levels of creosote. Also, wood burned to charcoal can glow for hours in an air-starved environment without giving off excessive creosote.

If you're connecting an airtight stove to an existing fireplace chimney, there's one possible problem you should be aware of. "From our research to date," says Maxwell, "we note a tendency for creosote to collect in flues to which airtight stoves are connected. This appears to occur because masonry flues, especially those located on an outside wall, are less insulated than a flue manufactured specifically for the stove. It may be very difficult for an airtight to generate enough exhaust products to heat up the chimney properly for a good draft."

other types of wood stoves

If you prefer the looks of a Franklin, potbelly or other style of stove that is not airtight, be reassured that these, too, can put out adequate heat for most applications. Base your judgment here on size, rather than efficiency. A large stove of low efficiency can produce just as much heat as a highly efficient one that's smaller. Also, a hot, clean fire tends to level off efficiencies for all types of wood stoves.

Radiant stoves discharge their heat directly through a single-wall firebox, warming a room by radiation. These include the Franklin, potbelly and most airtights. Circulator stoves have a double-wall construction that circulates heated air around an inner firebox, delivering it to the room through vents. Some have blowers to boost air circulation.

Circulator models give off less radiant heat than single-wall types, are somewhat cooler to the touch and can be safely placed closer to a combustible wall. Their efficiencies run high, though not as high as those for airtight designs. Many circulators have smartly styled modern enclosures that fit nicely into contemporary room settings—though they may lack the charm of traditional models.

If you buy a circular stove that offers forced-air circulation, check if it can be safely operated with the blower off in the event of a power failure. This also applies to prefab circulating fireplaces and to gas and oil heaters that use forced-air circulation. Some types, especially those that draw in outside combustion air, may not be recommended for power-off operation. This can be an important point if you're looking for blackout insurance.

are wood stoves safe?

Wood stoves are, generally, as safe as their installation and care. Studies made by the National Fire Protection Assn. (NFPA), the Consumer Products Safety Commission (CPSC) and other public-safety agencies indicate that the major hazards of stoves are improper installation, poor maintenance and careless use. No questions of faulty stove construction have been raised. It is vital, however, that safety standards for installation and operation be followed.

A PROPERLY MADE fire maximizes net B.T.U. gain, and minimizes creosote buildup in the chimney.

Get more heat from a space heater

By JOHN INGERSOLL

Whether you choose a wood stove or kerosene heater to supplement your central heating system, follow these guidelines for operating it efficiently

FOR WHATEVER reason you invested in a space heater, you're now a member of a sizable energy-saving group of converts who want to conserve central heat.

"Why spend good money to keep a bedroom used from 11:00 p.m. to 7:00 a.m. at a constant 68° F.?" asks one Columbus, Ind., space-heating enthusiast.

Why indeed? Space heaters, used judiciously, can save you cash. The key words are "used judiciously." For example, it makes little sense to get off oil- or gas-fired central heat, only to pour out hard cash for cord after cord of split logs to feed a voracious wood stove.

The common-sense principle of using a space heater to advantage is a matter of good timing. Quite simply, rooms not used for several hours during the day or night need not be heated to 68° F., as do areas of the home in constant use. Prime examples are upstairs bedrooms and bathrooms during the day. At night, while the family is asleep, the living room, kitchen, dining room and downstairs lavatory can be kept at 62° F., or less.

Space heaters have the additional bonus of being useful in an emergency. If your furnace gives out in the middle of a blustery December night, space heaters can save much grief. They are also handy for occasional demands, like heating a workshop or garage.

Space heaters used as zone heaters give you the option to save money. The rest is up to you. Here's a roundup of tips to gain maximum heat for the least investment:

heating with wood stoves

The picture series on the next page illustrates steps to take when breaking in a new wood stove. An airtight stove was used for the series, but the principles apply, with minor variations, to Franklins, potbellies and air-circulating stoves.

Information that manuals often don't include was gathered from industry researchers and veteran wood-stove users.

All the people I spoke to agreed that the toughest technique to learn is balancing air and fuel to (1) get a good burn, (2) use the least amount of fuel and (3) avoid depositing excessive creosote in the stove and flue.

"The most convenient, most efficient money-saving fire is one in a stove with a full charge of wood starved for air," says researcher John Allen of Battelle Memorial Labs, Columbus, Ohio. "That's also the way to produce a lot of creosote."

The straightforward way to avoid creosote (a chimney-fire risk) is to open the damper, give your fire plenty of air and allow it to burn briskly.

A hot fire tends to burn off creosote before it swirls up the flue with smoke. Second, the high heat warms the flue lining to a temperature at which creosote fails to condense.

But—and it's a big but—the fast-burn method runs up your wood-supply bill.

Are there solutions? Yes. Wendell Stickney

SEE ALSO
**Energy, saving . . . Fireplaces . . .
Heaters, portable . . . Heating systems, home . . .
Stoves, wood-burning . . . Winterizing, homes**

AVOID THESE HAZARDOUS PRACTICES

NEVER dry green or storm-soaked logs on top of a wood stove. They can reach their flash point quickly.

DO NOT BURN trash of any kind in your stove, *especially plastic-coated cartons.* Use your old newspapers for kindling.

CHEMICAL fire starters are not safe for use in a stove. The quick temperature rise may warp the firebox.

HOW TO BREAK IN A NEW STOVE

OPEN DAMPER on new stove completely. Also, open all windows and doors in the room to ventilate fumes and smoke from paint, oil and sealants.

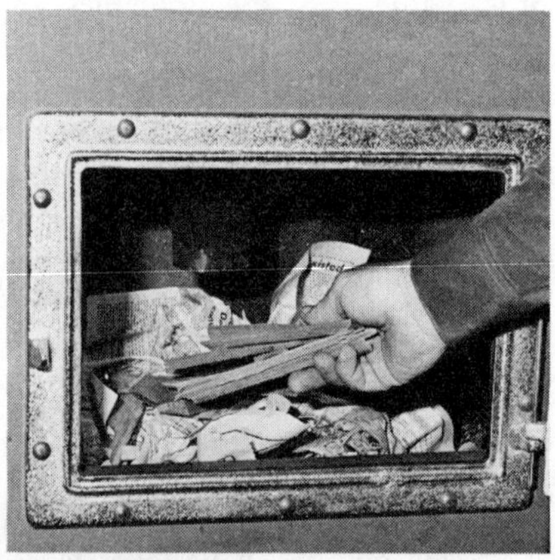

DO NOT START your first fire on a bare, metal stove bottom. Be sure to lay down 1½ in. of sand or cold ashes before adding kindling.

IGNITE KINDLING and burn it for about 60 seconds with door closed before adding three or four small logs. When embers form, add larger logs.

ADJUST AIR INTAKE to achieve steady, moderate flames. Too slow a fire will build up creosote and lots of ash. Using a shovel and scuttle, remove all but 1 or 2 in. of ash.

recommends a bed of ashes in which you bury live coals through the night.

This approach is also recommended by Allen and Dr. Jay Shelton, coauthor of *The Woodburner's Encyclopedia.*

"Let the wood charge burn to charcoal before you retire at night," says Allen, "and bury live coals in ashes; then shut down the damper completely. Some carbon monoxide (CO) will escape up the flue, but no bad hydrocarbons and almost no creosote."

When you arise in the morning, enough live coals will remain to fire up a small load of kindling. Then, on go fresh logs and, by adjusting the damper for a good burn, heat will come up rapidly.

Here's more advice on space heaters directly

from the professionals:

■ Hairline cracks in the stove metal or paint bubbles on the outer surface are a clear sign you're overfiring. Overfiring also accelerates corrosion of the stove's inside parts, whether steel or cast iron. The proper solution is to build smaller fires.

■ Dampers control the combustion air—and consequently the fire—on an airtight or circulator stove or wood furnace. There is only one way to control a fire in a Franklin, potbelly or any leaky stove: Limit the fuel.

■ Flashback—the instantaneous burst of flame from the firebox when a wood-stove door is opened—can be extremely dangerous. It happens when you open the door of an airtight stove or furnace that is totally damped down and in which a slow fire has been burning for hours. Atmospheric oxygen rushes in, ignites unburned gases, and flames leap toward the source of the oxygen—outside the stove door.

Anyone in the path of that fiery blast will be burned. Prevention is relatively simple: You just open the damper and leave it open for 20 to 30 seconds before you swing open the stove door (slowly).

■ Stoves with a grate, such as a Franklin, coal stove or solid-fuel furnace, need an air space between ashes and the metal grate. Hot embers in the ashes can cause the grate to rust, warp and break.

■ Invest in a Class A fire extinguisher and/or keep a bucket of sand close by a wood stove. Only *after* sand and chemical are spent, should you ever douse a red-hot stove with water. Instantly, water will turn to scalding-hot steam and may crack a cast-iron firebox.

■ Be certain to install a smoke alarm in the space heated by your wood stove.

using a coal stove

Burn the size coal for which your stove was intended. The manufacturer will specify pea, nut, stove or egg-size pieces. In general, the smaller the firebox, the smaller the coal size. Most grates are too open for pea coal, and large chunks leave clinkers that are inconvenient to remove.

Before starting a coal fire, open doors and slightly crack a window or two. You want plenty of combustion air, since coal produces considerable CO before it settles down to a slow burn. (This problem rules out a coal stove for use in a mobile home.) A good draft in the stack, plenty of room air and an open draft regulator send the initial release of CO up the flue.

With the draft slide open, start a coal fire with paper and dry kindling, just as you would a wood fire. When the flames peak, add a small charge of coal. Let it catch fully; then add more coal, but never an amount mounded higher than the firebrick lining. Once the charge has caught, close the draft regulator.

To recharge the stove, as you would for an overnight burn, shake the grate until a few red-hot coals drop down. Open the ash door—but slowly—to establish a draft, or you may get a puff of smoke billowing into the room.

Leave the door open until the coals fire up glowing red. Then add the new charge and close the ash door and the draft regulator.

Figure on emptying the ash drawer once a day and keep at least two ash cans handy for this purpose.

Does coal save cash? Often it is less expensive than many other fuels. But there's a catch; some communities don't permit coal-burners. Check before you buy and burn.

You can save money operating a coal-burner by letting the fire burn out during the day and relighting it the next morning. It's more maintenance work, but you do save money.

electric zone heaters

Electric heaters are pretty easy to operate: Flip the switch, and you have instant heat where you need it. There are, however, a few rules.

■ Don't place furniture in front of the heater, especially a radiant unit. You might end up with a charred chair, or worse.

■ Drapery material must be able to withstand 200° F. to hang over a baseboard heater. Check this out with the fabric manufacturer or dealer when buying drapes.

■ Never hang wet clothes over an electric heater. This is a fire hazard.

gas zone heaters

The same rules apply to gas heaters as for electrics. They have the same easy startup. Although unvented gas heaters labeled by the American Gas Assn. (AGA) are safe for indoor use, you'd still be wise to open a door to other spaces in the house, or crack a window slightly.

oil-fired zone heaters

Most oil heaters are rated for No. 1 oil or kerosene, generally stored in a raised tank outside the house. Units are also available with attached tanks, but these need refilling daily.

TIMELY MAINTENANCE KEEPS STOVES AND SPACE HEATERS IN TOP SHAPE

CREOSOTE buildup in the stove acts as an insulator. This can quickly reduce the stove's efficiency.

Every zone heater requires maintenance; no system works flawlessly forever. Solid-fuel burners call for upkeep on a steady basis. Other space heaters require less. Here's the rundown for each:

WOOD AND COAL STOVES

Getting rid of creosote wins top priority on your maintenance list for fireplace inserts and wood and coal stoves. When a stove's operation is ideal—hot fire, proper installation, insulated flue—only small deposits of creosote may collect. Owners of such stoves could get by with perhaps one chimney cleanout a year. But when conditions are bad, creosote can block a stovepipe opening completely in less than seven days of continuous fires. In its hardened or crusty state, creosote is flammable and the cause of many chimney fires.

A personal inspection is the best insurance against a chimney fire caused by creosote buildup. With the stove fire completely out, remove the stove-pipe connector, shine a light up the flue into the stove and check visually.

The cleanest, most convenient way to rid a system of creosote is by phone. Call in a professional chimney sweep and pay between $50 and $100 to have it done. (Pros charge the fee for each flue cleaned, not by the chimney structure.) If you want to do the job yourself, the tools you'll need include a steel-wire flue brush and extension rods, and a long-handled firebox brush. These will cost between $45 and $75. Other good aids include a shop vacuum, trouble light with long cord, shovel and metal pail.

How about tossing proprietary chemicals into the fire as a means of dispersing the creosote? Most pros agree that the chemicals help, but they disagree on how much. Some pros are concerned about the long-term corrosive effect of chemicals on metal and masonry joints. Don't try the Colonial-times trick of throwing salt on the fire. With moisture and heat, salt produces minute quantities of hydrochloric acid—a definite metal eater.

Here are a few more pointers:

- A hairline crack in cast iron will become a break. Welding is only a temporary solution; it's better to order a new part.
- A cracked seam on a steel stove can be welded, provided plates are not warped.
- Repaint or touch up a stove exterior with auto-engine paint having a heat tolerance of 1200° F.
- Stove smoke drifting into the room indicates poor draft. The trouble can stem from one or more of the following: (1) a clogged stovepipe or flue; (2) a stovepipe jutting too far into the flue; (3) too many elbows in the stove connector; (4) too little room air; (5) a flue undersized for the stove; or (6) high ever-green branches producing a downdraft in the flue.

If the solution doesn't show up readily, it would be best to seek help from the stove dealer.

GAS-FIRED SPACE HEATERS

Before starting up a gas heater each fall, remove the heater casing and vacuum the inside. A house vacuum is adequate. Use the upholstery-cleaning attachment to reach and clean any dusty crevices.

ELECTRIC SPACE HEATERS

Vacuum-clean an electric heater in the same way as a gas unit. Do it a couple of times during the heating season, too. "Baked" dust is what discolors wall paint or wall covering around an electric zone heater.

OIL-FIRED SPACE HEATERS

Carbon deposits will collect around an oil burner and may impede the flow of fuel if the carbon isn't cleaned or knocked out. Some burners have a cleanout device that loosens the carbon, which then is consumed in the flame. Pump the cleanout once a day. Also, it's wise to check the flue once a year for accumulated carbon. Clean it as you would clean a fireplace or stove flue.

PORTABLE KEROSENE HEATER

Clean the wick and flame spreader when you see carbon buildup in a kerosene heater. The easiest method is a dry cloth followed by a thorough vacuuming.

portable kerosene heaters

Ordinarily put into use for emergency heat, all kerosene space heaters must be fueled by hand to operate. As you would for an unvented gas heater, make certain the space in which the heater is located has plenty of fresh air.

The advantage of built-in oil, gas or electric heaters is wrapped up in the switch or starter—something coal and wood stoves lack. There are a lot more man-hours involved in running a wood stove for supplementary heat than in using an electric heater. Not only is an electric heater far more convenient, but you can easily control the hours of heat as opposed to those hours when no heat is needed. It is very easy to overfire a wood or coal stove and have more heat than you know what to do with.

In terms of cost per B.T.U., coal and gas space heaters are the cheapest to run. Electric heaters are generally the most expensive, but at least you don't have to refill them.

Of course, comparisons fall apart when you match wood you chop yourself against the price of electricity, oil, coal and gas.

Which course you take to supplement your central heating, and how much you save, is up to you.

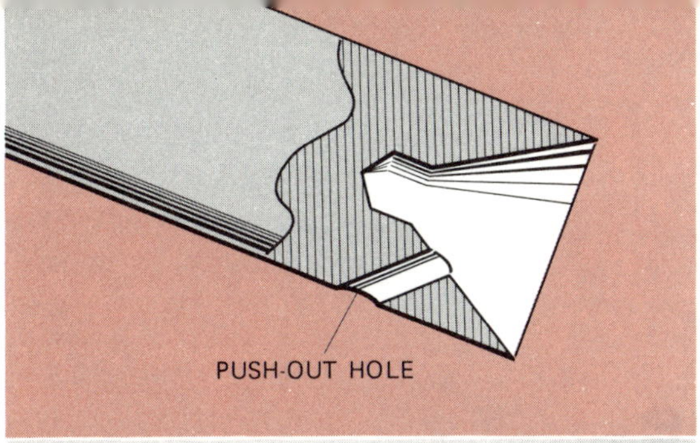

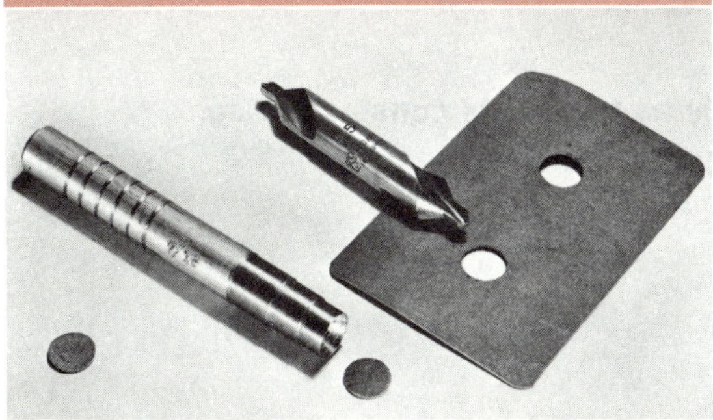

WHEN I NEEDED a gasket punch, I turned a piece of shafting to the desired punch diameter, then center-drilled it until the drill's cutting edge reached the shaft's o.d., making a knife edge. The fairly sharp taper of the hole helps slugs fall out, but you may want to drill a push-out hole.—*John Mallak, Silver Lake, MN.*

IF YOU LABEL brushes with their last previous use, it will tell you what solvent to use to soften the bristles if they have not been completely cleaned. Use a ballpoint pen on a strip of plastic-coated, cloth adhesive tape such as Mystik tape. Yellow is a highly visible tape color.—*Walter E. Burton, Akron, OH.*

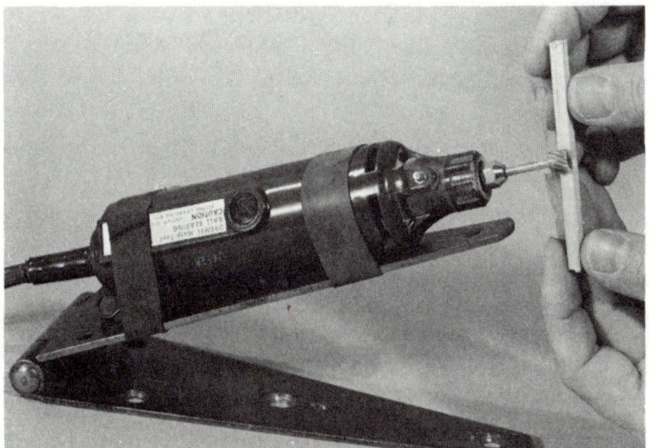

A SIMPLE adjustable stand for a small hand grinder can be made by fastening the tool to a large strap hinge with heavy rubber bands. Choose a hinge with stiff action or peen the pin with a hammer until the hinge will hold in any position. The stand should also help with "three-handed" soldering jobs.—*Ken Patterson, Regina, Sask.*

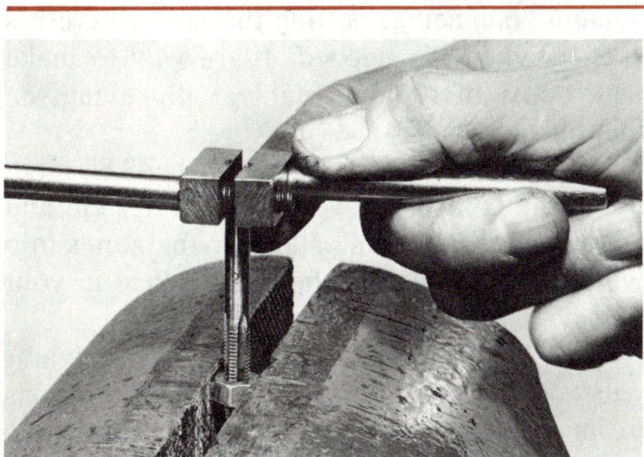

IF A NUT fits bolt threads too tightly, squeeze it in a vise while running a tap through it. This will enlarge the threaded hole more or less uniformly, often enough to assure a free-running fit. If the nut should be plated, it can be protected from vise marks with sheet-aluminum pads.—*W. B. May, Oak Park, IL.*

How to save money on heating your home

The cost of heating your home goes up constantly as fuel costs constantly rise. On these pages you'll find several unique and clever ideas to save heat, fuel and money in warming your home

Zoned heating: balanced comfort throughout your home

SEE ALSO
Boilers . . . Energy, saving . . . Fireplaces . . . Furnaces . . . House additions . . . Stoves, wood-burning . . . Winterizing, homes

■ WHAT IS ZONED heating? It's a way of using your present heating plant more efficiently, so that you can warm up chilly rooms without turning the rest of the house into an oven. It's dynamic balancing, putting the heat where it's needed when it's needed. It's a way to make your house more comfortable, with savings on fuel bills as well.

How is zoned heating accomplished? By modifying the controls of your present system and adding separate thermostats for the zones into which you will divide the living space in your home.

What kind of house can be made more livable with zoned heating? Almost any kind. Variations in sun and wind intensity on different sides of a house create different heating needs in rooms on those sides, and these needs will be more extreme if your house is elongated or shaped like a T, L or U. Additionally, your family occupies different parts of the house at various times of day and night; fuel used to heat unoccupied space is wasted.

A thermostat in every room, as is practical with electric baseboard heat, would be ideal, but you can usually achieve even temperatures throughout the house by dividing it into two or three zones.

How do you determine which rooms fall into which zones? It's generally worth the money to get a professional's help with this step. He will use either an occupancy-load method or a geographic-orientation method (which usually means adding a separate zone for rooms with northern exposure) to find your house's zones, and will be able to tell you where the extra equipment needed should be installed.

There are three ways to go with zoned heating. Where the existing system is of the forced-air type, thermostat-governed dampers are installed in ducts, or a plenum splitter with damper controlled by a second thermostat installed at the

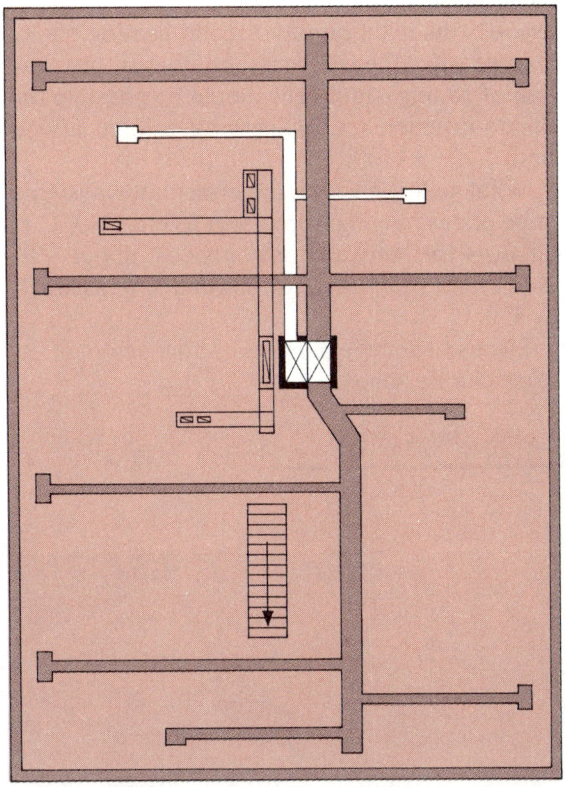

SECOND ZONE (white) has its own thermostat and supply duct running from the plenum.

DAMPERS INSTALLED in ducts near the plenum act to regulate the relative amounts of warm air sent to the two zones.

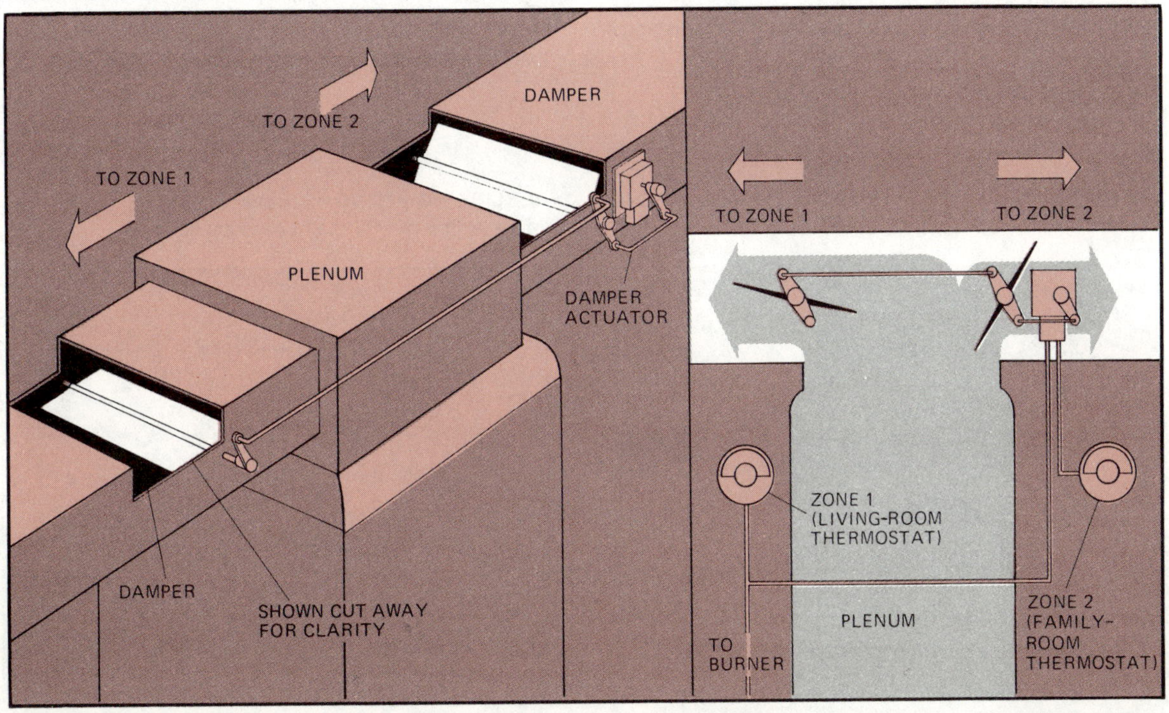

furnace plenum. With hot-water systems, zone valves or extra circulators can be used. The third method, most extreme but practical in some cases is the addition of a second heating plant. Except when the latter method is used, installation of zoning equipment should be possible for the do-it-yourselfer, but get professional advice first.

What will it cost? Damper-actuator systems have prices ranging from about $33 to $113. Circulators for hot-water systems cost about $60. And thermostats cost from around $7 to as much as $50.

Here are some examples of how heating systems can be zoned:

heating systems, continued

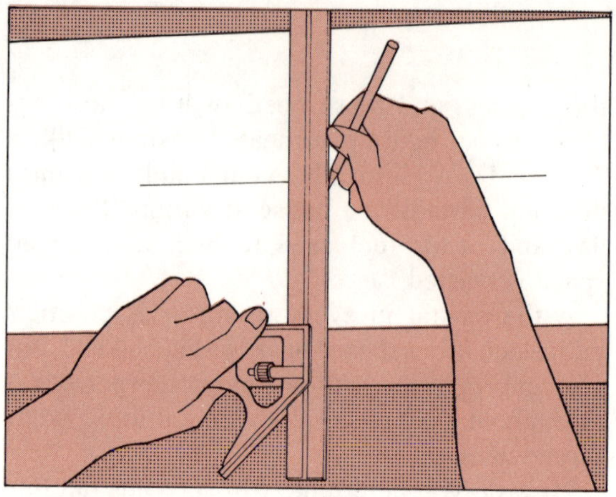

1. BEGIN BY locating center of the duct, front and back, where the zoning damper is to be installed.

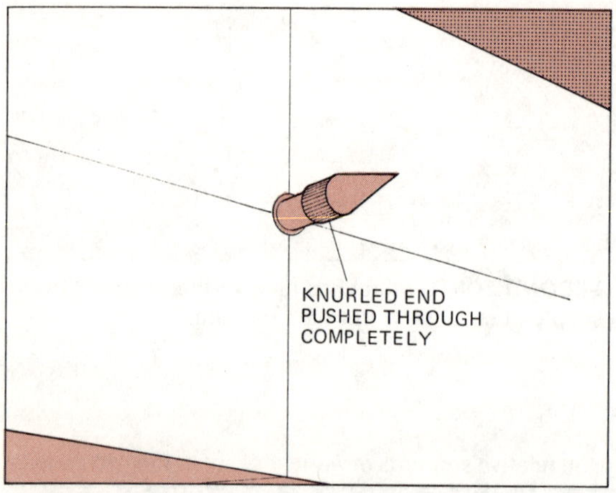

4. TEST TO SEE that the shaft rotates freely after pushing its knurled end all the way through the rear hole.

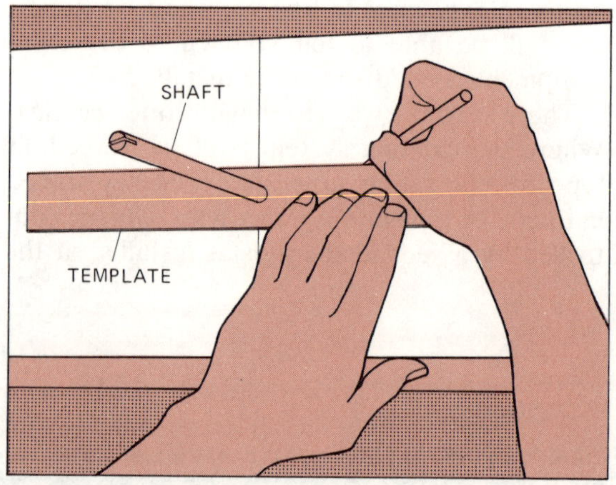

5. SLIDE TEMPLATE over shaft on front side of the duct and carefully scribe its outline onto the duct.

8. FASTEN BLADE onto the shaft and slip the assembly into the duct, reinserting the shaft.

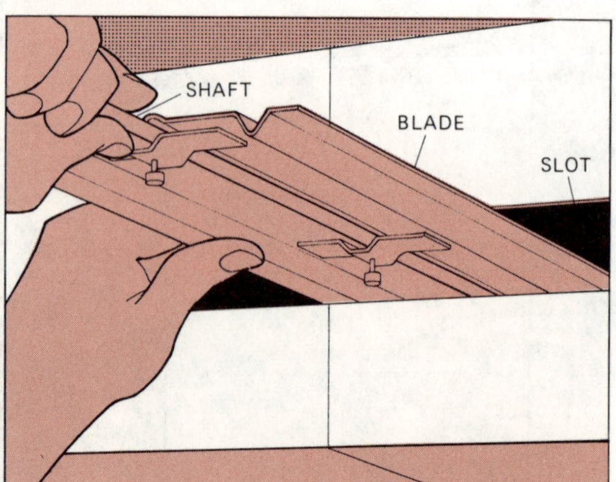

9. SLIDE MOUNTING plate over the shaft and fasten the plate to the duct with sheet-metal screws.

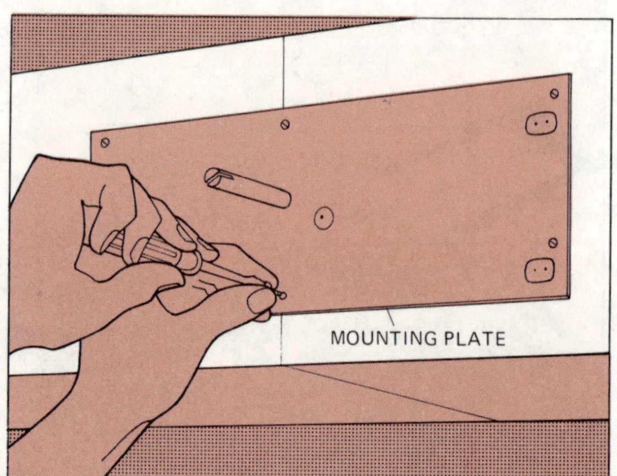

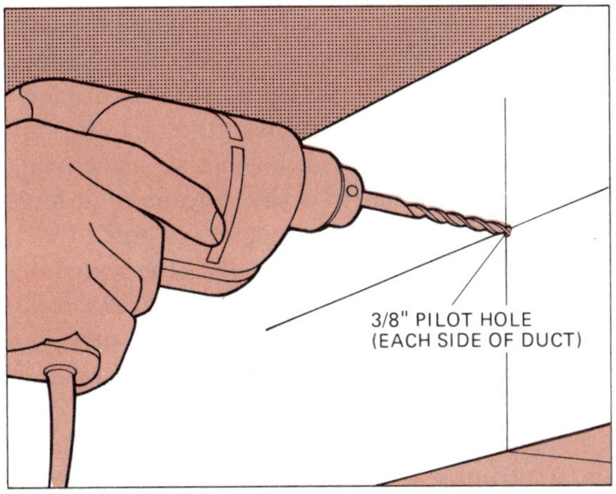

2. DRILL A ⅜-in.-diameter pilot hole through the center point on each side of the duct.

3. DRIVE THE DAMPER shaft through both of these holes from the front side of the duct.

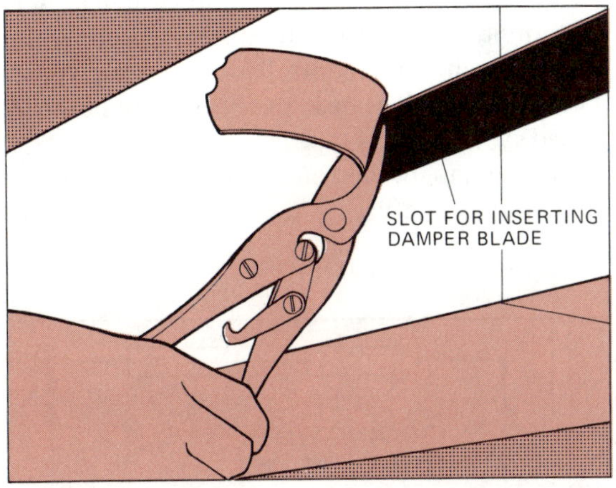

6. CUT SLOT for insertion of damper blade following template outline, after removing shaft from duct.

7. TRIM THE DAMPER blade to duct width, allowing for a ⅛-in. clearance at each of the ends.

continued

10. ATTACH THE DAMPER actuator securely to the mounting plate using sheet-metal screws.

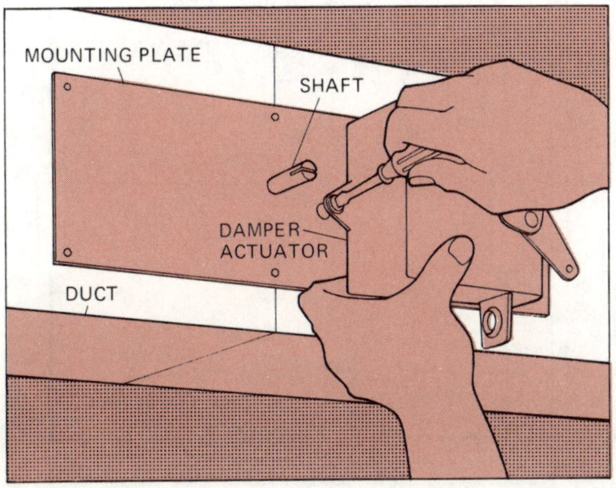

11. ADJUST ACTUATOR linkage for desired heat flow and tighten the crank on the damper shaft.

A basementless ranch house has living room and kitchen on one side, three bedrooms on the other and a forced-air heating plant in a central utility room. In this case, no additional ductwork is needed. Zoning requires no more than installing a splitter (a barrier in the plenum) if none is already there and two dampers. A living-room thermostat will operate the furnace and maintain temperature in living room and kitchen. A second thermostat in the sleeping area will control a single damper actuator to adjust settings of both dampers. Separate damper actuators could be used instead.

A more complex problem is that posed by a five-room house with a basement recreation room that needs heating. With a centrally located furnace, there could be two approaches. The less expensive way would be to use a single damper actuator and a splitter in the plenum to provide the means of installing a separate takeoff for the basement duct run. The alternative would be to install motorized dampers external to the furnace, one on either side, splitting the ground floor into two zones (living room and kitchen in one, bedrooms in the other). The basement could then be heated by overhead registers supplied by a duct in the basement ceiling, with airflow here controlled by a third motorized damper, installed in this duct near the furnace.

A larger installation turns out to be quite simple when air is supplied through separate trunk ducts to each area. In a seven-room split-level house, the living room, dining room and kitchen might be supplied by one trunk, the four bedrooms by a second and the recreation room below them by a third. Zoning here is merely a matter of installing a damper in each trunk and adding two thermostats. In cases where zones are heated through branch ducts running off one or two trunks, new ductwork might be needed; but when the heating plant is centrally located, such complications are rare.

There are two ways to zone a hot-water system. The more common one uses a single circulator, with hot water provided by the boiler through a common pipe. The hot-water flow is then divided to supply the different zones, the flow to each being controlled by a zone valve. These are installed near the branching point. A zoned system of this type is shown on page 1435.

The second method substitutes circulators for zone valves and uses a separate hot-water sup-

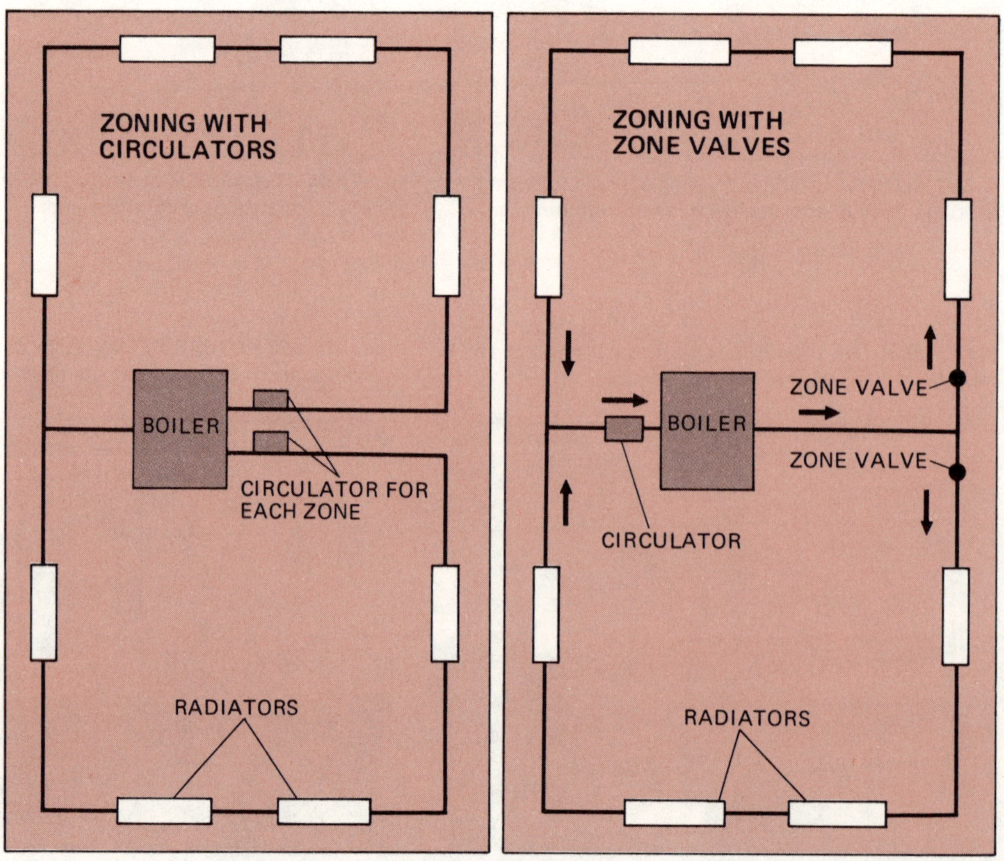

HOT-WATER SYSTEMS can be zoned with either circulators or zone valves. Extra circulators will be noisier and use more power than the valves.

ply pipe for each zone. Use of two circulators does produce more noise and requires more electricity than two zone valves.

Hot-water systems in one-story houses are easy to zone when the boiler is located near the center of the basement, with each half of the house served by a separate set of pipes. Zoning is accomplished here by splicing a zone valve onto the boiler side of each circuit; the valves and their thermostats are connected to a relay that operates burner controls. The arrangement in a case like this is as shown at the bottom of the page.

A two-story house with hot-water heat presents a greater problem, because both floors will probably use the same set of supply pipes. To zone such a system, it would be necessary to install a separate set of feed and return pipes. You can, however, add zone controls to one or two single radiators to shut off the supply of hot water to them. These controls must not be inserted directly in the line or they will shut off the entire system; a diverting line must be provided wherever a zone valve is used to control an individual radiator. This method is set up as shown schematically at the right.

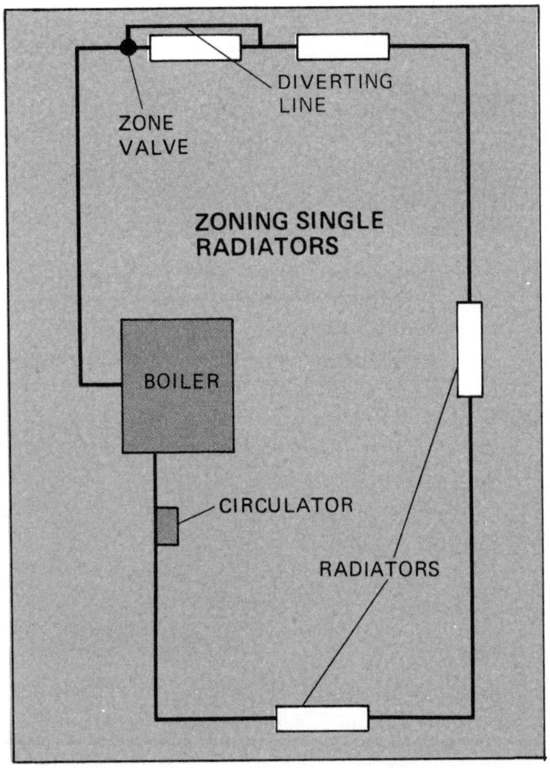

THERMOSTAT-RUN valve on an individual radiator can also provide a zoning action in your home.

continued

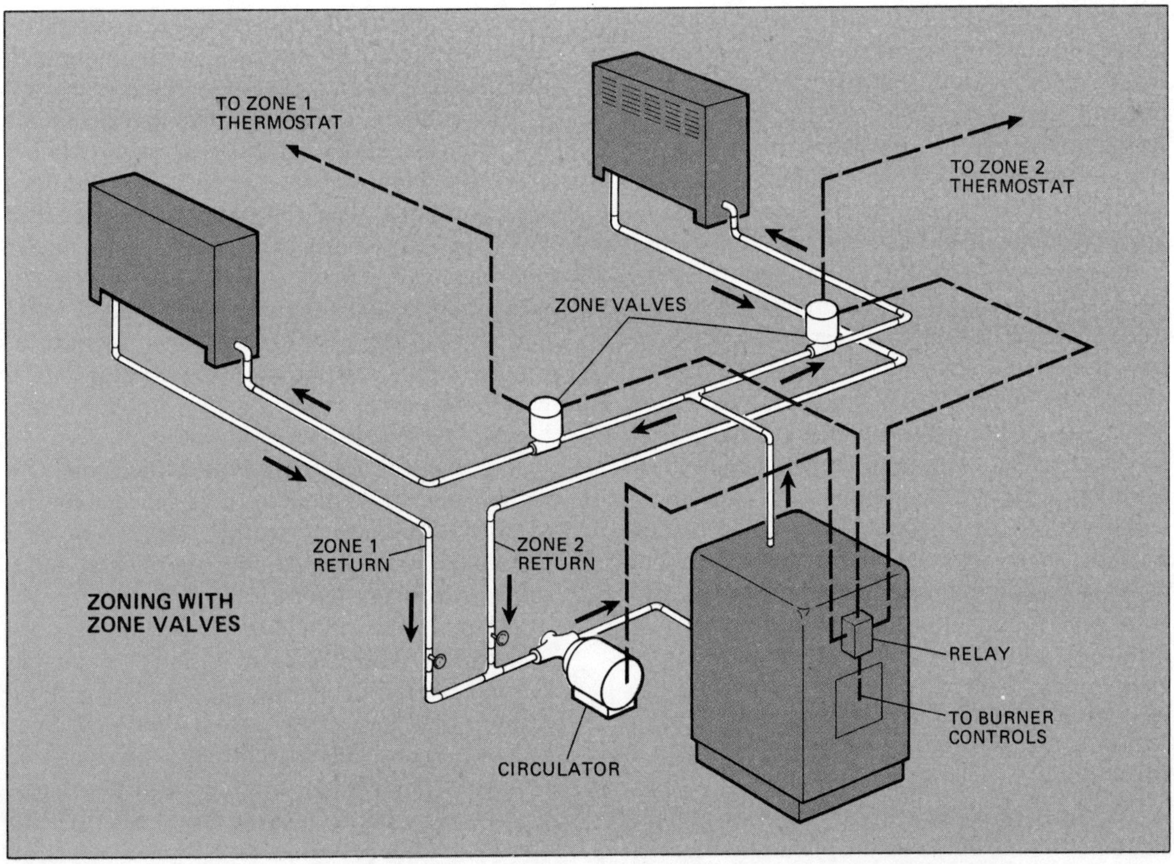

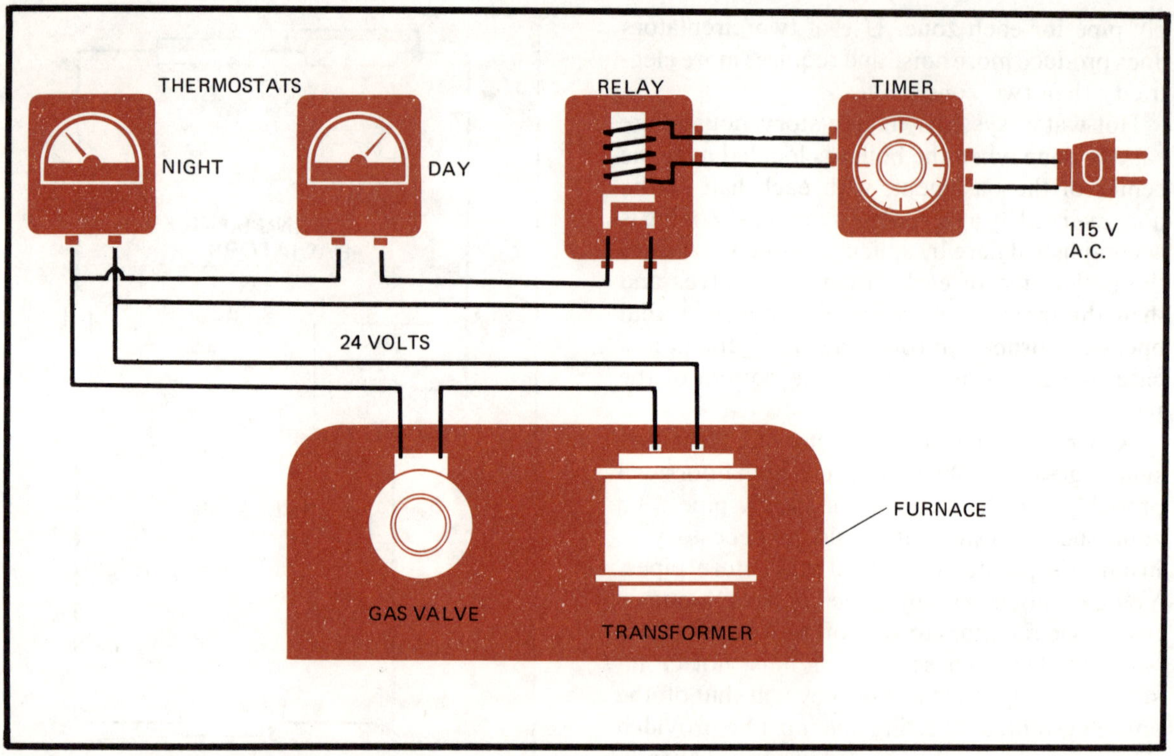

Save fuel with this thermostat timer

■ DESIGNED BY TWO MEN who work together at a power company, this homemade fuel-saver is, basically, two thermostats wired so one will control daytime settings and the other the night temperature. Its inventors say that if it is set to automatically lower the thermostat by 5° each night, it could save eight or nine percent of a home heating bill and pay for itself in months.

Inventors Morris Zuver and Matthew L. Bruce of Jackson, Mich., assembled the control using three basic items—a thermostat, 24-hour house timer and 115-v. relay. These can be purchased for about $15, they say. That is very little money to spend for the amount you will save.

They decided to utilize a simple 24-hour timer (used for turning a lamp on and off) and small surplus relay from an electronic circuit (rated 115 v.). Coil and contact points capable of about a 600-milliampere carrying capacity were used to work with the timer to make it safe electrically and not harm the 24-v. furnace-control transformer. With two indicator lights wired into the circuit, and using the regular house thermostat set at 73° F., the extra stat will maintain a night temperature of 60° F.

The timer-relay is connected in series with the daytime thermostat, and the nighttime thermostat is parallel to the load side of the relay. The nighttime thermostat is operative all the time in this manner. When the temperature is above 65° F., the contacts are open in this thermostat.

The nighttime thermostat is open all day because the day thermostat is operative and does the controlling when the timer reactivates it at 6:00 a.m. The house temperature being higher than the night setback temperature renders the night thermostat inoperative above 65° F. The system alternates between daytime thermostat for 16½ hours and nighttime thermostat for 7½ hours. The timer repeats daily without anyone having to touch it once it is set up.

If cooling is on the daytime thermostat, a higher summer daytime setting is needed for the system to operate correctly. Adjustment of a combination heating/cooling thermostat functions with the system.

All materials should be available in your community. The placement of timer-relay-night thermostat can be camouflaged behind a floral arrangement on a table near the daytime thermostat. Almost-transparent 24-v. wires can be connected into the daytime thermostat to complete the circuit, and you are ready to save energy and money.

■ YOUR BIGGEST INCENTIVE for checking out ways to cut your fuel bill is the price of the fuel itself. Heating bills are now higher than ever, and it's safe to say that we'll never again pay for fuel what we did a few years ago. On this page are three common-sense ideas to help you stretch the heat you are paying for. Cost to duplicate them is low; heat savings should recoup the cash outlay in one heating season.

Three stunts to get more of the heat that's there

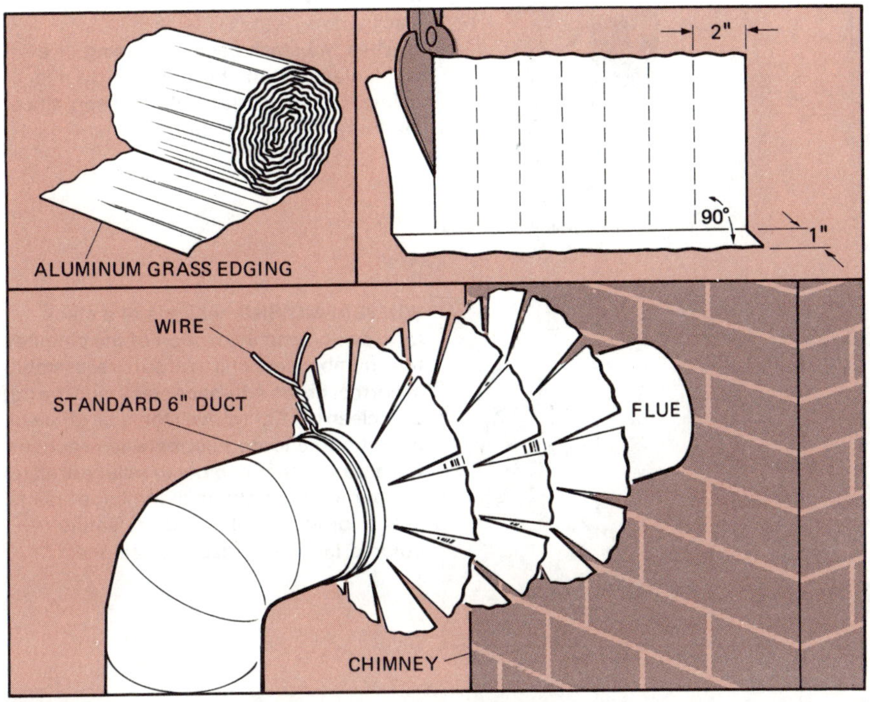

IF YOU were foolhardy and put your hand on the stack pipe between furnace and chimney, you'd get a good idea of the amount of heat that escapes unused. To trap some of it, purchase a roll of aluminum lawn edging.

CUT ALUMINUM edging in sections long enough to encircle stovepipe (find length using cardboard). Then bend down one side about an inch wide to form a collar. Using tin snips, cut the long side all around at 2 in. intervals.

SHAPE THE COLLARS around a tin can or pail about the size of the furnace pipe. Fit it snug to the latter and hold it secure with wire. Attach as many flanges as space allows; you'll be surprised how much heat you'll trap.

continued

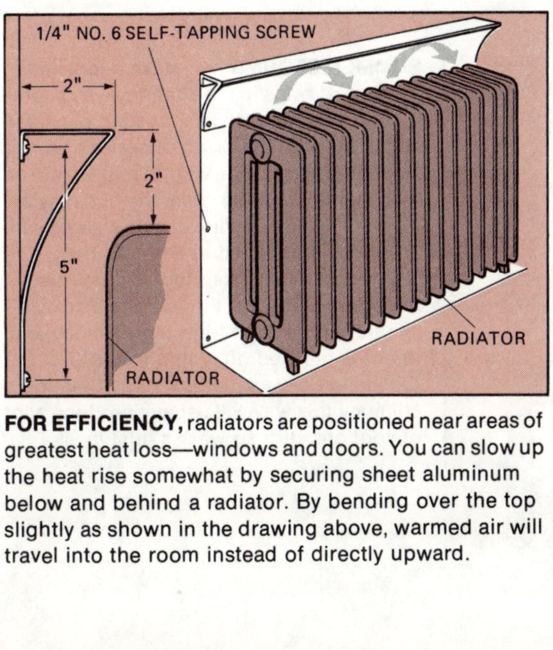

FOR EFFICIENCY, radiators are positioned near areas of greatest heat loss—windows and doors. You can slow up the heat rise somewhat by securing sheet aluminum below and behind a radiator. By bending over the top slightly as shown in the drawing above, warmed air will travel into the room instead of directly upward.

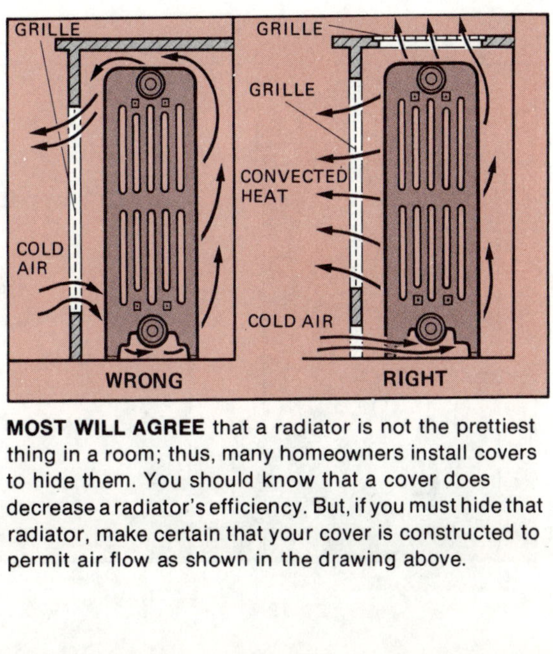

MOST WILL AGREE that a radiator is not the prettiest thing in a room; thus, many homeowners install covers to hide them. You should know that a cover does decrease a radiator's efficiency. But, if you must hide that radiator, make certain that your cover is constructed to permit air flow as shown in the drawing above.

What you can do to keep your heating system efficient

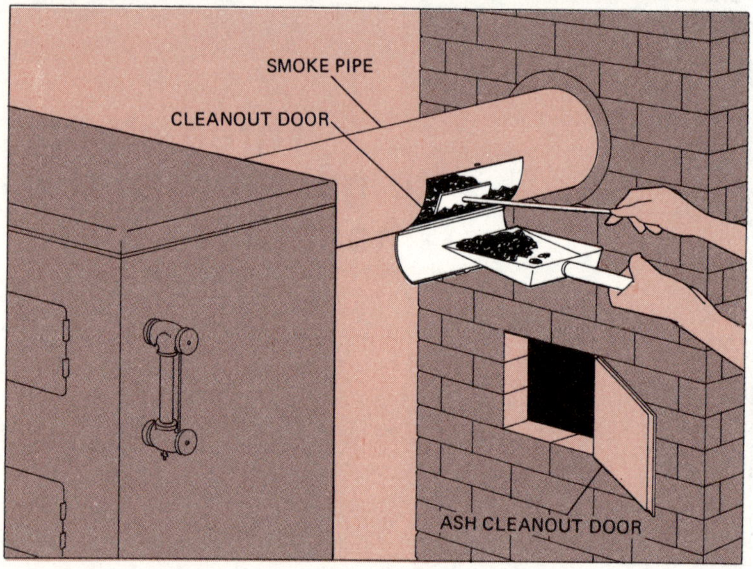

FOR EFFICIENCY, your furnace stack (smoke pipe between furnace and chimney flue) must be kept clean. Start of the heating season is also a good time to clean out the fireplace ashpit, where accumulations could interfere with furnace operation. Inspect the stack; holes are not worth patching—they show that it's time to replace the stack. Remove a worn-out stack by pulling it out gently (it should be press-fitted in place) and take it to a tinsmith for use as a pattern in assembling a new stack.

When the stack needs replacing or even just a cleaning, the best time to do it is before the start of the heating season, since the furnace must be shut down.

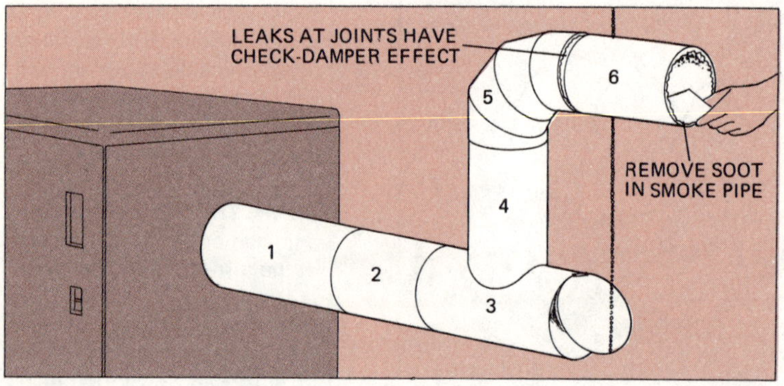

WHEN REMOVING sections of a stack for cleaning and inspection of the chimney flue, number sections to assure reassembly in correct order. A furnace stack must be not only clean but tight as well for most efficient operation—a loose joint between sections will act as a check damper to reduce draft to the burner. If careful realignment of joints fails to produce tight fit, use aluminum-colored fabric duct tape to seal them.

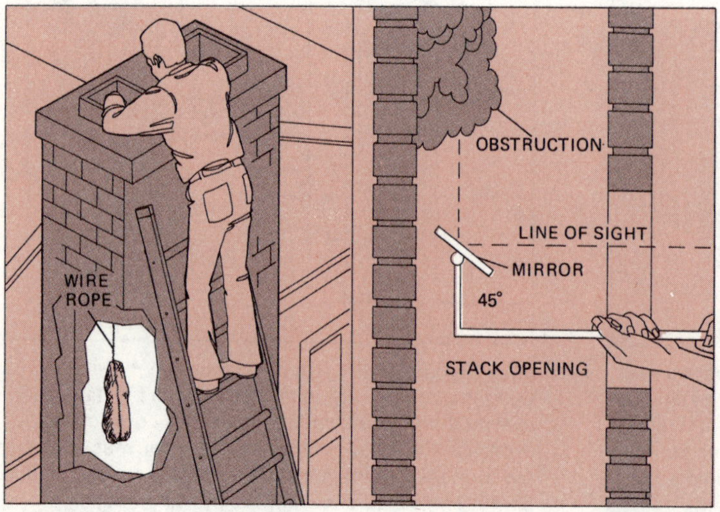

SUMMER STORMS may have deposited leaves and twigs in the chimney—and some birds prefer chimneys as nesting places. A chimney with little or no offset can be inspected from inside with an angled mirror. If daylight cannot be seen, the flue may be blocked. A blocked flue can be cleared with a tire chain wrapped in a burlap bag, lowered carefully from top. Before this operation is begun, the furnace stack should be removed from the chimney and the hole blocked off with a wad of dampened newspapers or rags. Clearing a chimney this way will usually produce a lot of soot and dirt, so wear a dust mask.

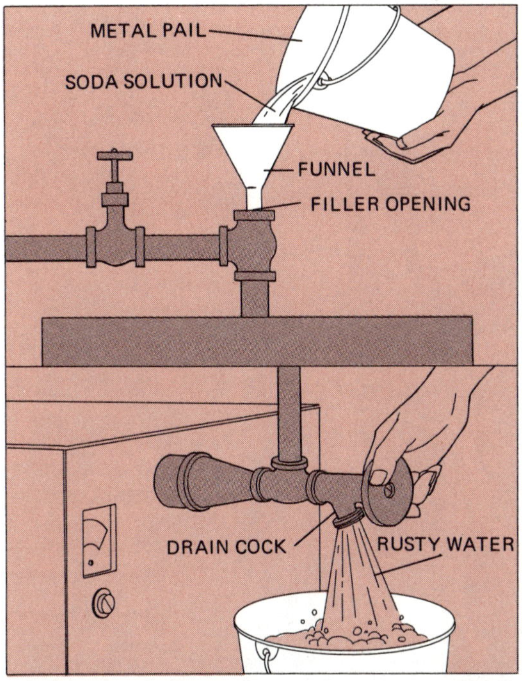

A BOILER that has a clean-out (filler) opening can be cleaned with a soda solution. You can buy the cleaner in powder form from a plumbing supply house or use auto radiator cleaner. A hot-water system should be purged of rusty water at start of heating season, refilled with fresh water.

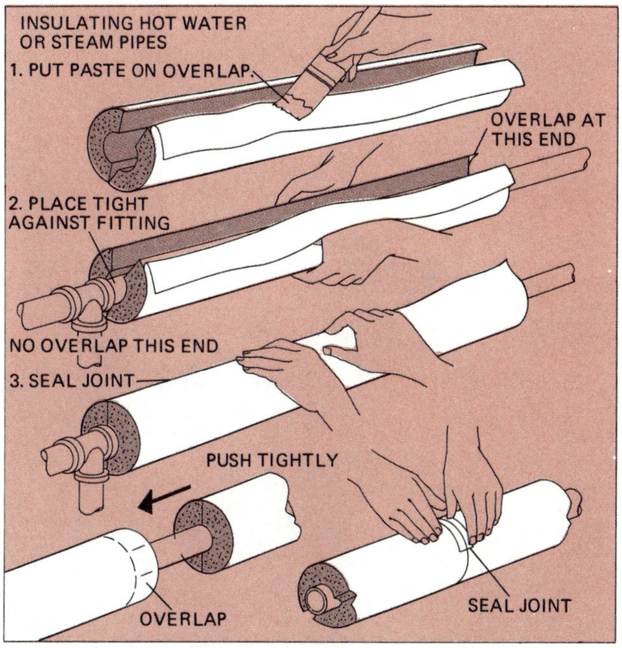

STEAM and hot-water pipes, especially where they run through unheated spaces, should be insulated. Ready-made sections of pipe insulation are applied as shown above; lengths of slit urethane foam tubing are also available. Runs of warm-air duct through unoccupied spaces should also be insulated to cut losses; use wraparound batts taped in place.

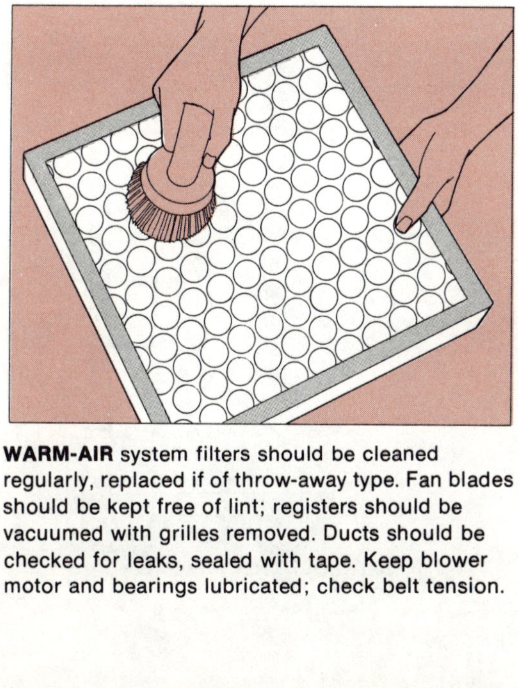

WARM-AIR system filters should be cleaned regularly, replaced if of throw-away type. Fan blades should be kept free of lint; registers should be vacuumed with grilles removed. Ducts should be checked for leaks, sealed with tape. Keep blower motor and bearings lubricated; check belt tension.

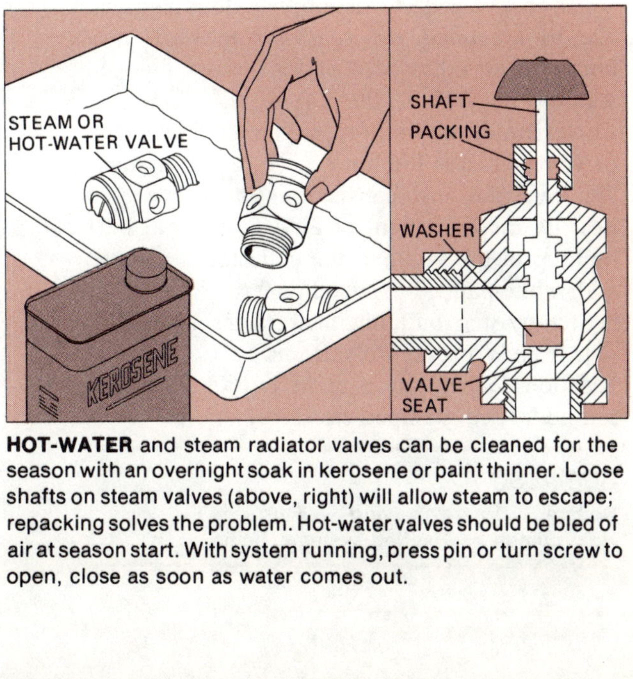

HOT-WATER and steam radiator valves can be cleaned for the season with an overnight soak in kerosene or paint thinner. Loose shafts on steam valves (above, right) will allow steam to escape; repacking solves the problem. Hot-water valves should be bled of air at season start. With system running, press pin or turn screw to open, close as soon as water comes out.

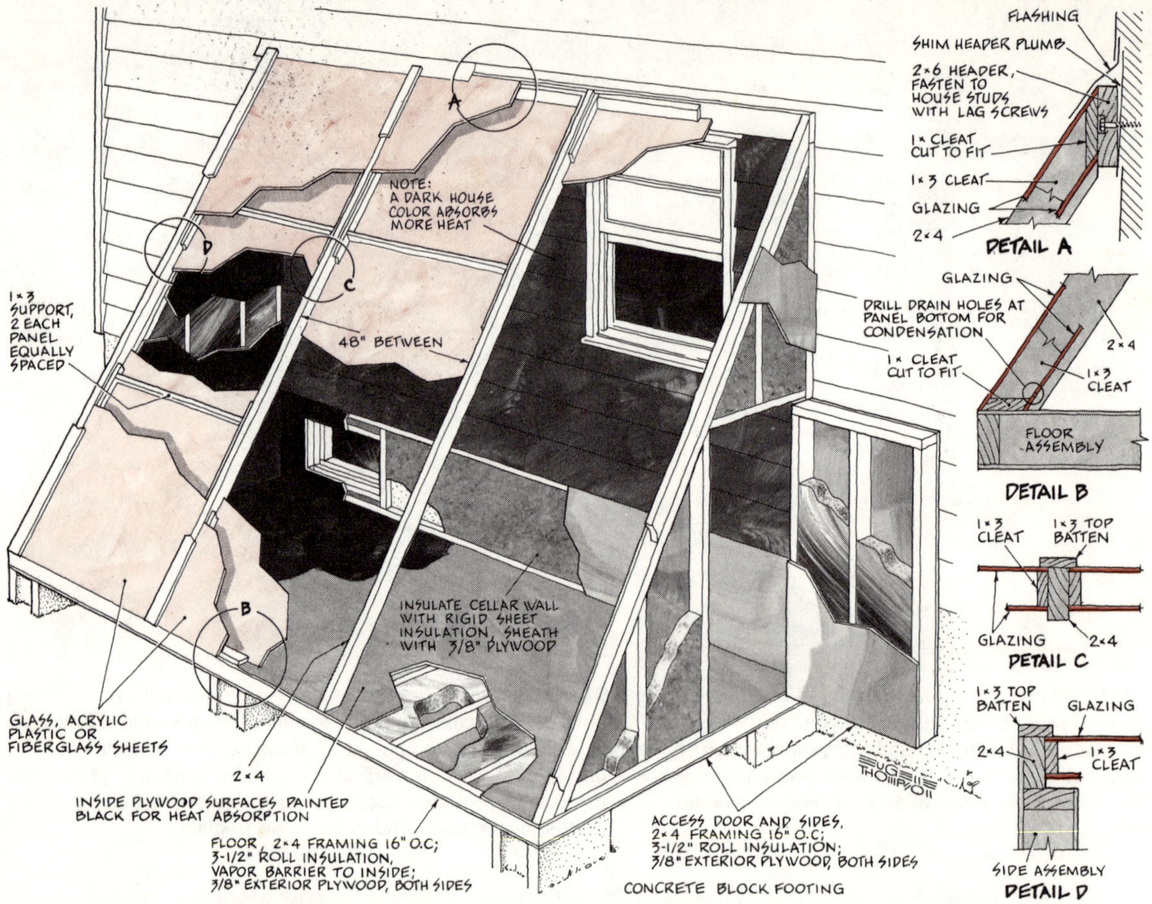

A solar collector anyone can build

A SOLAR COLLECTOR with a payback period of only two years? That's how long Prof. Bruce McQuarrie of Worcester Polytechnic Institute estimates it took before he received free B.T.U.s from the sun.

His passive collector is simply a double-glazed lean-to adjoining the south-facing wall of a house. As air is heated, it passes through an open window or vent at the top of the enclosure. Cooler air, drawn in through a basement window or vent, replaces the hot air. No active systems are involved—just convection (the transfer of heat by the movement of air). To prevent heat buildup in the summer, the collector is covered with white-painted plywood panels.

Step-by-step building instructions are available from Worcester Polytechnic Institute, Public Relations Dept., Worcester, MA 01609. Enclose a self-addressed, stamped envelope.

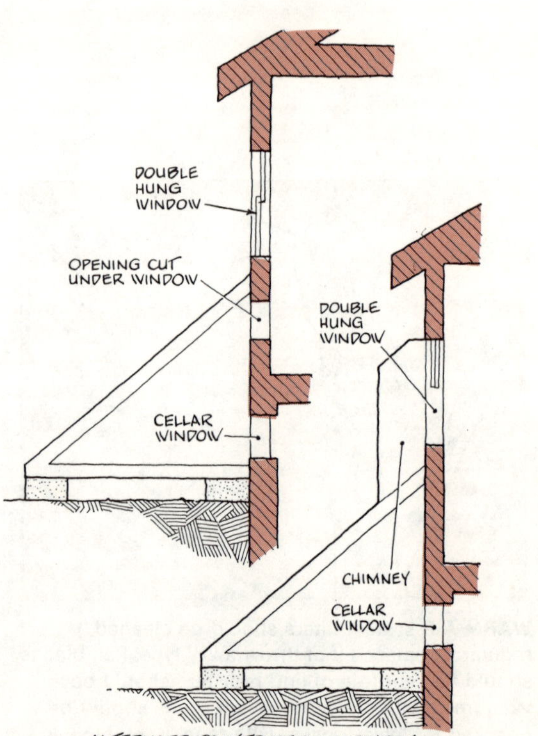

ALTERNATE CONSTRUCTION METHODS

SEE ALSO

**Boilers . . . Energy, saving . . . Furnaces . . .
Heat pumps . . . Heating systems, home . . .**

METRIC CONVERSION

Conversion factors can be carried so far they become impractical. In cases below where an entry is exact it is followed by an asterisk (*). Where considerable rounding off has taken place, the entry is followed by a + or a - sign.

CUSTOMARY TO METRIC

Linear Measure

inches	millimeters
1/16	1.5875*
1/8	3.2
3/16	4.8
1/4	6.35*
5/16	7.9
3/8	9.5
7/16	11.1
1/2	12.7*
9/16	14.3
5/8	15.9
11/16	17.5
3/4	19.05*
13/16	20.6
7/8	22.2
15/16	23.8
1	25.4*

inches	centimeters
1	2.54*
2	5.1
3	7.6
4	10.2
5	12.7*
6	15.2
7	17.8
8	20.3
9	22.9
10	25.4*
11	27.9
12	30.5

feet	centimeters	meters
1	30.48*	.3048*
2	61	.61
3	91	.91
4	122	1.22
5	152	1.52
6	183	1.83
7	213	2.13
8	244	2.44
9	274	2.74
10	305	3.05
50	1524*	15.24*
100	3048*	30.48*

1 yard =
.9144* meters
1 rod =
5.0292* meters
1 mile =
1.6 kilometers
1 nautical mile =
1.852* kilometers

Fluid Measure

(Milliliters [ml] and cubic centimeters [cc or cu cm] are equivalent, but it is customary to use milliliters for liquids.)

1 cu in = 16.39 ml
1 fl oz = 29.6 ml
1 cup = 237 ml
1 pint = 473 ml
1 quart = 946 ml
= .946 liters
1 gallon = 3785 ml
= 3.785 liters
Formula (exact):
fluid ounces × 29.573 529 562 5*
= milliliters

Weights

ounces	grams
1	28.3
2	56.7
3	85
4	113
5	142
6	170
7	198
8	227
9	255
10	283
11	312
12	340
13	369
14	397
15	425
16	454

Formula (exact):
ounces × 28.349 523 125* =
grams

pounds	kilograms
1	.45
2	.9
3	1.4
4	1.8
5	2.3
6	2.7
7	3.2
8	3.6
9	4.1
10	4.5

1 short ton (2000 lbs) =
907 kilograms (kg)
Formula (exact):
pounds × .453 592 37* =
kilograms

Volume

1 cu in = 16.39 cubic centimeters (cc)
1 cu ft = 28 316.7 cc
1 bushel = 35 239.1 cc
1 peck = 8 809.8 cc

Area

1 sq in = 6.45 sq cm
1 sq ft = 929 sq cm
= .093 sq meters
1 sq yd = .84 sq meters
1 acre = 4 046.9 sq meters
= .404 7 hectares
1 sq mile = 2 589 988 sq meters
= 259 hectares
= 2.589 9 sq kilometers

Kitchen Measure

1 teaspoon = 4.93 milliliters (ml)
1 Tablespoon = 14.79 milliliters (ml)

Miscellaneous

1 British thermal unit (Btu) (mean)
= 1 055.9 joules
1 calorie (mean) = 4.19 joules
1 horsepower = 745.7 watts
= .75 kilowatts
caliber (diameter of a firearm's bore in hundredths of an inch)
= .254 millimeters (mm)
1 atmosphere pressure = 101 325* pascals (newtons per sq meter)
1 pound per square inch (psi) = 6 895 pascals
1 pound per square foot = 47.9 pascals
1 knot = 1.85 kilometers per hour
25 miles per hour = 40.2 kilometers per hour
50 miles per hour = 80.5 kilometers per hour
75 miles per hour = 120.7 kilometers per hour